I0032995

MANUAL ON THE SIMPLE LINEAR ACTUARIAL MODEL

Hiddo A. Huitzing, Xylee Javier, Rouselle F. Lavado, and Ammar Aftab

DECEMBER 2020

ADB

ASIAN DEVELOPMENT BANK

Creative Commons Attribution 3.0 IGO license (CC BY 3.0 IGO)

© 2020 Asian Development Bank
6 ADB Avenue, Mandaluyong City, 1550 Metro Manila, Philippines
Tel +63 2 8632 4444; Fax +63 2 8636 2444
www.adb.org

Some rights reserved. Published in 2020.

ISBN 978-92-9262-651-8 (print); 978-92-9262-652-5 (electronic); 978-92-9262-653-2 (ebook)
Publication Stock No. TIM200426-2
DOI: http://dx.doi.org/10.22617/TIM200426-2

The views expressed in this publication are those of the authors and do not necessarily reflect the views and policies of the Asian Development Bank (ADB) or its Board of Governors or the governments they represent.

ADB does not guarantee the accuracy of the data included in this publication and accepts no responsibility for any consequence of their use. The mention of specific companies or products of manufacturers does not imply that they are endorsed or recommended by ADB in preference to others of a similar nature that are not mentioned.

By making any designation of or reference to a particular territory or geographic area, or by using the term "country" in this document, ADB does not intend to make any judgments as to the legal or other status of any territory or area.

This work is available under the Creative Commons Attribution 3.0 IGO license (CC BY 3.0 IGO) https://creativecommons.org/licenses/by/3.0/igo/. By using the content of this publication, you agree to be bound by the terms of this license. For attribution, translations, adaptations, and permissions, please read the provisions and terms of use at https://www.adb.org/terms-use#openaccess.

This CC license does not apply to non-ADB copyright materials in this publication. If the material is attributed to another source, please contact the copyright owner or publisher of that source for permission to reproduce it. ADB cannot be held liable for any claims that arise as a result of your use of the material.

Please contact pubsmarketing@adb.org if you have questions or comments with respect to content, or if you wish to obtain copyright permission for your intended use that does not fall within these terms, or for permission to use the ADB logo.

Corrigenda to ADB publications may be found at http://www.adb.org/publications/corrigenda.

Notes:
1. In this publication, "USD" refers to United States dollar, and "AMD" refers to Armenian dram.
2. Tables and figures without explicit sources are those of Microsoft.

On the cover: Healthcare service delivery in Central and West Asia (photos by ADB).

Cover design by Josef Ilumin.

Contents

Tables and Figures

Acknowledgments

The Simple Linear Actuarial Model was developed by Hiddo A. Huitzing, health specialist of the Social Sector Division (CWSS) of the Central and West Asia Department of the Asian Development Bank (ADB).

The manual was written by Xylee Javier, consultant, and Hiddo A. Huitzing. The Simple Linear Actuarial Model and Manual is part of an actuarial costing study led by Rouselle F. Lavado (senior health specialist, CWSS), and composed of George Schieber, health financing consultant; Ammar Aftab, actuarial consultant; and Saro Tsaturyan, health policy consultant.

Contributions were received from Susann Roth (principal knowledge sharing and services specialist, Sustainable Development and Climate Change Department, ADB); Eduardo Banzon (principal health specialist, Sustainable Development and Climate Change Department); and Grigor Gyurjan (senior economics officer, Armenia Resident Mission, ADB).

Gladys Ann R. Maravilla, Cristina Lim, Madeline Dizon, Dennis Von Custodio, and Mary Jane F. Carangal-San Jose provided support in preparing the report.

Funding for this report was obtained from Armenia Transaction Technical Assistance and Regional Technical Assistance on Innovation, headed by Susann Roth.

The team is indebted to the management for their support: Rie Hiraoka, director, CWSS; Shane Rosenthal, country director, Georgia Resident Mission, ADB; and Paolo Spantigati, country director, Armenia Resident Mission, ADB.

Abbreviations

ADB	–	Asian Development Bank
AMD	–	Armenian dram
IMF	–	International Monetary Fund
IPD	–	inpatient day
OPD	–	outpatient day
SLAM	–	Simple Linear Actuarial Model
SLM	–	Simple Linear Model
VBA	–	Visual Basic for Applications

CHAPTER I

Introduction

Actuarial analysis is a form of statistical analysis typically conducted using health-related financial cost data in the context of calculating insurance premium rates or otherwise determining expenditure needs. It entails estimation of average healthcare expenditures of a risk pool so that financing needs can be estimated to ensure that revenues balance expected outlays. Costs are estimated from a consumption approach and takes the production of health services largely as a given. Actuarial analysis probabilistically determines utilization and associated expected expenditures that would be needed to finance healthcare from a pool of financial resources. (Cichon et al. 1999; Cotlear 2015; Wang et al. 2012).

This manual serves as a detailed guide to using the Microsoft Excel version of the Simple Linear Actuarial Model (SLAM). Specifically, Chapter II of this manual describes SLAM, including its limitation, potential data issues, and applicable baseline scenarios. Chapter III provides an overview of the SLAM file, for its intended users, to opening the file, and then guide to its contents. Chapter IV provides details on how to use the data input worksheets of the SLAM file, while Chapter V provides guidance on how to view the results of the modeling. Sensitivity analyses using the SLAM file are also discussed in this manual, and then concluded by a summary of the tool's use and potential.

The SLAM was developed for assessing the financial sustainability of national and local micro- health insurances in select countries in the South Caucasus region, Africa, Southeast Asia, and Central and West Asia. As an actuarial model, the SLAM should calculate and, at a glance, present the actuarial projections and financial key indicators to support the management in assessing the financial sustainability of health insurance programs. Updates envisaged include enrollment numbers (i.e., uptake, retention, and dropout rates), changes in healthcare costs, changes in profiles of members, and changes in health utilization.

The goal was to have an actuarial model that the management of the health insurance programs nationwide and at local levels could update themselves without the need of frequently contracted intervention of actuarial experts[1] and use for day-to-day management of the health insurance schemes.

---

[1] For more in-depth assessments and/or reviews of health insurance programs, health insurance and actuarial experts would still be needed. The SLAM is a tool that could considerably speed up the review process and increasing the transparency from one actuarial expert to the next.

CHAPTER II

The Simple Linear Actuarial Model

This chapter describes the Simple Linear Actuarial Model (SLAM) as a tool and provides insights to its limitation and potential data issues. Toward the end of the chapter, baseline assumptions required from the users before using the tool are also discussed.

A. Description

The SLAM is a tool that will permit using a present policy and make projections to assess the financial sustainability of health insurance operations. The actuarial projections derived from the model can show whether continuing business-as-usual operations is an option for health insurance schemes.

The Simple Linear Model (SLM) was used to estimate the costs and set a premium for health events that will be included in SLAM analysis. The SLM assumes that the total claim amount, called "pure premium," is equal to the sum of the individual claims multiplied by their frequency of the event taking place.

The estimation of premium needed to covered medical expenses involves identifying the correlated costs of healthcare events covered by the insurance scheme. For instance, the associated correlating costs of a vehicular accident include X-ray use to assess whether bones are broken, and possible minor or major surgery, which might then be succeeded by hospitalization for an overnight stay. In the case of a complicated pregnancy, an emergency transport to a health facility might be needed. In the health facility where caesarian section is performed, the newborn might need premature care.

The SLAM was designed to be user-friendly, foolproof, have a high usability, and function as a decision-making tool to aid the management in their decision-making process in updating benefit packages, enrollment and eligibility criteria, while assessing the medium- to long-term financial sustainability and outlook of the health insurance program.

B.   Limitation

The SLAM, at present, only looks at the pure premium, also called risk premium, which does not include operational expenses, although profit margins, risk loading , and administrative cost loading can be added. Moreover, questions on willingness-to-pay and ability-to-pay are not part of the model. Another aspect not covered by SLAM are the running costs of implementing the health insurance programs.

C.   Potential Data Issues

For potential data issues of SLAM, some data sources (e.g., health insurance claims database) may have open format data entries leading to services provided being described inconsistently. Multiple services could also be entered in one field. This could lead to some services be excluded in the actuarial analysis.

Also, there could be incorrect recording of members who have availed themselves of health services. This can happen when a child (dependent) is admitted but the name of the parent is entered as the member. Another example is services provided to the newborn registered under the name of the mother. This will lead to incorrect linking of the type of membership and the health services provided, leading to errors in estimating costs per type of member.

Lastly, changes in the membership type that are not reflected in the final claims data could lead to incorrect calculation of length of enrollment.

D.   Baseline Scenario

The SLAM recommends that expected costs and future trends for the provision of medical and nonmedical services for the insured populations be based on assumptions with regard to characteristics of the target population, incidences and prevalence of communicable diseases and chronic diseases, health-related events, and demographic and healthcare utilization trends.

The following text discusses baseline assumptions that users must identify before using the tool. Stepwise guides to setting up this required information are detailed in Chapter IV in Microsoft file.

1.   General Assumptions

Assumption 1: Number of Periods

The SLAM permits defining different periods, e.g., months, quarters, and years, to be used in the number of periods of projections. The number of periods can be set at 5, 10, or 15.

Assumption 2: Inflation for Expenditures

The inflation for expenditures corresponds to the inflation of the costs of the health insurance program for health expenditures of its members, i.e., payouts to health facilities used by its covered members. SLAM users may base their inflation assumptions on the data from the International Monetary Fund (IMF).[2]

Assumption 3: Inflation for Revenues

The inflation for revenues is the increase in premiums paid by enrolled members. In the baseline scenario, SLAM users are advised to set the premiums as increasing once annually with the inflation based on the IMF published data, or they may set the inflation for revenues to zero while keeping the inflation of expenditures increasing based on *Assumption 2*. The analyst should also check existing laws and program mandates that allow or restrict premium increases, if any.

2. Risk Loading, Administrative Loading, and Profit Margin Assumptions

Risk loading represents the uncertainty of actuarial estimates: the probability and size of the estimate being smaller than the actual payout. It also shows how big the risk the insurer is willing to run, and is typically defined as a percentage of the expected health payouts. The increases in the premium are meant to offset increases in the health expenditures because of the higher risk of not knowing the health needs of the target population.

Administrative loading meanwhile represents the administrative costs of running the health insurance program. It is typically defined as a percentage of the expected health payouts, a fixed amount, or a combination of both.

The profit margin represents the profit of health insurance program. It is typically defined as a percentage of the expected health payouts or a percentage of the positive operational cash flow.

Assumptions 4, 5, and 6: Risk Loading, Administrative Loading, and Profit Margins

All three are assumed to be zero in the Baseline Scenario.

3. Target Population and Member Assumptions

Assumption 7: Target Population

The target population refers to the population intended to be covered by the health insurance programs.

---

[2] International Monetary Fund (IMF). IMF DataMapper. Inflation rate, average consumer prices. https://www.imf.org/external/datamapper/PCPIPCH@WEO/OEMDC (28 September 2020).

Assumption 8: Maximum Size of the Target Population and of the Health Insurance Program

The maximum size of the target population is also the assumed maximum size of the health insurance program if all members of the target population will be enrolled in the program.

Assumption 9: Member Group—Children

These numbers represent the persons who belong to the "Children" subgroup of the target population with age range from 0 to 7 years old.

Assumption 10: Member Group—Formal Sector

These numbers represent the persons who belong to the "Formal Sector" subgroup of the target population with age range from 18 to 63.

Assumption 11: Member Group—Disabled

These numbers represent the persons who belong to the "Disabled" subgroup of the target population with age range from 18 to 63.

Assumption 12: Member Group—Pensioners

These numbers represent the persons who belong to the "Pensioners" subgroup of the target population with ages 64 and above.

Assumption 13: Member Group—State Order—Others

These numbers represent the persons who belong to the "State Order – Others" subgroup of the target population with age range from 18 to 63.

Assumption 14: Member Group—Everyone Else

These numbers represent the persons who belong to the "Everyone Else" subgroup of the target population.

Assumption 15: Mutually Exclusive Member Groups

The SLAM user and/or analyst is expected to define whether member groups defined in Assumptions 9 to 14 are mutually exclusive or not. That is, if a member can only belong to one subset of target member population. For purposes of clarity, it is recommended that only one mutually exclusive group be used.

Assumption 16: Member Groups Order of Precedence

In case a member defined in *Assumptions 9 to 14* is part of several subsets, the SLAM user is expected to define an order of precedence to be followed in the actuarial model. For instance if a member is registered as a "Formal Sector," but at the same time grouped as "State Order – Others," then in the SLAM it will be assumed that the member belongs to "State Order – Others" if the order of precedence in the analysis is "Disabled" > "State Order – Others" > "Formal Sector." Similarly, if a member of the formal sector is also registered as being disabled, then in the SLAM it will be assumed that the member is solely part of the group of "Disabled."

4.   Population Growth Rates

Assumption 17: Growth Rates of Subpopulations

The SLAM analysis requires defining growth percentages for the target population and its subgroups. The growth rates should not yet factor in dropout rates in the enrollment of these targeted member groups.

5.   Health Categories and Health Services

The SLAM makes a distinction between "Health Services" and "Health Categories." "Health Services" are the services provided to the members of the health insurance. All health services are then part of a subgroup or a "Health Category," which could be "General Surgery," "Cardiology," "Gynecology," or "Oncology," among others.

Assumption 18: Health Categories

The "Health Services" that are covered by health insurance packages must be grouped into "Health Categories." The SLAM allows for listing the same health services under more than one health category.

6.   Health Needs, Health Services, and Health Service Costs

"Health Needs" are the latent needs of the population in terms of healthcare services they need. While some health needs will be obvious, such as the need for a delivery at the end of a pregnancy, other health needs may not be apparent (for example the need for tuberculosis treatment for a patient unaware of his/her condition).

Since there is no information on the actual "Health Needs" as earlier described, the SLAM will assume that the "Health Services" represent the health needs of the insured household members.

To estimate the probability of a "Health Service" occurring, the Law of Large Numbers is applied in the SLAM analysis. The Law of Large Numbers or the related Central Limit Theorem states that in a large population (of insured) members, the probability of an event taking place and the height of the resulting claim will be close to the expected values. In practice, this means that to estimate the probability and value of future claims, past incidences and claim values could be used.

For each "Health Service" that is included in the benefit packages of health insurance scheme, costs, prices, and tariff of providers will be used by the SLAM program to predict the expected value of future claims from current and future health insurance program members.

Assumption 19: Predicting Future Health Needs

To estimate the probability and expected value of future claims of the current and future members of the health insurance program, it would be ideal to have a similar population of insured persons and multiple years of claims data.

To obtain "similar" groups, the "Members" should not only be disaggregated according to subgroups as defined in *Assumptions 9 to 14*, but also according to sex and age groups as seen relevant by the SLAM users and decision makers.

This means that one looks at how many of the similar persons needed a specific health service, say in 2018, and divide this by the number of periods these similar persons were insured in the same year.

In the SLAM, the modeling of future "Health Needs" is done per "Health Service" as defined in *Assumption 18* for each of the periods defined in Assumption 1 and standardized per 1,000; 10,000; or 100,000 members, per "Member Subpopulations" (i.e., subgroups defined in Assumptions 9 to 14).

Assumption 20: Stable Incidences and Prevalence Under the Baseline Scenario

In the Baseline Scenario, it is assumed that the incidences and prevalence of conditions do not change over time.

7.   Benefit Packages

The benefit packages are those that define what services are covered at which healthcare facilities, what approvals are needed to obtain insurance benefits, and the limitation of the insurance coverage, among others.

In the SLAM analysis, it should be determined if there is a distinction in terms of the services the members may avail, if any. The differences in terms of the premium contributions from various types of members should also be considered.

8.   Revenues from Premiums

The actuarial modeling requires the determination whether members are enrolled as individuals or part of a group enrollment. In the SLAM, the revenues are specified per sex and per age group by member subpopulations.

9.   Uptake and Retention

The uptake or enrollment rates is defined as 100% of the growth rate of the target populations defined in *Assumption 17*. The SLAM analysis requires users to determine renewal rates, which the SLAM will then automatically use to compute for retention rates and dropout rates.

CHAPTER III

Getting Started with the Simple Linear Actuarial Model in Microsoft Excel

This chapter provides an overview of the SLAM file, for its intended users, to opening the file, and then guide to the SLAM file contents. Details on how to use the data input worksheets are discussed in Chapter IV, while details on how results are derived and viewed are discussed in Chapter V.

In this chapter, variables and parameters are denoted in *blue italics*, buttons are described in **red underlined**, while emphasized information are in **black underlined**.

A. Users

Countries working toward Universal Health Coverage are direct users of the Microsoft Excel-based SLAM. Project processing teams supporting client countries will also benefit from having a readily-available tool for making projections to assess the financial sustainability of health insurance operations.

B. The File

The SLAM has been developed to be intuitive and user-friendly in their use, yet elaborate and versatile enough to deal with most issues faced in actuarial modeling.

SLAM software has been programmed into Microsoft Excel, while the calculations have been programmed into the Visual Basic for Applications (VBA). To prevent user errors, VBA functionality is also used with regard to automatic changes to the layout and adding and/or deleting estimation items (e.g., type of service categories).

This manual recommends the SLAM Excel file to follow the naming convention *Country_SLAM_File_version date* where the version date is in *YYYYMMDD* format. This manual, however, makes use of a Microsoft Excel File: **"SLAM - MANUAL version."** It has prefilled settings for the country *Armenia* with a few exemplary health categories, health services, and sample benefit packages as well. It is nested into one main folder (Figure 1).

Figure 1: Sample View of the SLAM Main Folder

May 2020

SLAM = Simple Linear Actuarial Model.

For organizational purposes, this manual recommends that the SLAM file be located in one main folder bearing the current version's month and year. The location and name of the folder may vary but the SLAM Excel file must not be renamed. If the SLAM Excel file is updated on a different date, save as a new file bearing the new version date. The main folder thus can contain multiple SLAM files bearing different date stamps. It is highly recommended to update the SLAM file one time after another to prevent overlapping of files. Also, it is recommended to have a "File Manager" that keeps tabs on SLAM file updates, as well as for consolidation, in case updating of input sheets would be assigned to multiple personnel.

C. Opening the SLAM in Microsoft Excel

To start the SLAM File, users must double click the file (Figure 2). Opening the file may take some time due to its large size.

Figure 2: Opening the SLAM File

SLAM - MANUAL version

SLAM = Simple Linear Actuarial Model.

If opened for the first time, a yellow Message Bar with **Protected View** prompt will appear (Figure 3). This information is provided by Microsoft for every file that originated from an internet source, which could be unsafe (i.e., obtained by sharing the file over the internet). Files from the internet and from other potentially unsafe locations can contain viruses, worms, or other kinds of malware, which can harm your computer. By using Protected View, users can read a file and inspect its contents while reducing the risks that can occur.

Closing the "protected view" prompt would make the file to remain protected where editing is restricted but viewing is allowed.

Figure 3: Protected View Message Bar

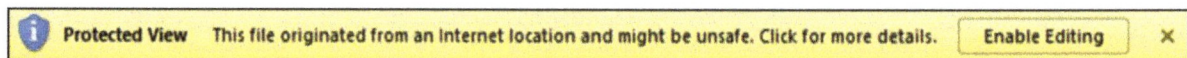

| ⓘ Protected View | This file originated from an Internet location and might be unsafe. Click for more details. | Enable Editing | ✕ |

To continue opening the file, click the **Enable Editing** button and another message bar with a **security warning** prompt will appear (Figure 4). This information is provided by Microsoft for every file that has active content (e.g., data connections, macros, among others) that may also contain viruses and other security hazards that could harm user's computer or network. If the source of the file is trusted or that the active content is known to be secure, enable the file's active content and click the **Enable Content** button. This makes the file a trusted document. Thus, when the file is reopened, the message bar does not appear.

Figure 4: Security Warning Message Bar

| ⚠ Security Warning | Macros have been disabled. | Enable Content | ✕ |

ⓘ FOR YOUR INFORMATION

In Microsoft Excel, Visual Basic for Applications (VBA) operates via add and delete buttons in specific inputs worksheets (i.e., 1.2A Service Categories and 1.2B Health Needs) to prevent users from making mistakes if they try to add or remove variables. The model that has been programmed in Excel is fairly complex and inadvertently adding or removing a row or column manually (without using VBA buttons) on one sheet has consequences on the formulas written on multiple other sheets.

As noted, the buttons to add or remove data fields in the Simple Linear Actuarial Model (SLAM) have been programmed in VBA. For SLAM to work, the macros embedded in the file must then be enabled. More details on VBA buttons are found in the Legend worksheet (Chapter III-D).

In addition, if the file is saved on a network location or in the Cloud, a different **Security Warning** message window (Figure 5). The user must then press <u>Yes</u> to proceed.

Figure 5: Security Warning Message Window

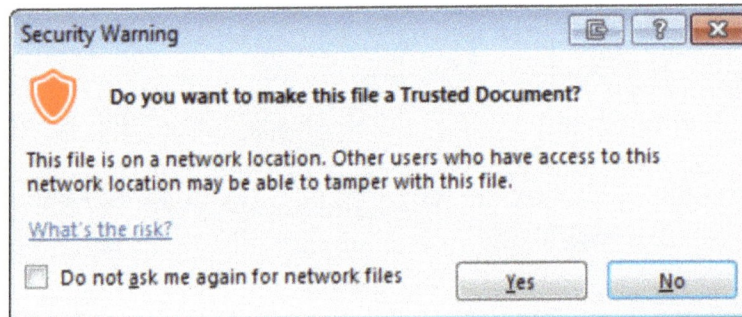

> **TAKE NOTE**
>
> In the event that the Security Warning prompt was not displayed, it is probably necessary to check or redefine the general security settings of the Excel program (Appendix, pp. 135–137).

Depending on the general security settings, the user may already be able to work with the opened SLAM Excel file. The easiest way to check if editing is already allowed is to try a button, for instance, to add an item in worksheet 1.2A Service Categories. To do this: (A) type in a sample category under *"Add a Service Category"* in **cell B8** and then (B) click <u>Add Item</u>. A message window (C) showing the input will be displayed and click <u>OK</u> (D) to continue (Figure 6).

Figure 6: Checking the Opened SLAM File for Allowed Editing Permission (Part 1)

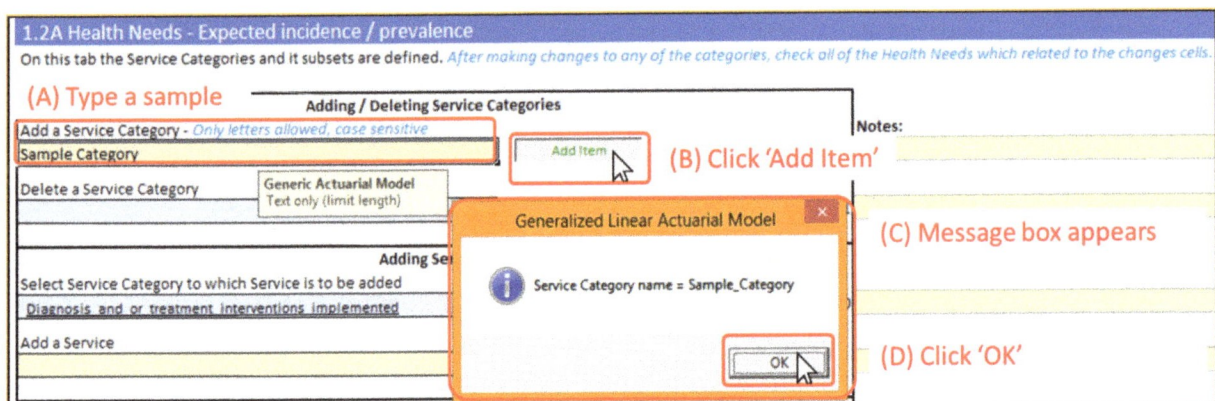

SLAM = Simple Linear Actuarial Model.

Note: Screenshot is from the 1.2A Service Categories worksheet.

A Message Box to assign a 3-character code to the new Service Category will be displayed. Input the desired code (e.g., "SAM") and click OK (Figure 7).

Figure 7: Checking the Opened SLAM File for Allowed Editing Permission (Part 2)

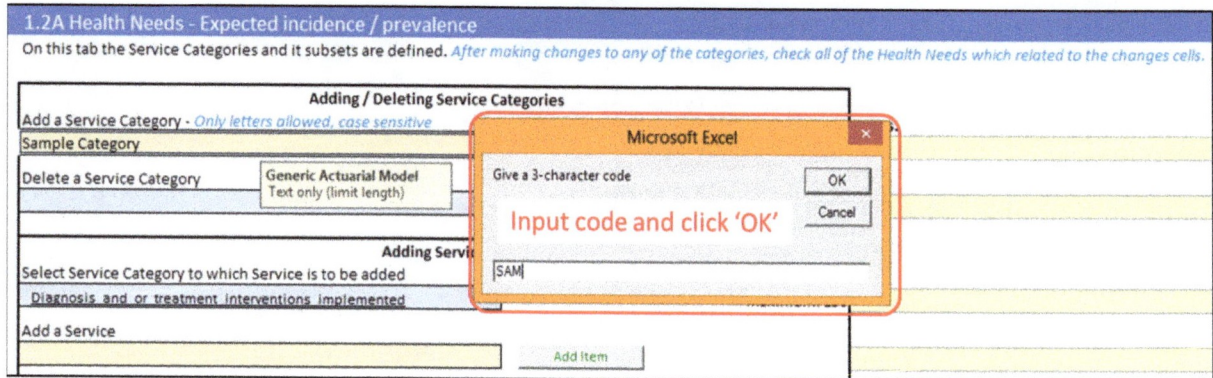

SLAM = Simple Linear Actuarial Model.

Note: Screenshot is from the 1.2A Service Categories worksheet.

The new service category will then be added at the bottom of the table, row 666 or line number 608 in the sample Figure 8 below.

Figure 8: New Row for Added Health Service

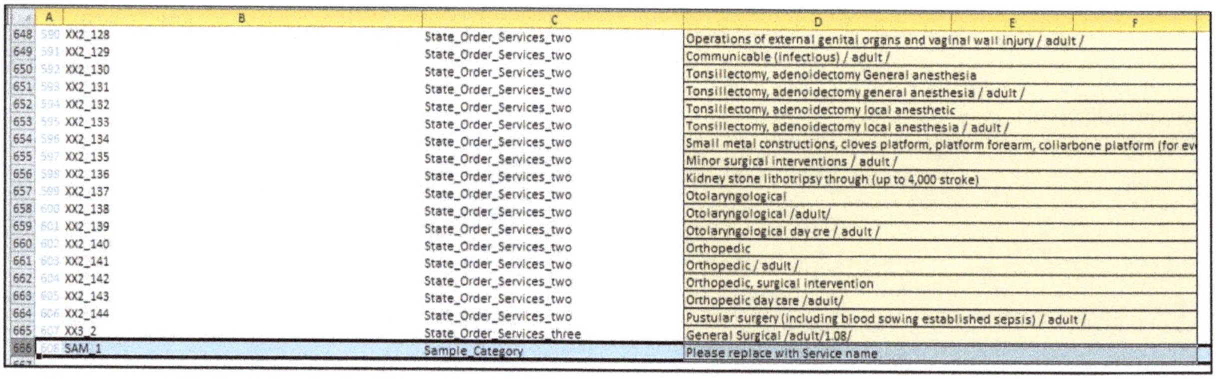

		A	C	D
648	590	XX2_128	State_Order_Services_two	Operations of external genital organs and vaginal wall injury / adult /
649	591	XX2_129	State_Order_Services_two	Communicable (infectious) / adult /
650	592	XX2_130	State_Order_Services_two	Tonsillectomy, adenoidectomy General anesthesia
651	593	XX2_131	State_Order_Services_two	Tonsillectomy, adenoidectomy general anesthesia / adult /
652	594	XX2_132	State_Order_Services_two	Tonsillectomy, adenoidectomy local anesthetic
653	595	XX2_133	State_Order_Services_two	Tonsillectomy, adenoidectomy local anesthesia / adult /
654	596	XX2_134	State_Order_Services_two	Small metal constructions, cloves platform, platform forearm, collarbone platform (for ev
655	597	XX2_135	State_Order_Services_two	Minor surgical interventions / adult /
656	598	XX2_136	State_Order_Services_two	Kidney stone lithotripsy through (up to 4,000 stroke)
657	599	XX2_137	State_Order_Services_two	Otolaryngological
658	600	XX2_138	State_Order_Services_two	Otolaryngological /adult/
659	601	XX2_139	State_Order_Services_two	Otolaryngological day cre / adult /
660	602	XX2_140	State_Order_Services_two	Orthopedic
661	603	XX2_141	State_Order_Services_two	Orthopedic / adult /
662	604	XX2_142	State_Order_Services_two	Orthopedic, surgical intervention
663	605	XX2_143	State_Order_Services_two	Orthopedic day care /adult/
664	606	XX2_144	State_Order_Services_two	Pustular surgery (including blood sowing established sepsis) / adult /
665	607	XX3_2	State_Order_Services_three	General Surgical /adult/1.08/
666	608	SAM_1	Sample_Category	Please replace with Service name

Note: Screenshot is from the 1.2A Service Categories worksheet.

TAKE NOTE

Undo or CTRL +Z does not work with most VBA buttons. The Delete button must be used to remove entries in worksheets where macros are used.

> **SUMMARY REMINDERS IN OPENING THE SLAM EXCEL FILE**
>
> **The SLAM file is located in one main folder bearing** the current version's month and year (e.g., May 2020). The location and name of the folder may vary.
>
> **The naming convention of the SLAM Excel file** follows *Country_SLAM_file_version date* where version date is in *YYYYMMDD* format.
>
> **The SLAM Excel file must not be renamed.** Save as a new file bearing the new version date.
>
> **Make sure** that the file being used is the latest version to date by checking the details of the file such as its *Name, Date modified, Type,* and *Size.*

D.   Guide to File Contents

The SLAM file is composed of 13 color-coded worksheet tabs grouped as follows:

- **Information tab** refers to the Legend worksheet, which explains the formatting of entries, cells, buttons, and tabs in the SLAM Excel file. This sheet is detailed in this section.
- **Input tabs refer** to worksheets 1.0 General Assumptions–1.6 Uptake and Retention, where data are encoded and parameters are set. These sheets are detailed in Chapter IV.
- **Result tabs** refer to worksheets Dashboard and 3.1 Results, where actuarial modeling results are shown. These sheets are detailed in Chapter V.

The worksheets from left to right of the File tabs are summarized in Table 1. Tab colors, on the other hand, are summarized in Table 2 and are also discussed in the succeeding Legend worksheet.

Table 1: Description of Worksheets and Color Tabs in the SLAM File

Worksheet Name	Description
Legend	Provides help or explanation in terms of the texts, cells, buttons, and tabs in the file.
Dashboard	Contains a quick overview of the SLAM Output, using tabular and graphical presentation of the results.
1.0 General Assumptions	Allows setting up the name and number of periods of projections; currency and exchange rate used for projections. inflation for expenditures and revenues, risk and administrative loading, profit margin, and discount rate.
1.1A Target Populations	Allows setting up of up to six target groups by age and sex distriution.
1.1B Growth Target Populations	Allows setting up growth rates of the specific sex and age brackets of people in each target group, per specified period.

continued on next page

Table 1 *continued*

Worksheet Name	Description
1.2A Service Categories	Allows for adding, deleting, and defining service categories (e.g., inpatient/outpatient) and respective subservices (e.g., wound dressing/twin delivery).
1.2B Health Needs	Allows setting up code; rate per population; group, sex, and age bracket of target group; incidence/prevalence; and inpatient days (if applicable), per health service.
1.3 Health Supply - Costs	Allows setting up cost, prices, and tariffs of providers per health service.
1.4 Benefit Packages	Allows setting up benefit package definition in terms of health service provider; and whether the benefit is for inpatient, outpatient, or both.
1.5 Revenues	Allows setting up premiums per age bracket and sex of target groups for individual or set group rates.
1.6 Uptake and Retention	Allows for setting up number or percentage of members of the target population that are new enrollees and re-enrolls at the end the specified period of enrollment.
2.0 Generate Results	Provides a "Generate Results" button that updates the 3.1 Results worksheet.
3.1 Results	Shows the time series of results in tabular format for population projection; health needs; enrollment projections; expenditures projections; revenue projections inclusive and exclusive of risk loading/profit margin/premium increase; cash flow projections; discounted cash flow; expenditures per enrollee; revenues per enrollee; cash flow per enrollee; cash flow as % of revenues; and cash flow as % of expenditures.

SLAM = Simple Linear Actuarial Model.

Table 2: Color-Coding of Worksheet Tabs in the SLAM File

Tab Color	Worksheet Description
Green	Accessible worksheet that provides results in a dashboard interface.
Gray	Accessible worksheet that provides help and explanations.
Light Gold	Accessible worksheets that provide assumptions on general input.
Light Orange	Accessible worksheets that provide assumptions on benefit packages.
Dark Orange	Locked worksheet that enables updating the results worksheet.
Light Green	Locked worksheet that provides results in tabular form.

SLAM = Simple Linear Actuarial Model.

The Legend Worksheet

To serve as a guide, a Legend worksheet (Figure 9) was created as the default worksheet (i.e., first sheet of the SLAM file) to explain the basic contents (e.g., How the texts and numeric entries are formatted in the succeeding worksheets, among others).

Figure 9: Preview of the Legend Worksheet

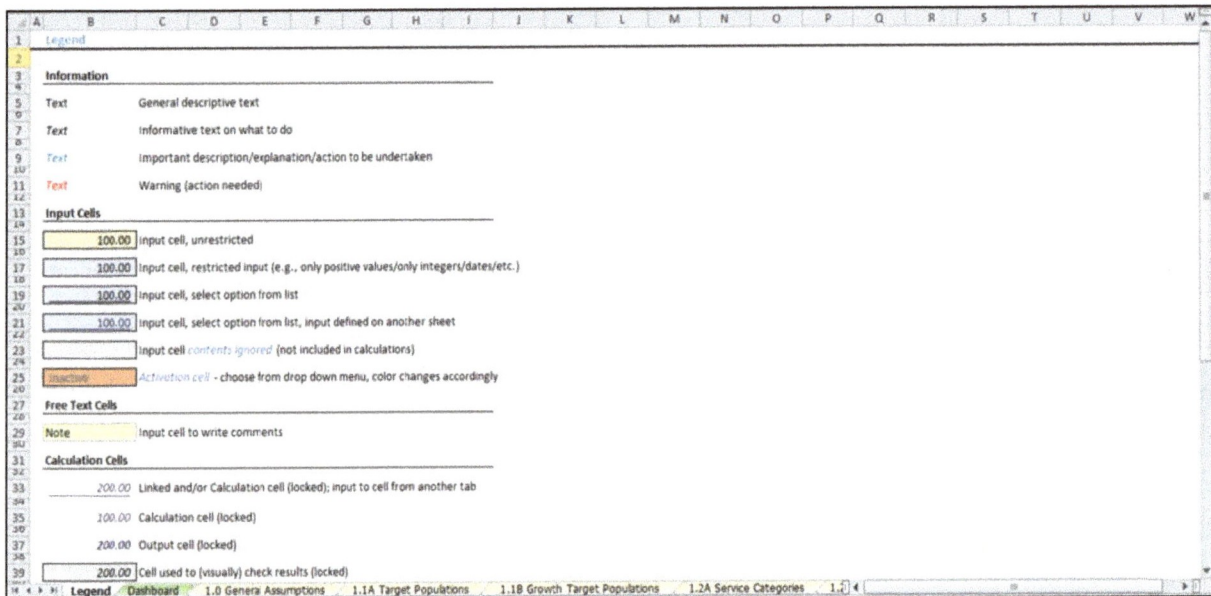

Item blocks in this worksheet are about (i) information, (ii) input cells, (iii) free text cells, (iv) calculation cells, (v) buttons, and (vi) tabs, as explained below. Contents of this worksheet will also be shown in message boxes for subsequent sections, where applicable, to better appreciate stepwise details in navigating and using SLAM.

Information

Color-coding of informative texts used throughout the SLAM worksheets is shown in Figure 10. Explanatory texts, mostly in black font are provided in white background (see Figure 11 for samples). Important description, explanation, or actions to be undertaken are in blue font (see Figure 12 for sample). "Warning" texts are provided in red to highlight if there is an action needed that may result in error if not correctly inputted (see Figure 13 for sample). Some cells will also change color if certain inputs are contradictory or not allowed in the default settings.

Figure 10: Guide to Information Texts in the Legend Worksheet

INFORMATION	
Text	General descriptive text
Text	Informative text on what to do
Text	Important description / explanation / action to be undertaken
Text	Warning (action needed)

Figure 11: Sample Explanatory Texts

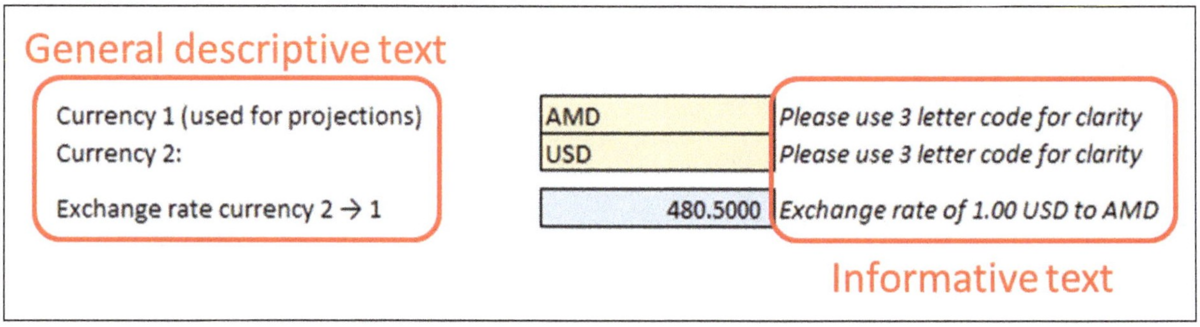

General descriptive text

Currency 1 (used for projections)	AMD	*Please use 3 letter code for clarity*
Currency 2:	USD	*Please use 3 letter code for clarity*
Exchange rate currency 2 → 1	480.5000	*Exchange rate of 1.00 USD to AMD*

Informative text

Note: The screenshot above is from the "1.0 General Assumptions" worksheet.

Figure 12: Sample of Important Description, Explanation, or Actions to be Undertaken

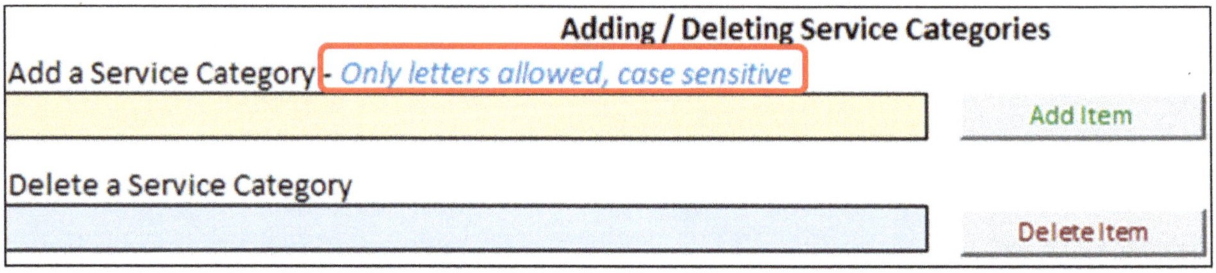

Adding / Deleting Service Categories

Add a Service Category - *Only letters allowed, case sensitive*

| | Add Item |

Delete a Service Category

| | Delete Item |

Note: Screenshot from the 1.2A Service Categories worksheet.

Figure 13: Sample Warning Text

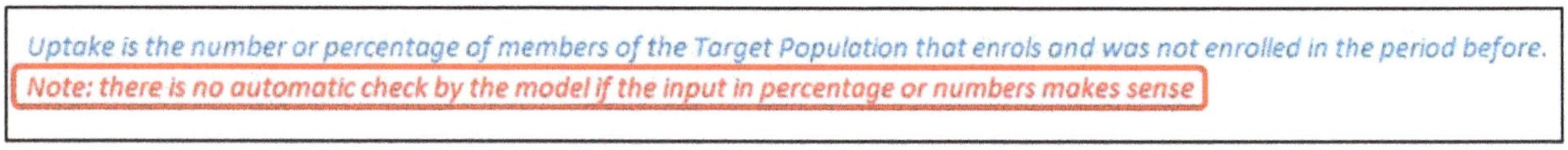

Uptake is the number or percentage of members of the Target Population that enrols and was not enrolled in the period before.
Note: there is no automatic check by the model if the input in percentage or numbers makes sense

Note: Screenshot from the 1.6 Uptake and Retention worksheet.

Input Cells

Color-coding of input cells for encoding and setting up of data is illustrated in Figure 14. These input cells can either be unrestricted, provided in orange background (see Figure 15 for sample); or restricted, provided in blue background. Restrictions in the input cells may include encoding only positive numeric values, integers, dates, and others, in black font (see Figure 16 for sample) or selection from a drop-down list in an underlined black font (see Figure 17 for sample). Furthermore, if the input to the drop-down list is defined on another worksheet (to the left of the current tab being used), it is shown using an underlined navy blue font (see Figure 18 for sample).

Figure 14: Guide to Input Cells Texts in the Legend Worksheet

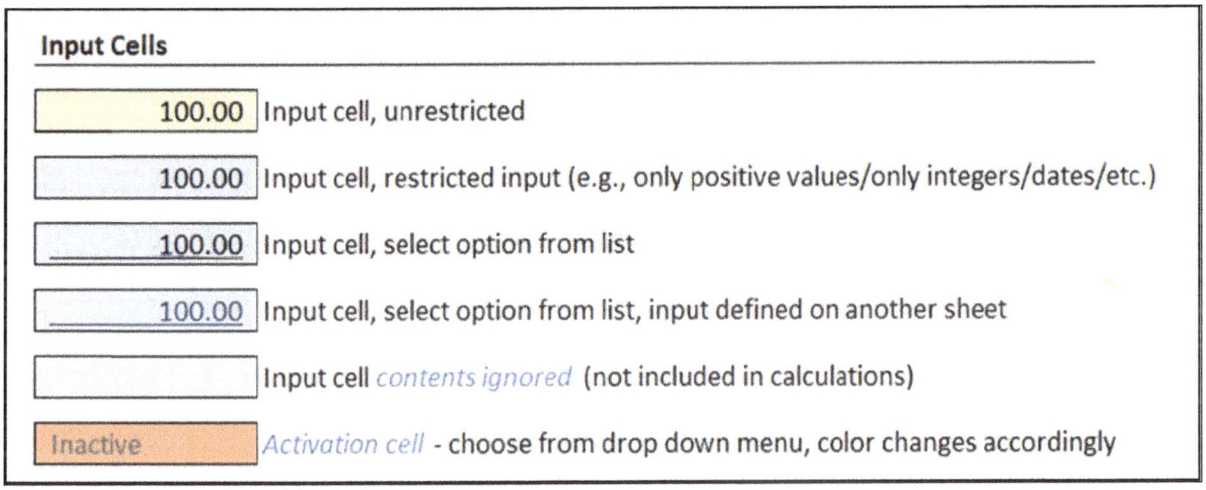

Input Cells

100.00	Input cell, unrestricted
100.00	Input cell, restricted input (e.g., only positive values/only integers/dates/etc.)
100.00	Input cell, select option from list
100.00	Input cell, select option from list, input defined on another sheet
	Input cell *contents ignored* (not included in calculations)
Inactive	*Activation cell* - choose from drop down menu, color changes accordingly

Figure 15: Sample Unrestricted Input Cells

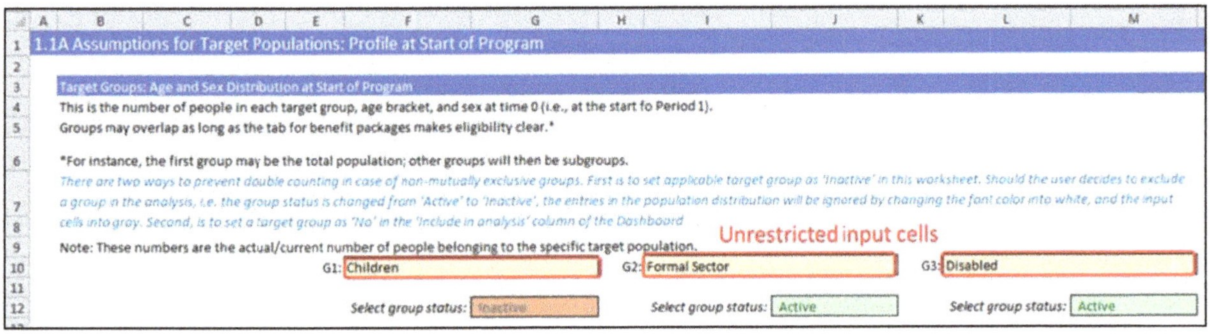

Note: Screenshot from the 1.1A Target Populations worksheet.

Figure 16: Sample Restricted Input Cells

Various samples of restricted input cells

A

Inflation, by Period

	Expenditures	Revenues
1	0.917%	0.917%
2	2.522%	2.522%

B

Note: these are the 'living' people, not the numbers of (potentially) enrolled members

G1: **Children**

Select group status: **Active**

	≥ Lower Bound	Upper Bound
1	0	1
2	2	7

	Females	Males
	39,060	44,238
	116,431	132,242

Note: Screenshot A is from the 1.0 General Assumptions worksheet, while screenshot B is from the 1.1A Target Populations worksheet.

Figure 17: Sample Input Cell Restricted with Drop-Down List

Input cell restricted with dropdown list

Select number of Periods: **15.00** ▾ *te: with this number the Number of Periods of Projections is also defined*

5
10
15

ost often the period will be equal to a year or a month

Note: Screenshot is from the 1.0 General Assumptions worksheet.

Figure 18: Sample Input Cell where Input is Defined from Another Sheet

	A	C	D	E	F	G	H	I
3		1.2B Health Needs - Expected incidence / prevalence						
4							Sensitivity factc	
5		Specify item (row number)			Specify number items to be added / deleted	Periods of projection		
6			Add 1 Item		1	Add Multiple Items		
7			Delete 1 Item		1	Delete Multiple Items		
8		14568	: Current number of items (max 20,000)					
9					Sample input cell where entries are defined in another worksheet			
10		Service		per 1,000 / 10,000 Specify sub target population				
11		Service Category	Service provided	/ 100,000	Target population		Age LB Age UB	
13	1	Burn	Burn treatment cases	100,000	G2: Formal Sector	Simple Linear Actuarial Model Defined on '1.1A Target Populations'		
14	2	Cardiology	Coronary geography (including contrast material cost of anes	100,000	G2: Formal Sector			
15	3	Cardiology	Drug eluted 2 stent stenting (in the State)	100,000	G2: Formal Sector			
16	4	Cardiology	One Drug eluted stent two non medical eluted stent	100,000	G2: Formal Sector	Female	18	24
17	5	Cardiology	Stenting with drug eluted 3 stent	100,000	G2: Formal Sector	Female	18	24
18	6	Cardiology	Stenting with drug eluted 4 stent	100,000	G2: Formal Sector	Female	18	24
19	7	Cardiology	Magistral and peripheral artery stenting, the stent	100,000	G2: Formal Sector	Female	18	24
20	8	Cardiology	Coronary artery balloon dilatation using one cylinder	100,000	G2: Formal Sector	Female	18	24

Note: Screenshot from the 1.2B Health Needs worksheet.

The use of restriction in the input cells minimizes erroneous entries that the programmed SLAM file cannot understand or prevents the contents from being accidentally deleted. For instance, following Figure 16 and setting negative values to expenditures and sex as an example will prompt error reminders shown in Figure 19. The use of drop-down list in Figure 17, on the other hand, ensures that the parameter has the required information.

Figure 19: Sample Message Prompts for Encoding Incorrect Entries in Restricted Input Cells

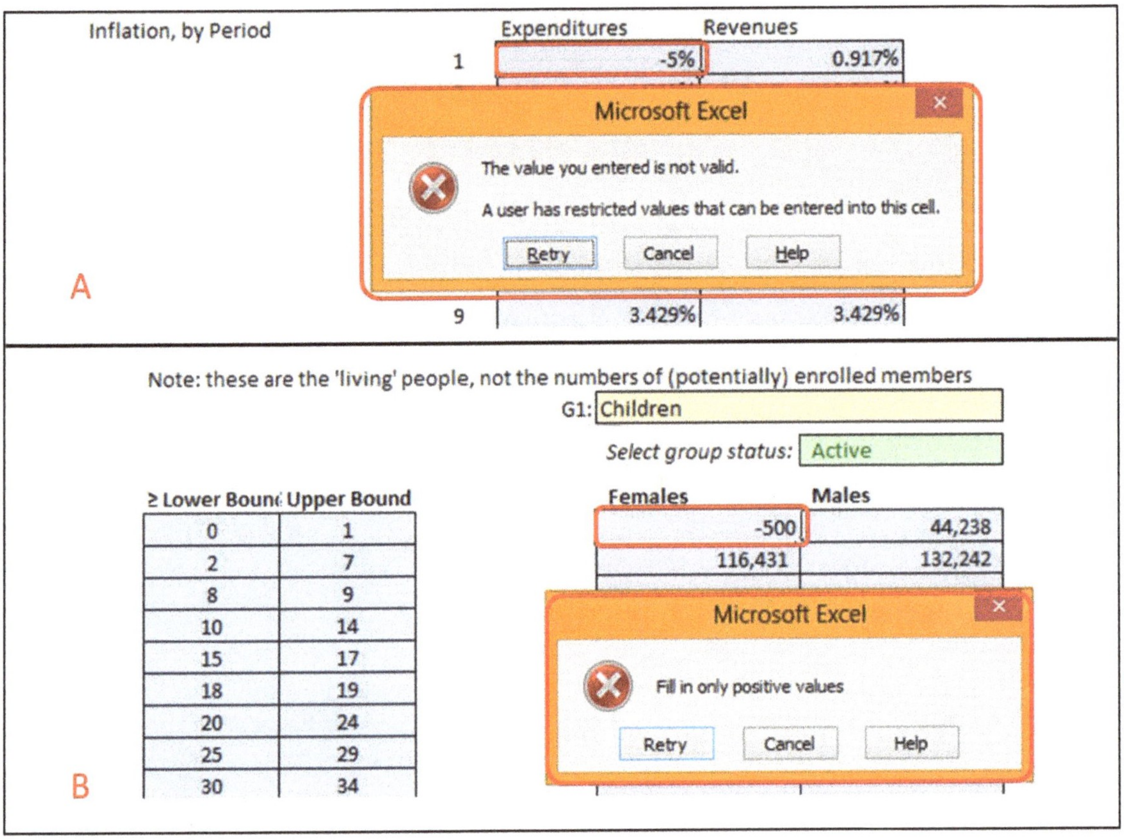

Note: Screenshot A is from the 1.0 General Assumptions worksheet, while screenshot B is from the 1.1A Target Populations worksheet.

Other input cells defined by SLAM are the ignored and activation cells. Activation cells the set status of a variable or an indicator from active (i.e., included in the projections), denoted by a green input cell, or inactive (i.e., not taken into account), denoted by a red input cell. Inactivated entries where input values are ignored are denoted by a gray input cell with white texts. Screenshot B of Figure 19 shows an active status for sample subgroup *Children*, provided in green background. This means that the identified subgroup is included in the analysis. Figure 20, on the other hand, shows an example where the same subgroup, *Children*, is inactivated and ignored.

Figure 20: Sample Inactivated and Ignored Input Cells

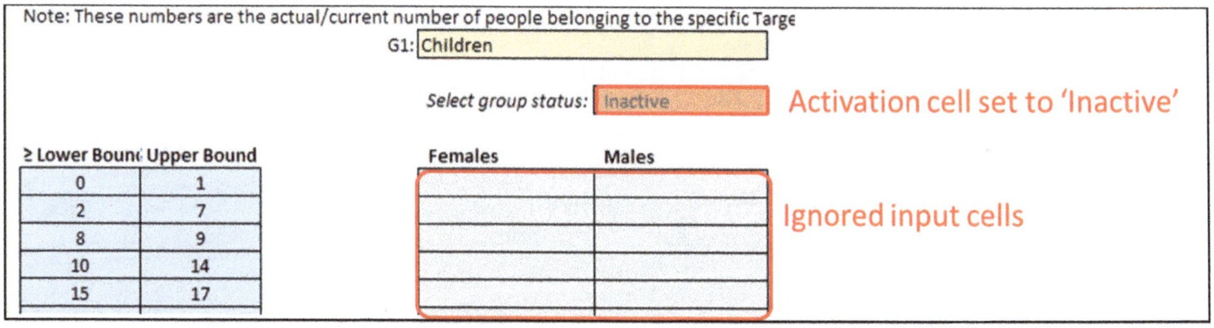

Note: Screenshot from the 1.1A Target Populations worksheet

Free Text Cells

Each row where data can be entered has a corresponding free text cell for adding explanations, comments, sources, or other helpful texts (Figure 21). These are needed so that other managers and users can understand the data.

Figure 21: Guide to Free Text Cells in the Legend Worksheet

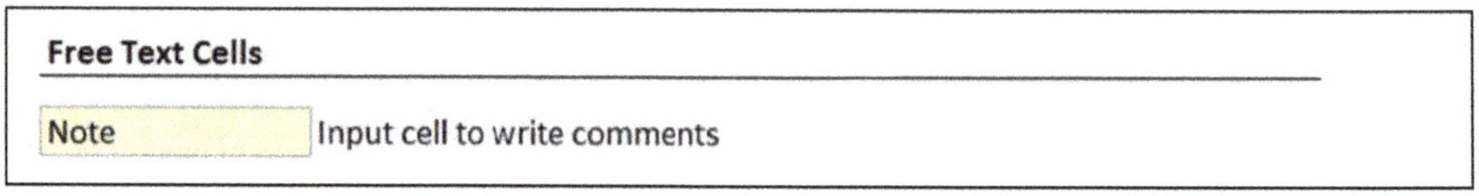

These notes in yellow background are not used in the calculations and are commonly located at the right side of the screen, next to the input cells (Figure 22). They can also be located above or below group of input cells (Figure 23).

Figure 22: Sample Free Text Cells Located Next to Input Cells

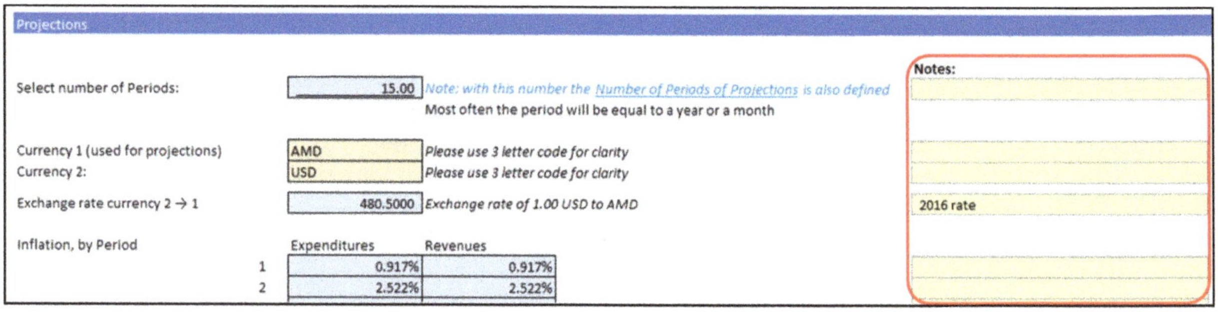

Notes: AMD = Armenian dram, USD = United States dollar. Screenshot is from the 1.0 General Assumptions worksheet.

Figure 23: Sample Free Text Cells Located Above or Below Group of Input Cells

		G1: Children		G2: Formal Sector	
		Select group status: Active		*Select group status:* Active	
≥ Lower Boun(	Upper Bound	Females	Males	Females	Males
0	1	39,060	44,238		
2	7	116,431	132,242		
8	9				
10	14				
15	17				
18	19			17,317	19,405
20	24			59,033	57,374
25	29			74,666	69,402
30	34			70,613	64,468
35	39			57,969	52,752
40	44			49,957	43,380
45	49			47,935	40,064
50	54			57,832	47,403
55	59			62,419	51,250
60	63			38,056	29,586
64	69				
70	74				
75					
		155,491	*176,480*	*535,797*	*475,083*

Notes: Notes:

A

G1: Children

Group status *Active* Notes:

Females

Age bracket	Period 1	Period 2	Period 3	Period 4	Period 5	Period 6	Period 7	Period 8
[0 - 1]	-2.71%	-2.78%	-2.86%	-2.95%	-2.47%	-2.53%	-2.60%	-2.67%
[2 - 7]	-1.38%	-1.42%	-1.46%	-1.50%	-2.22%	-2.27%	-2.33%	-2.38%
[8 - 9]	-0.05%	-0.05%	-0.05%	-0.05%	-1.97%	-2.01%	-2.05%	-2.10%
[10 - 14]	2.99%	2.91%	2.82%	2.75%	0.73%	0.73%	0.72%	0.71%
[15 - 17]	-1.04%	-1.05%	-1.07%	-1.08%	3.09%	3.00%	2.91%	2.83%

Age bracket	Period 9	Period 10	Period 11	Period 12	Period 13	Period 14	Period 15
[0 - 1]	-2.74%	-2.19%	-2.24%	-2.29%	-2.35%	-2.40%	-1.06%
[2 - 7]	-2.44%	-2.33%	-2.39%	-2.45%	-2.51%	-2.57%	-1.63%
[8 - 9]	-2.14%	-2.47%	-2.54%	-2.60%	-2.67%	-2.74%	-2.20%
[10 - 14]	0.71%	-1.97%	-2.01%	-2.06%	-2.10%	-2.14%	-2.48%
[15 - 17]	2.75%	0.74%	0.73%	0.73%	0.72%	0.72%	-1.99%

B

Note: Screenshot A is from the 1.1A Target Populations worksheet, while screenshot B is from the 1.1B Growth Target Populations worksheet.

Calculation Cells

The cells containing formulas where calculations take place are also color-coded as shown in (Figure 24). Locked cells mean that the contents cannot be altered without a password to unlock the sheet. This is to prevent accidental changes in the formulas that can have a great impact on the estimated outcomes. See Figures 25 to 27 for samples in the SLAM Excel file.

Figure 24: Guide to Calculation Cells in the Legend Worksheet

Calculation Cells

200.00 Linked and/or Calculation cell (locked); input to cell from another tab

100.00 Calculation cell (locked)

200.00 Output cell (locked)

200.00 Cell used to (visually) check results (locked)

Figure 25: Sample Linked and/or Calculation Cell (Locked)

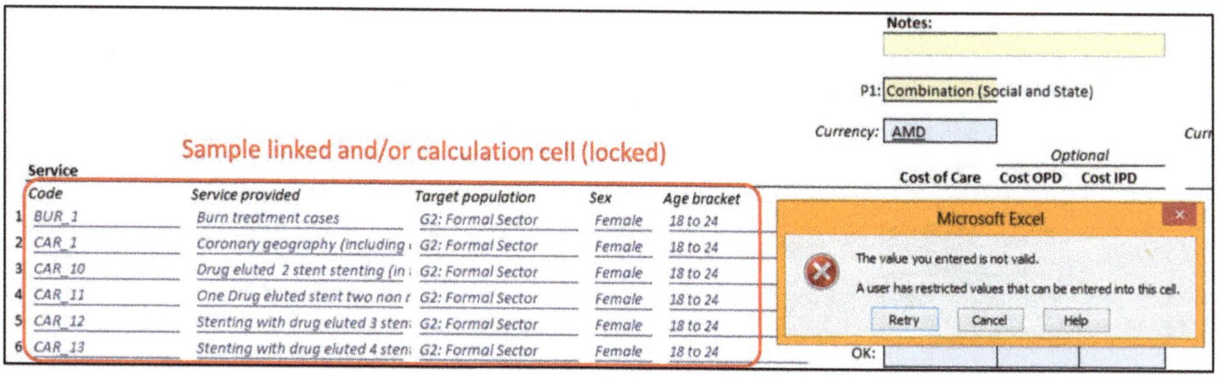

Note: Screenshot is from the 1.3 Health Supply—Costs worksheet..

Figure 26: Sample Output Cell (Locked)

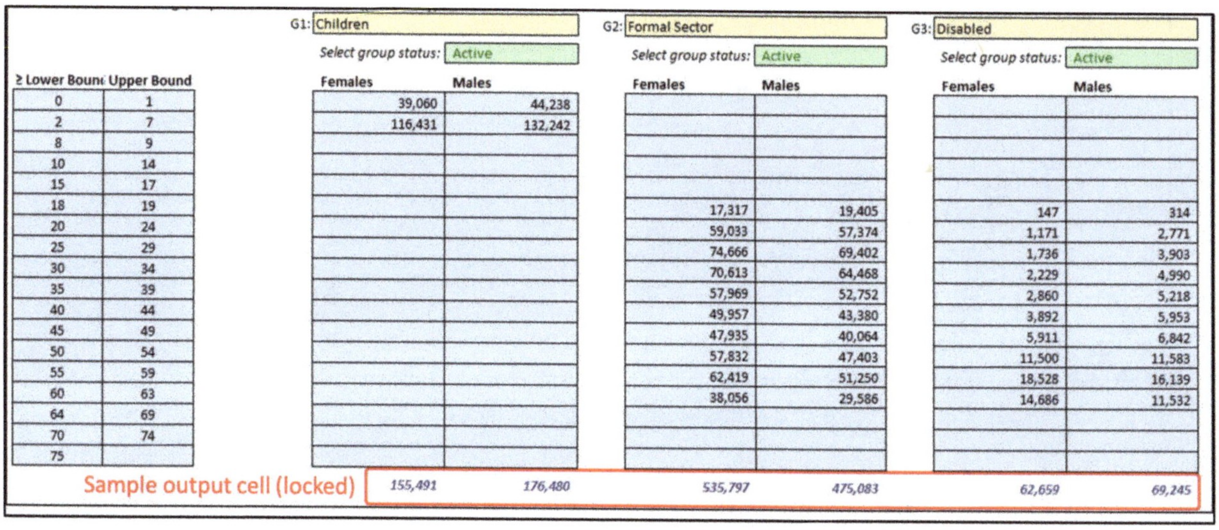

Note: Screenshot from the 1.1A Target Populations worksheet.

Figure 27: Sample of Cells Used to Visually Check Results (Locked)

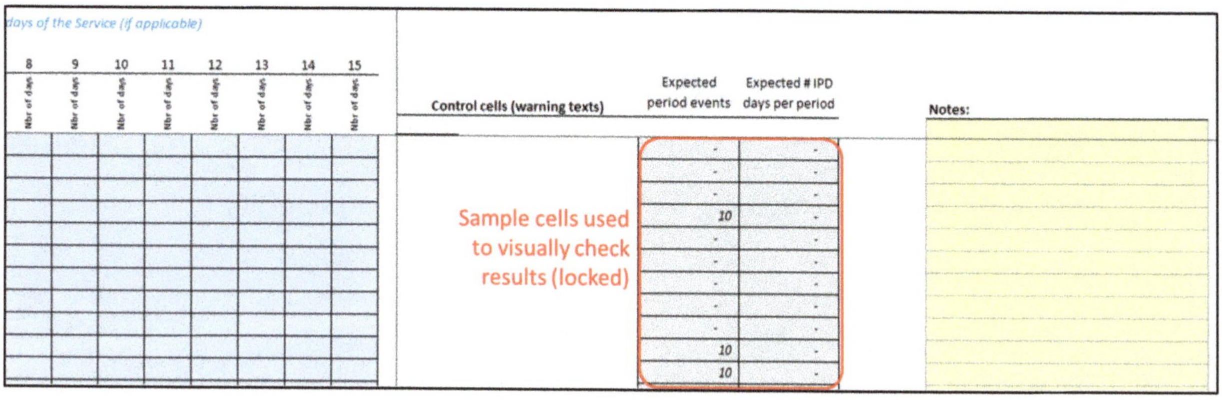

Note: Screenshot from the 1.2B Health Needs worksheet.

Buttons

Buttons in the SLAM file are also color-coded (Figure 28). Bold italics in orange means an action must be performed, for instance after cell values have been changed. Green text on a button means to add an item, and red text means to delete an item (see Figure 29 for sample buttons). Blue text on a button, meanwhile, means an option may be selected or an optional action may be performed (see Figure 30 for sample buttons).

Figure 28: Guide to Buttons in the Legend Worksheet

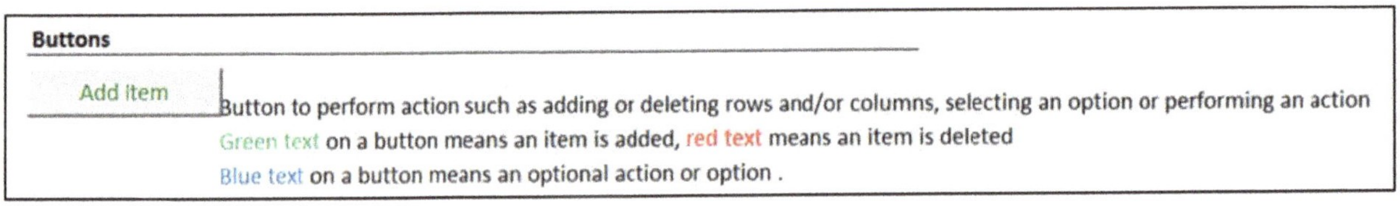

Buttons

Add Item	Button to perform action such as adding or deleting rows and/or columns, selecting an option or performing an action
	Green text on a button means an item is added, red text means an item is deleted
	Blue text on a button means an optional action or option .

The **add** and **delete** buttons (Figure 29) in specific inputs sheets (i.e., 1.2A Service Categories and 1.2B Health Needs) are programmed using the Microsoft Excel Visual Basic for Applications (VBA). These VBA-operated buttons prevent users from making mistakes if they were to add or remove variables themselves. The model that has been programmed in Excel is fairly complex and inadvertently adding or removing a row or column manually (without the use of VBA buttons) on one sheet has consequences on the formulas written on multiple other sheets.

Figure 29: Sample Add and Delete Buttons in Visual Basic for Applications

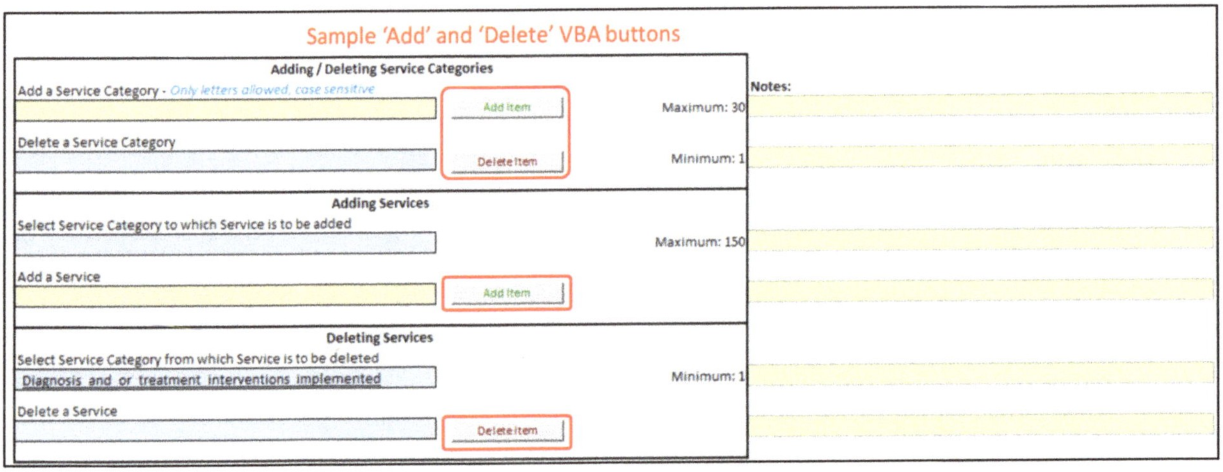

Note: Screenshot from the 1.2A Service Categories worksheet.

On the other hand, an **apply** button (Figure 30) found in 1.5 Revenues worksheet allows users to implement a simple distribution over age groups.

Figure 30: Sample Apply Buttons in Visual Basic for Applications

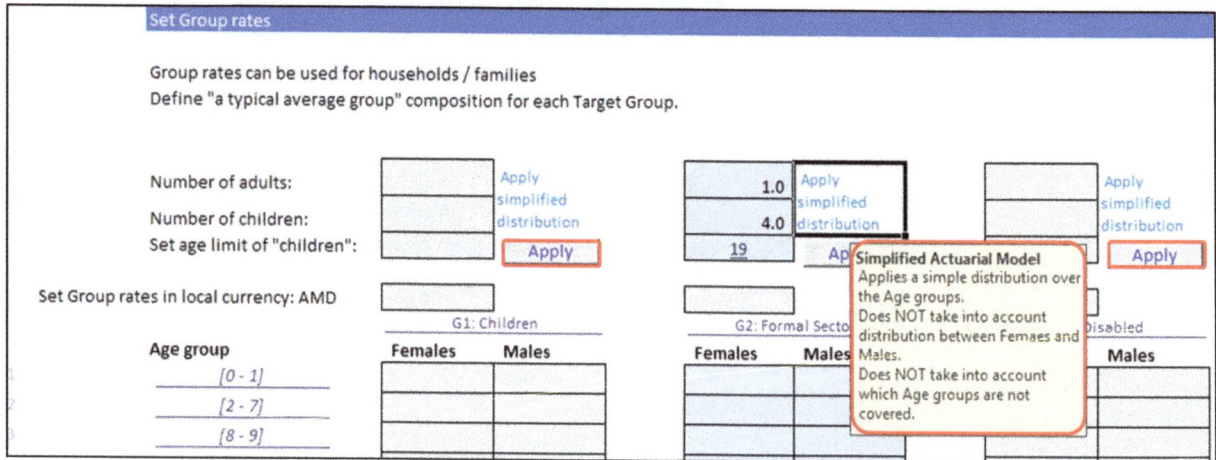

Note: Screenshot from the 1.5 Revenues worksheet.

Tabs

Last, a guide to worksheet tabs is shown in Figure 31 and summarized in Table 2. The gray tab refers to the Legend sheet; the green tab refers to the Dashboard results; the light gold tabs refer to assumptions on general input; the light orange tabs are for assumptions on benefit packages; dark orange tabs refer to generate results; and light green tabs refer to results in tabular form.

Figure 31: Guide to Tabs in the Legend Worksheet

Grouped Rows and Columns

In some worksheets, range of cells can be tied together so they can be collapsed or expanded. Selected rows and/or columns can be grouped using the Data > Outline > Group tab in Microsoft Excel (Figure 32).

Figure 32: The Data > Outline > Group Tab in Microsoft Excel

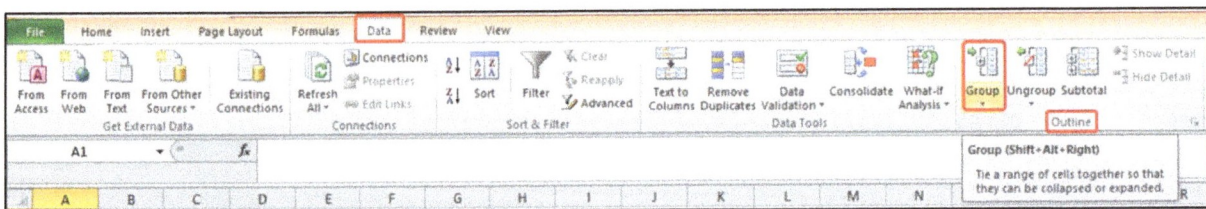

A worksheet has grouped cells if outline symbols `1 2`, `+`, and/or `−` are present in column or row headings of the worksheet window. In the SLAM Excel file, this is applicable to worksheets 1.2A Service Category (Figure 33), 1.2B Health Needs (Figure 34), 1.3 Health Supply–Costs (Figure 35), and 1.4 Benefit Packages (Figure 36). This is preferred as an alternative to hiding rows or columns as it remains visible where rows or columns have been grouped and hidden from view.

Figure 33: Grouped Cells in the 1.2A Service Category Worksheet

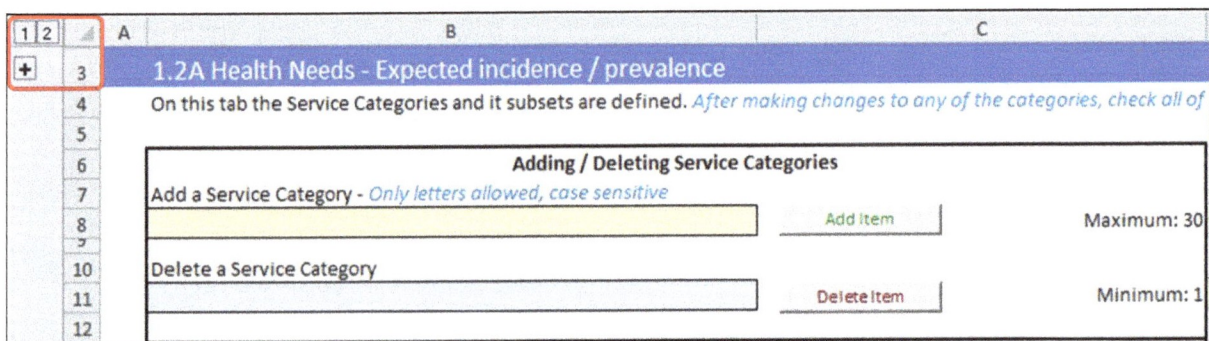

Figure 34: Grouped Cells in the 1.2B Health Needs Worksheet

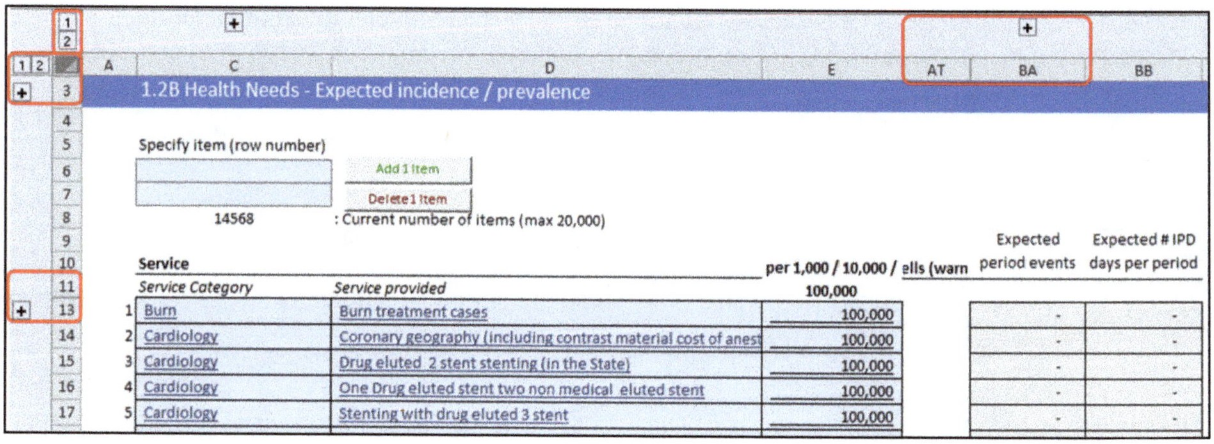

Note: Screenshot contains hidden rows for illustration purposes only.

Figure 35: Grouped Cells in the 1.3 Health Supply—Costs Worksheet

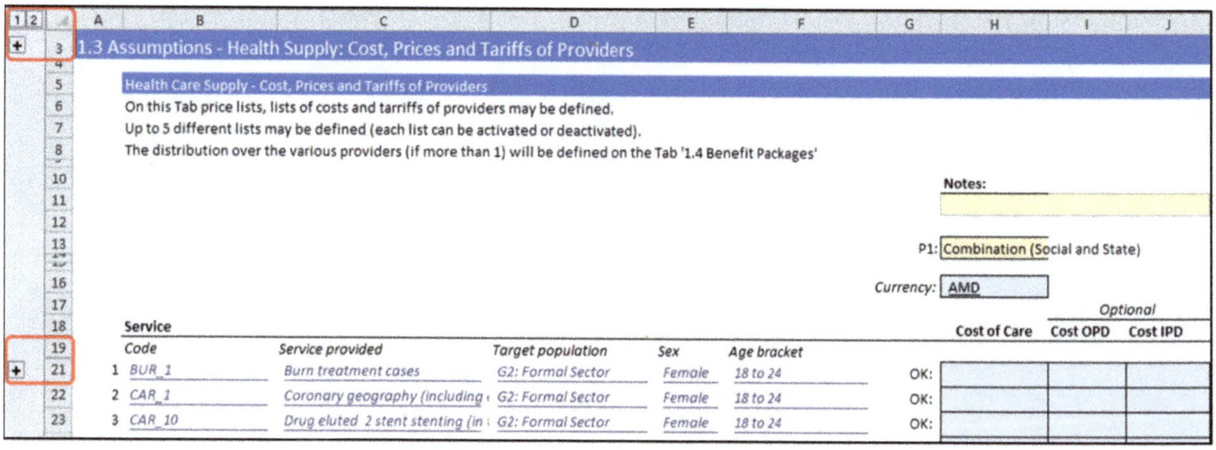

Figure 36: Grouped Cells in the 1.4 Benefit Packages Worksheet

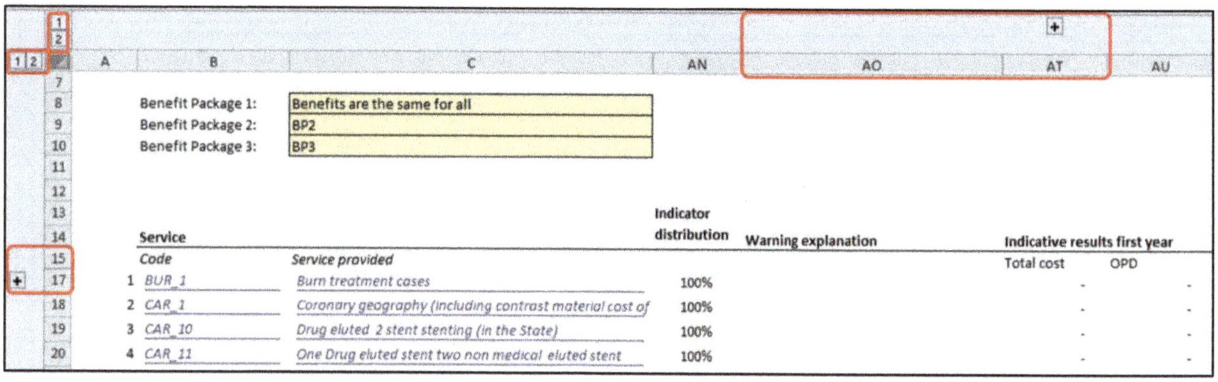

Note: Screenshot contains hidden rows for illustration purposes only.

These hidden rows and columns are used only in programming purposes and are locked from the user's access (Figure 37).

Figure 37: Collapsed Cells Locked for Programming Purposes

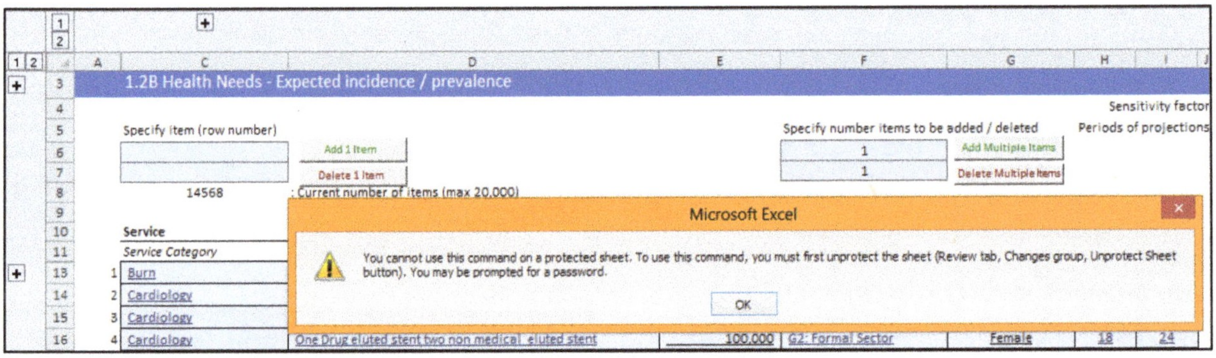

Note: Screenshot is from the 1.2B Health Needs worksheet.

CHAPTER IV

Using the SLAM File

This chapter explains the steps on using the SLAM File per corresponding worksheet, from setting up general assumptions, choosing the target population, and up to setting up uptake and retention parameters. Viewing results, summary tables, and charts of estimates are discussed in Chapter V. Meanwhile, overview up to opening of the file is discussed in Chapter III.

The data should first be entered on the sheets on the left (excluding the Legend and the Dashboard worksheet), while working toward the sheets on the right. Specifically, the first sheet where data must be entered is the 1.0 General Assumptions worksheet and the last input sheet is the 1.6 Uptake and Retention worksheet. It is important to follow this rule working from left to right, as sheets on the right are dependent on the information entered on the sheets to the left.

In this chapter, variables and parameters are denoted in *blue italics*, buttons are described in **red underlined**, while emphasized information are in **black underlined**.

A.   The 1.0 General Assumptions Input Sheet

This worksheet (Figure 38) allows setting up the *Name* and *Number of Periods* of projections, *Currencies and Exchange Rate* used for projections, *Inflation for Expenditures* and *Inflation for Revenues, Risk Loading* and *Administrative Loading, Profit Margin,* and *Discount Rate. Specifically,* this worksheet provides for inputting the following assumptions described in *Chapter II-D*:

- Assumption 1: Number of periods.
- Assumption 2: Inflation for expenditures.
- Assumption 3: Inflation for revenues.
- Assumption 4: Risk loading.
- Assumption 5: Administrative loading.
- Assumption 6: Profit margins.

Figure 38: Preview of the 1.0 General Assumptions Worksheet

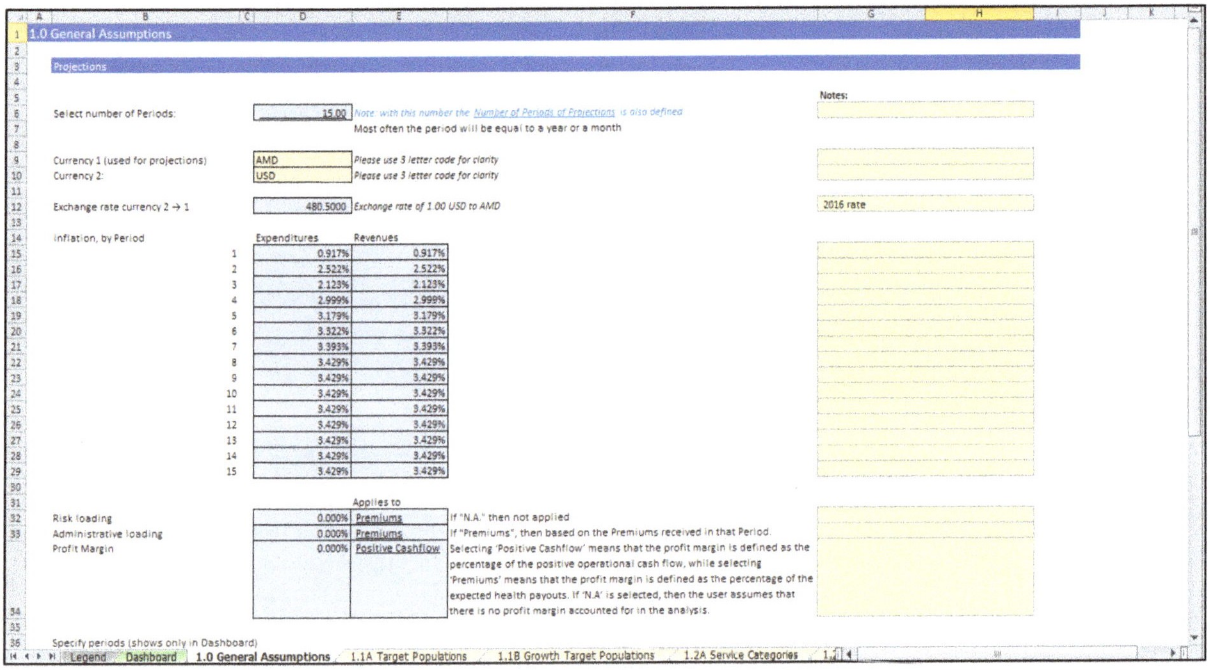

FOR YOUR INFORMATION

Cells found in this worksheet include:

Input Cells

100.00	Input cell, unrestricted
100.00	Input cell, restricted input (e.g., only positive values/only integers/dates/etc.)
100.00	Input cell, select option from list

Free Text Cells

Note	Input cell to write comments

- Unrestricted input cells that accept alphanumeric keys;
- Restricted input cells for encoding only positive numeric values;
- Restricted input cells for selection from a drop-down list; and
- Free text cells next to input cells, for adding corresponding explanations, comments, sources, or other helpful texts pertaining to encoded information.

Number of Periods

Cell D6 allows users to *select number of periods* (Assumption 1) (Figure 39). A drop-down menu is provided for the selection of the number of periods (5, 10, or 15) that will be used in the SLAM analysis. The cell is restricted so that user will not be able to type in any values apart from those included in the drop-down list.

Figure 39: Input Cell for Select Number of Periods in the 1.0 General Assumptions Worksheet

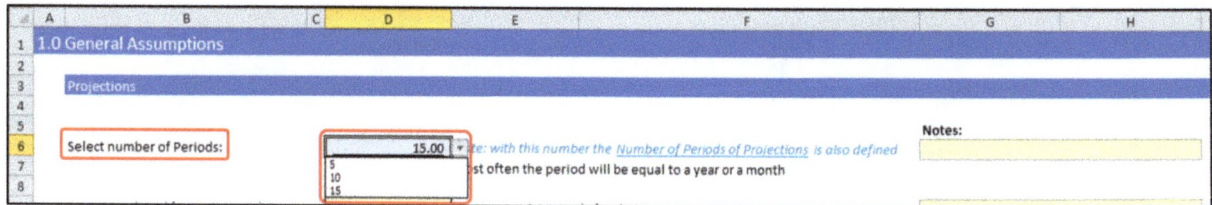

The number selected in cell D6 will be equal to the number of periods of projections that will be used in the SLAM analysis. The user must indicate in the *Notes* column (Figure 40) the definition of the period (e.g., whether in months, quarters, or years).

Figure 40: Input Cell for Notes on Select Number of Periods in the 1.0 General Assumptions Worksheet

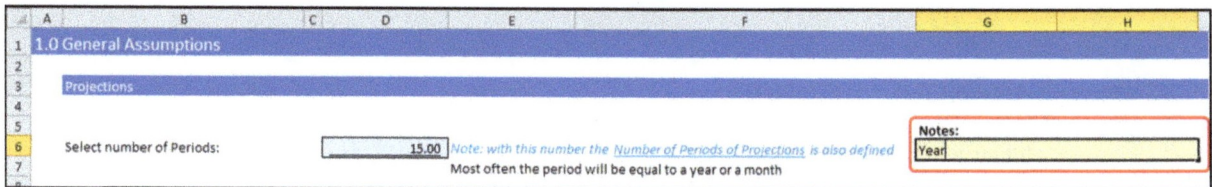

Currencies

The currency that will be used for projections (*Currency 1*) must be inputted in **cell D9**; another currency that can be used for conversion (*Currency 2*), if needed, must be inputted in **cell D10**. See Figure 41 for illustration.

Figure 41: Input Cells for Currencies in the 1.0 General Assumptions Worksheet

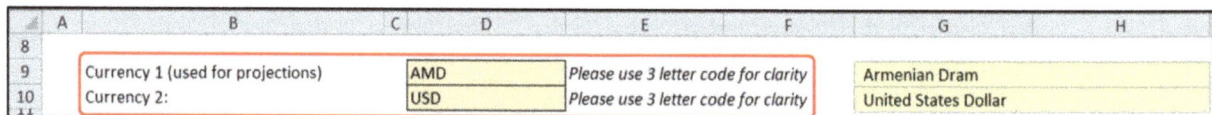

The input cells for currencies are unrestricted but it is recommended to input only the standard three-letter currency code, while document in the *Notes* column (Figure 42) the name of the currencies.

Figure 42: Input Cells for Notes on Currencies in the 1.0 General Assumptions Worksheet

A	B	C	D	E	F	G	H
8							
9	Currency 1 (used for projections)		AMD	*Please use 3 letter code for clarity*		Armenian Dram	
10	Currency 2:		USD	*Please use 3 letter code for clarity*		United States Dollar	

Exchange Rate

The official *Exchange Rate* between currencies must be inputted in **cell D12** (Figure 43), with the date of the exchange rate recorded in **cell G12** (Figure 44). The source of the data must also be entered in the *Notes* for complete documentation. Note that as per programming of restricted input cells, cell D12 will only accept numeric entries.

Figure 43: Input Cell for Exchange Rate in the 1.0 General Assumptions Worksheet

A	B	C	D	E	F	G	H
11							
12	Exchange rate currency 2 → 1		480.5000	*Exchange rate of 1.00 USD to AMD*		2016 rate	
13							

Figure 44: Input Cell for Notes on Exchange Rate in the 1.0 General Assumptions Worksheet

A	B	C	D	E	F	G	H
11							
12	Exchange rate currency 2 → 1		480.5000	*Exchange rate of 1.00 USD to AMD*		2016 rate	
13							

Inflation for Expenditures and Revenues

The expected *Inflation of Expenditures* (*Assumption 2*) that corresponds to the inflation of costs of the health expenditures must be inputted in **cells D15 to D29** (Figure 45). As discussed in Chapter II-D1, users may base their assumption on inflation for expenditures based on the data from the International Monetary Fund (IMF).

Figure 45: Input Cells for Inflation of Expenditures in the 1.0 General Assumptions Worksheet

			Expenditures	Revenues			
	A	B	C	D	E	F	G	H
14	Inflation, by Period			Expenditures	Revenues			
15			1	0.917%	0.917%			
16			2	2.522%	2.522%			
17			3	2.123%	2.123%			
18			4	2.999%	2.999%			
19			5	3.179%	3.179%			
20			6	3.322%	3.322%			
21			7	3.393%	3.393%			
22			8	3.429%	3.429%			
23			9	3.429%	3.429%			
24			10	3.429%	3.429%			
25			11	3.429%	3.429%			
26			12	3.429%	3.429%			
27			13	3.429%	3.429%			
28			14	3.429%	3.429%			
29			15	3.429%	3.429%			

Meanwhile, the expected *Inflation of Revenues* (Assumption 3) or inflation on the premiums to be paid by enrolled members must be recorded in cells **E15 to E29** (Figure 46). In the baseline scenario, it is recommended to set the premiums as increasing once per year, with the inflation based on the IMF data used in the assumed inflation for expenditures. SLAM users may also opt to set the inflation revenues to zero while keeping the inflation of expenditures increasing. The decision here should be dependent on the national laws governing the rate premium setting, if any.

Figure 46: Input Cells for Inflation of Revenues in the 1.0 General Assumptions Worksheet

	A	B	C	D	E	F	G	H
14	Inflation, by Period			Expenditures	Revenues			
15			1	0.917%	0.917%			
16			2	2.522%	2.522%			
17			3	2.123%	2.123%			
18			4	2.999%	2.999%			
19			5	3.179%	3.179%			
20			6	3.322%	3.322%			
21			7	3.393%	3.393%			
22			8	3.429%	3.429%			
23			9	3.429%	3.429%			
24			10	3.429%	3.429%			
25			11	3.429%	3.429%			
26			12	3.429%	3.429%			
27			13	3.429%	3.429%			
28			14	3.429%	3.429%			
29			15	3.429%	3.429%			

Input cells for inflation expenditures and revenue are restricted to accept only numeric entries. Data sources, on the other hand, must be encoded under the *Notes* column (Figure 47). Since periods are labeled as "1" for the first period, "2" for the second period, and so on, it is recommended that the actual corresponding year/quarter/month also be recorded in the *Notes* column for complete documentation.

Figure 47: Input Cells for Notes on Inflation of Expenditures and Revenues
in the 1.0 General Assumptions Worksheet

Figure 47: Input Cells for Notes on Inflation of Expenditures and Revenues
in the 1.0 General Assumptions Worksheet

	A	B	C	D	E	F	G	H
14		Inflation, by Period			Expenditures	Revenues			
15				1	0.917%	0.917%			
16				2	2.522%	2.522%			
17				3	2.123%	2.123%			
18				4	2.999%	2.999%			
19				5	3.179%	3.179%			
20				6	3.322%	3.322%			
21				7	3.393%	3.393%			
22				8	3.429%	3.429%			
23				9	3.429%	3.429%			
24				10	3.429%	3.429%			
25				11	3.429%	3.429%			
26				12	3.429%	3.429%			
27				13	3.429%	3.429%			
28				14	3.429%	3.429%			
29				15	3.429%	3.429%			

Risk Loading

The *risk loading* (*Assumption 4*) estimate is the increase in premium that is meant to offset increases in the health expenditures of the insurance program due to the higher risk of not knowing the actual health needs of its target population. **Cell D32** allows the users to input the expected percentage of risk loading to the premiums (Figure 48).

Figure 48: Input Cell for Risk Loading in the 1.0 General Assumptions Worksheet

	A	B	C	D	E	F	G	H
31					Applies to			
32		Risk loading		0.000%	Premiums	If "N.A." then not applied		

The default setting in the SLAM File is 0.000%, which is applied to premiums as defined in the drop-down menu in **cell E32** (Figure 49). A user, however, may opt to input a positive value in cell D32 and apply it to premiums. The user may decide later to change the baseline scenario and not apply the risk loading value inputted on cell D32. Instead of deleting the risk loading value, the user may in turn select "N.A." in cell E32.

Figure 49: Input Cell for Application of Risk Loading
in the 1.0 General Assumptions Worksheet

	A	B	C	D	E	F	G	H
31					Applies to			
32		Risk loading		0.000%	Premiums	"N.A." then not applied		
		Administrativ		0	N.A.	"Premiums", then based		
33					Premiums	the Premiums received		

The basis of the risk loading assumption must then be recorded in the *Notes* column (Figure 50)

Figure 50: Input Cell for Notes on Risk Loading in the 1.0 General Assumptions Worksheet

	A	B	C	D	E	F	G	H
31					Applies to			
32		Risk loading		0.000%	Premiums	If "N.A." then not applied		

Administrative Loading

Administrative Loading (Assumption 5) is typically defined as a percentage of the expected health payouts, a fixed amount, or a combination of both. SLAM only allows users to represent the administrative costs of running the health insurance program as a percentage of premiums. Similar to the risk loading assumption, the percentage must be recorded in **cell D33** (Figure 51) and the premium must be selected from the drop-down menu provided in **cell E33** (Figure 52). The user may also choose "N.A." if the administrative loading factor will not be included in the analysis.

Figure 51: Input Cell for Administrative Loading in the 1.0 General Assumptions Worksheet

	A	B	C	D	E	F	G	H
31					Applies to			
32		Risk loading		0.000%	Premiums	If "N.A." then not applied		
33		Administrative loading		0.000%	Premiums	If "Premiums", then based on the Premiums received in that Period.		

Figure 52: Input Cell for Application of Administrative Loading in the 1.0 General Assumptions Worksheet

	A	B	C	D	E	F	G
31					Applies to		
32		Risk loading		0.000%	Premiums	If "N.A." then not applied	
33		Administrative loading		0.000%	Premiums	Premiums", then based on the Premiums received in that Period.	
		Profit Margin		0.000%	N.A. / Premiums	ecting 'Positive Cashflow' means that the profit margin is defined as the percentage of the positive operational cash flow, while selecting 'Premiums'	

The basis of the administrative loading assumption must then be recorded in the *Notes* column (Figure 53).

Figure 53: Input Cell for Notes on Administrative Loading in the 1.0 General Assumptions Worksheet

	A	B	C	D	E	F	G	H
31					Applies to			
32		Risk loading		0.000%	Premiums	If "N.A." then not applied		
33		Administrative loading		0.000%	Premiums	If "Premiums", then based on the Premiums received in that Period.		

Profit Margin

The *Profit Margin* (*Assumption 6*) must be recorded as a percentage in **cell D34** (Figure 54), while the factor on how it is defined and calculated must be selected from the drop-down menu in **cell E34** (Figure 55). Cells D32 to D34 are restricted to only accept numeric entries, while cells E32 to E34 are limited to the options listed in the drop-down menus.

Figure 54: Input Cell for Profit Margin in the 1.0 General Assumptions Worksheet

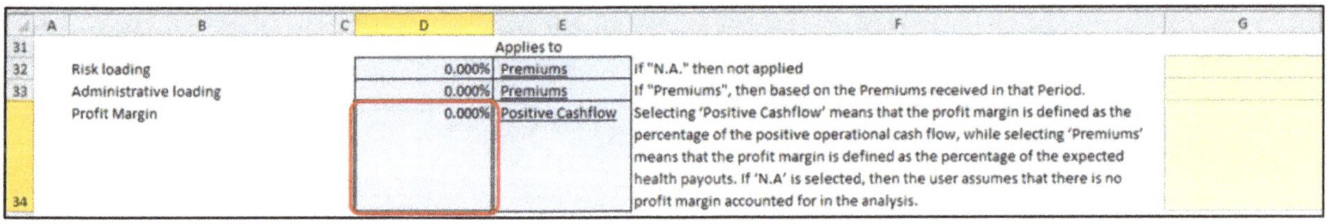

Figure 55: Input Cell for Application of Profit Margin in the 1.0 General Assumptions Worksheet

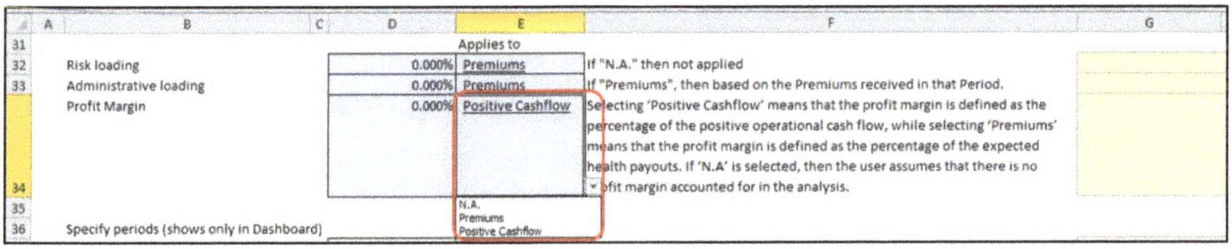

Selecting positive cashflow means that the profit margin is defined as the percentage of the positive operational cash flow, while selecting premiums means that the profit margin is defined as the percentage of the expected health payouts. If "N.A." is selected, then the user assumes that there is no profit margin accounted for in the analysis.

The basis of the profit margin assumption must then be recorded in the *Notes* column (Figure 56).

Figure 56: Input Cell for Notes on Administrative Loading in the 1.0 General Assumptions Worksheet

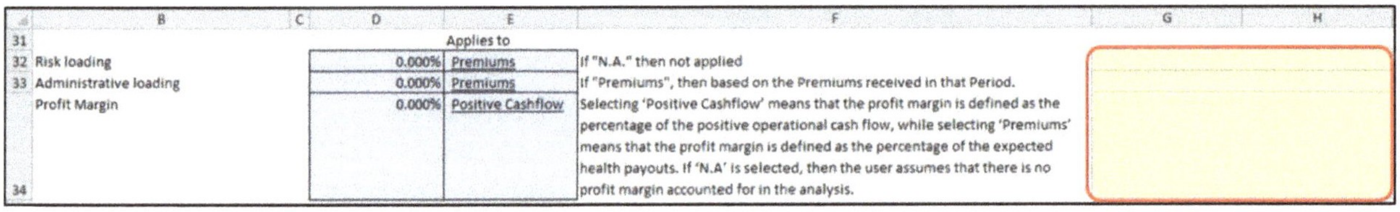

Name of Period

The *Name of Period* that will be used to define periods 1–15 must be recorded in **cells D37 to D51** (Figure 57). The identified labels will be displayed only in the Dashboard.

Figure 57: Input Cells for Name of Period in the 1.0 General Assumptions Worksheet

	A	B	C	D	E	F	G	H
36		Specify periods (shows only in Dashboard)						
37			1	2017				
38			2	2018				
39			3	2019				
40			4	2020				
41			5	2021				
42			6	2022				
43			7	2023				
44			8	2024				
45			9	2025				
46			10	2026				
47			11	2027				
48			12	2028				
49			13	2029				
50			14	2030				
51			15	2031				

Further details and information about the label of periods must then be recorded in the *Notes* column for documentation (Figure 58).

Figure 58: Input Cells for Notes on Name of Period in the 1.0 General Assumptions Worksheet

	A	B	C	D	E	F	G	H
36		Specify periods (shows only in Dashboard)						
37			1	2017				
38			2	2018				
39			3	2019				
40			4	2020				
41			5	2021				
42			6	2022				
43			7	2023				
44			8	2024				
45			9	2025				
46			10	2026				
47			11	2027				
48			12	2028				
49			13	2029				
50			14	2030				
51			15	2031				

Discount Rate

For the scenario analysis (see Chapter VI), users may set a *Discount Rate* to estimate discounted cash flows in reviewing insurance premiums. **Cell D53** (Figure 59) provides the input cell to define the said discount rate.

Figure 59: Input Cell for Discount Rate in the 1.0 General Assumptions Worksheet

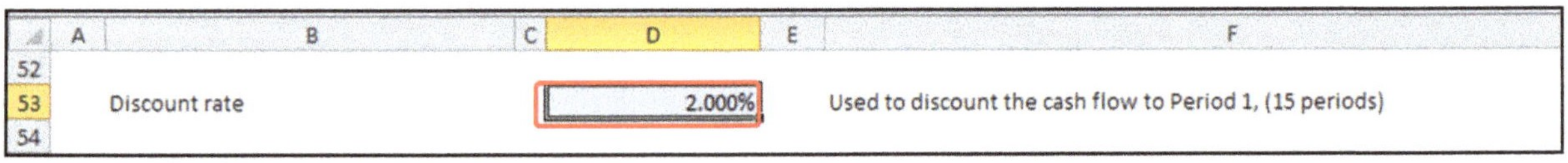

	A	B	C	D	E	F
52						
53		Discount rate		2.000%		Used to discount the cash flow to Period 1, (15 periods)
54						

The 1.1A Target Populations Input Sheet

This worksheet allows for the definition of the profile of the population that is considered for the insurance coverage (Figure 60). It provides setting up of up to six *target groups* by *age bracket* and *sex*. Specifically, this worksheet provides for inputting the following assumptions described in Chapter II-D:

- Assumption 7: Target Population
- Assumption 9: Member Group (Children)
- Assumption 10: Member Group (Formal Sector)
- Assumption 11: Member Group (Disabled)
- Assumption 12: Member Group (Pensioners)
- Assumption 13: Member Group (State Order–Others)
- Assumption 14: Member Group (Everyone Else)
- Assumption 15: Mutually Exclusive Member Groups
- Assumption 16: Member Groups Order of Precedence.

Figure 60: Preview of the 1.1A Target Populations Worksheet

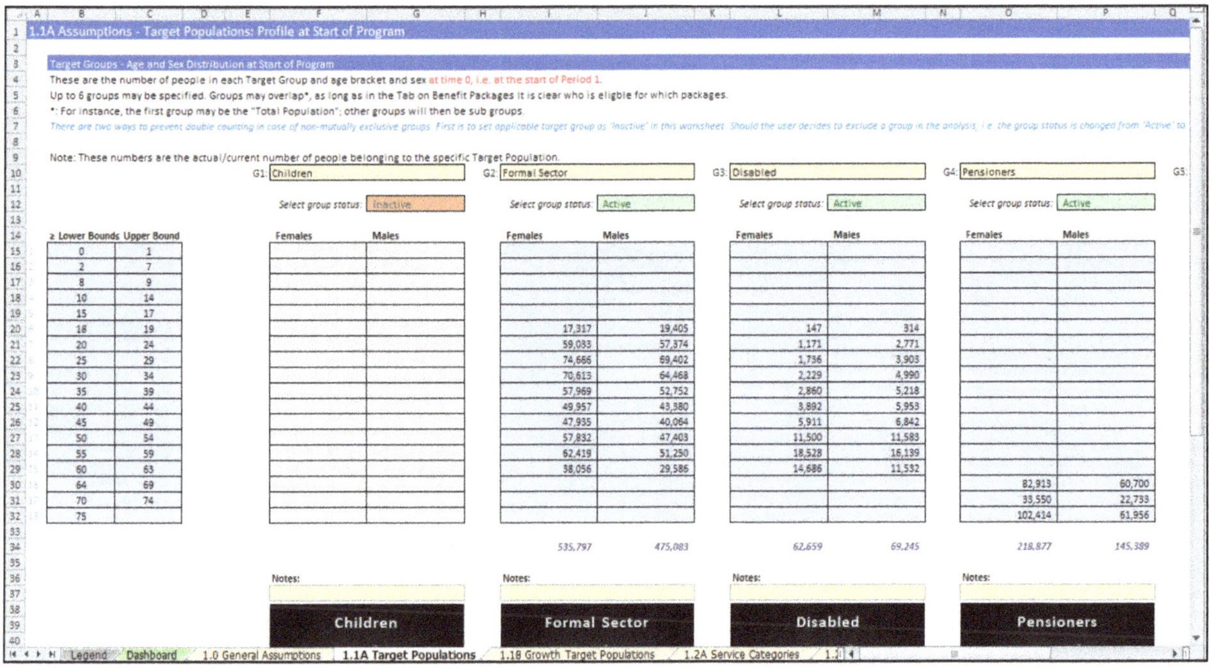

FOR YOUR INFORMATION

Cells found in this worksheet include:

Input Cells

100.00	Input cell, unrestricted
100.00	Input cell, restricted input (e.g., only positive values/only integers/dates/etc.)
	Input cell *contents ignored* (not included in calculations)
Inactive	*Activation cell* - choose from drop down menu, color changes accordingly

Free Text Cells

Note	Input cell to write comments

Calculation Cells

100.00	Calculation cell (locked)

- Unrestricted input cells that accept alphanumeric keys;
- Restricted input cells for encoding only positive numeric values;
- Ignored input cells where entries are not considered in calculations and analyses;
- Activation cells which activate or inactive parameters;
- Free text cells, below input cells, for adding corresponding explanations, comments, sources, or other helpful texts pertaining to the encoded information; and
- Output cells that are locked for editing and show results of calculations within the worksheet.

Target Groups and Status

Row 10 provides the input cells for Assumptions 9–14 to define the name of the *target groups* that belong to the target population identified in Assumption 7 (Figure 61). Up to six Target Population groups may be specified. The following groups are specified in the current SLAM Excel file:

- Group 1: Children
- Group 2: Formal Sector
- Group 3: Disabled
- Group 4: Pensioners
- Group 5: State Order–Others
- Group 5: Everyone Else

Figure 61: Input Cells for Name of Target Groups in the 1.1A Target Populations Worksheet

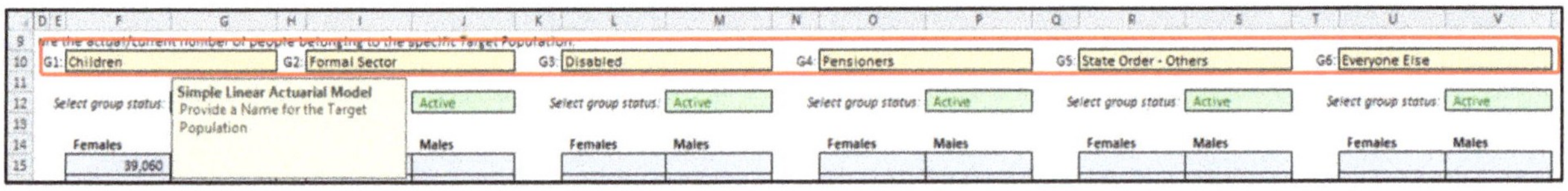

Row 12, meanwhile, allows for the determination of *Group Status* (Figure 62) and whether the said target group will be included in the projections (active) or not taken into account (inactive).

Figure 62: Input Cells for Group Status of Target Groups in the 1.1A Target Populations Worksheet

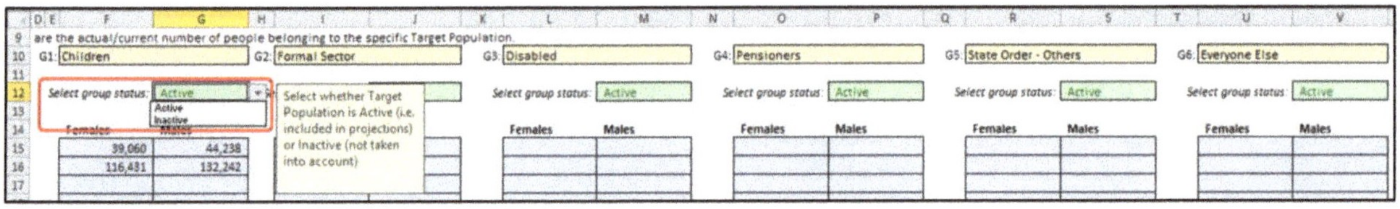

As discussed in Assumptions 15 and 16, target groups may also overlap. The analyst, however, must make it clear in the 1.4 Benefit Packages worksheet (Figure 63; *pg. 78* for discussion) who is eligible for which health insurance packages. For example, the user may define that the formal sector group can include the disabled State Order (others).

Figure 63: Selection of Target Population per Service in 1.4 Benefit Packages Worksheet

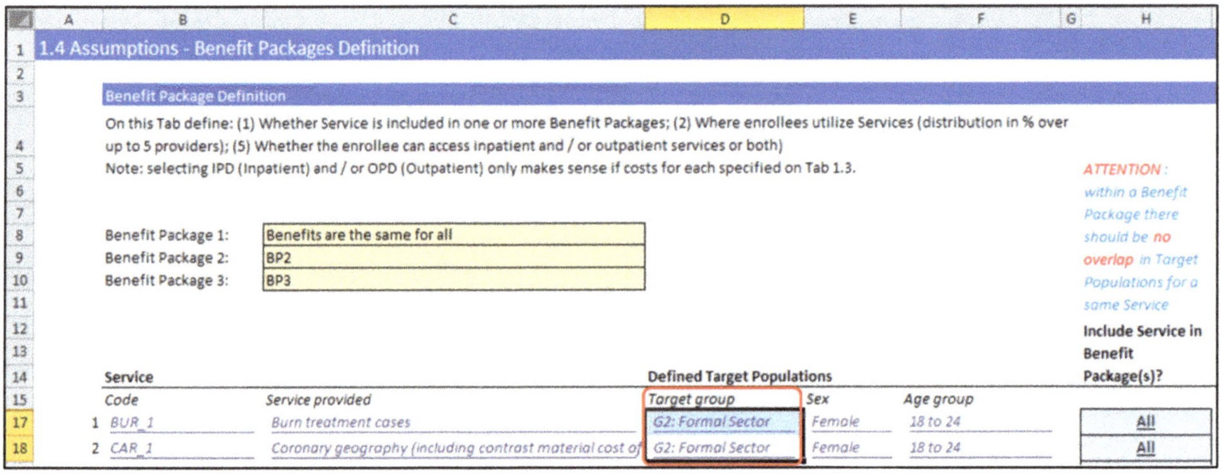

There are two ways to prevent double counting in case of nonmutually exclusive groups. First is to set applicable target group as inactive in this worksheet (Figure 64). Should the user decide to exclude a group in the analysis (i.e., the group status is changed from active to inactive), the entries in the population distribution will be ignored by changing the font color into white, and the input cells into gray.

Figure 64: Inactivation of a Target Population 1.1A Target Populations Worksheet

Note: These numbers are the actual/current number of people belonging to the specific Target Population.

		G1: Children		G2: Formal Sector		G3: Disabled		G4: Pensioners		G5: State Order - Others	
		Select group status: Inactive		Select group status: Active		Select group status: Active		Select group status: Active		Select group status: Active	
≥ Lower Bound	≤ Upper Bound	Females	Males	Females	Males	Females	Males	Females	Males	Females	Males
0	1										
2	7										
8	9										
10	14										
15	17										
18	19			17,317	19,405	147	314			3,226	3,615
20	24			59,033	57,374	1,171	2,771			10,997	10,688
25	29			74,666	69,402	1,736	3,903			13,909	12,929
30	34			70,613	64,468	2,229	4,990			13,154	12,009
35	39			57,969	52,752	2,860	5,218			10,799	9,827
40	44			49,957	43,380	3,892	5,953			9,306	8,081
45	49			47,935	40,064	5,911	6,842			8,930	7,463
50	54			57,832	47,403	11,500	11,583			10,773	8,830
55	59			62,419	51,250	18,528	16,139			11,628	9,547
60	63			38,056	29,586	14,686	11,532			7,089	5,511
64	69							82,913	60,700		
70	74							33,550	22,733		
75								102,414	61,956		
				535,797	475,083	62,659	69,245	218,877	145,389	99,811	88,501

Second, set a target group as "No" in the "Include in analysis" column of the Dashboard (Figure 65; see pg. 115 for discussion).

Figure 65: Inactivation of a Target Population in the Dashboard Worksheet

Target Population Projections

		Target Group Size (end of period)	
Target Groups	***Include in analysis?***	**2017**	**2031**
G1: Children	No	326,075	235,641
G2: Formal Sector	Yes	1,000,786	923,925
G3: Disabled	Yes	131,408	123,081
G4: Pensioners	Yes	371,696	538,484
G5: State Order - Others	Yes	186,432	172,114
G6: Everyone Else	Yes	0	0
		2,016,397	1,993,244

Age Bracket

Up to 18 *age brackets* or groups (Figure 66) may be defined in cells **B15–B32** (for lower bound age) and **C15–C32** (for upper bound age).

Figure 66: Input Cells for Age Groups in the 1.1A Target Populations Worksheet

Age under column B is restricted to ensure there is no conflict with the upper bound of the previous age group in the (Figure 67).

Figure 67: Restrictions to Lower Bound of Age Groups in the 1.1A Target Populations Worksheet

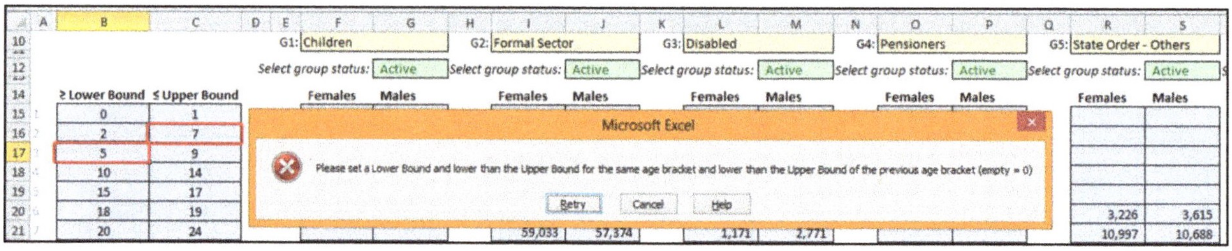

Meanwhile, the cells in column C are restricted to ensure that the upper bound of an age group is not lower than the recorded lower (Figure 68).

Figure 68: Restrictions to Upper Bound of Age Groups in the 1.1A Target Populations Worksheet

	A	B	C	D E	F	G	H	I	J	K	L	M
10					G1: Children			G2: Formal Sector			G3: Disabled	
12					Select group status: Active			Select group status: Active			Select group status: Active	
14		≥ Lower Bound	≤ Upper Bound		Females	Males		Females	Males		Females	Males
15	1	0	1									
16	2	2	7									
17	3	8	7									
18	4	10	14									
19	5	15	17									
20	6	18	19								147	314
21	7	20	24					59,033	57,374		1,171	2,771

Microsoft Excel

Please set an Upper Bound and higher than the Lower Bound (empty = over 100)

Retry   Cancel   Help

Sex

The population distribution by identified *Age Bracket* and *Sex* must be recorded in **rows 15–32** (Figure 69), specifically **cells F and G** for *Target Group 1*; **cells I and J** for *Target Group 2*; *cells L and M* for *Target Group 3*; **cells O and P** for *Target Group 4*; **cells R and S** for *Target Group 5*; and **cells U and V** for *Target Group 6*. These input cells which must be consistent with Assumptions 9 to 14 are restricted to accept positive numeric values only. For example, a pregnant women group should only be limited to women of reproductive age (15–49 years), or "Seniors" should be restricted to persons at least 60 years old.

Figure 69: Input Cells for Population Distribution by Age Group and Sex in the 1.1A Target Populations Worksheet

	F	G	I	J	L	M	O	P	R	S	U	V
9	ple, not the numbers of (potentially) enrolled members											
10	G1: Children		G2: Formal Sector		G3: Disabled		G4: Pensioners		G5: State Order - Others		G6: Everyone Else	
12	Select group status: Active		Select group status: Active		Select group status: Active		Select group status: Active		Select group status: Active		Select group status: Active	
14	Females	Males	Females	Males	Females	Males	Females	Males	Females	Males	Females	Males
15	39,060	44,238										
16	116,431	132,242										
17												
18												
19												
20			17,317	19,405	147	314			3,226	3,615		
21			59,033	57,374	1,171	2,771			10,997	10,688		
22			74,666	69,402	1,736	3,903			13,909	12,929		
23			70,613	64,468	2,229	4,990			13,154	12,009		
24			57,969	52,752	2,860	5,218			10,799	9,827		
25			49,957	43,380	3,892	5,953			9,306	8,081		
26			47,935	40,064	5,911	6,842			8,930	7,463		
27			57,832	47,403	11,500	11,583			10,773	8,830		
28			62,419	51,250	18,528	16,139			11,628	9,547		
29			38,056	29,586	14,686	11,532			7,089	5,511		
30							82,913	60,700				
31							33,550	22,733				
32							102,414	61,956				
34	155,491	176,480	535,797	475,083	62,659	69,245	218,877	145,389	99,811	88,501	-	-

The *Population totals by sex per group* are then automatically computed in **row 34** (Figure 70).

Figure 70: Population Totals by Sex per Target Group in the 1.1A Target Populations Worksheet

On the other hand, **row 37** provides for space where users can indicate *Notes* per target group. Automatic graphs for the defined target populations showing the breakdown by age group and by sex are also available below the *Notes* section. See Figure 71 for illustration.

Figure 71: Notes and Graphs on Population of Target Groups in the 1.1A Target Populations Worksheet

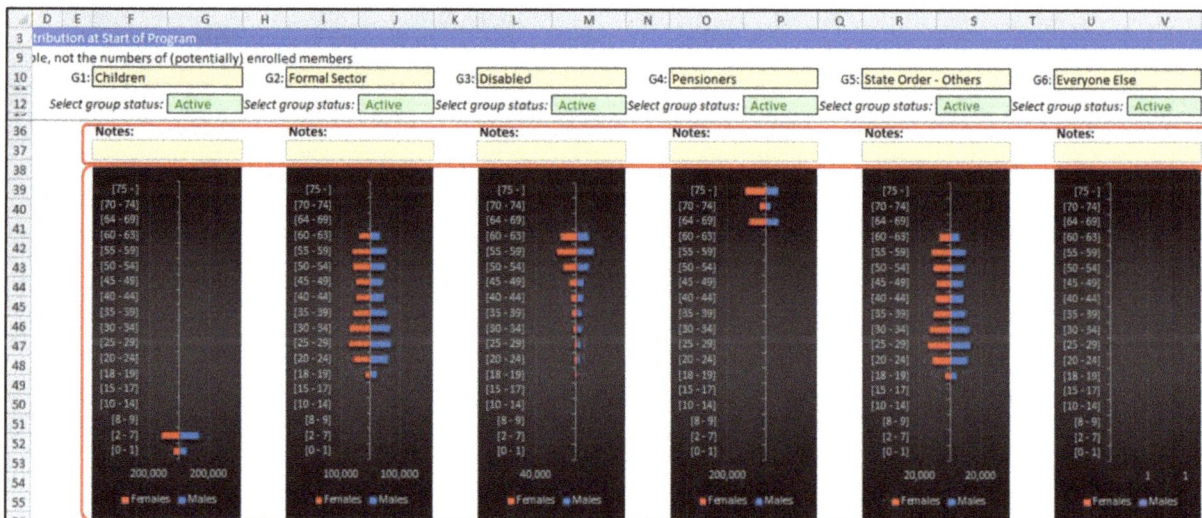

B.   The 1.1B Growth Target Populations Input Sheet

This worksheet allows setting up of *Growth Rates* of the specific *Age Bracket* and *Sex* of people in each Target Group for all periods to be included in the projections (Figure 72). Specifically, this worksheet provides for inputting *Assumption 17 (Growth Rates of Subpopulations)* described in Chapter II-D.

As noted in Chapter II-D4, these rates should not yet include dropout rates in the membership of these targeted groups. Growth rates in Period 1 will be applied to project the population size at the end of Period 1, and so forth.

Figure 72: Preview of the 1.1B Growth Target Populations Worksheet

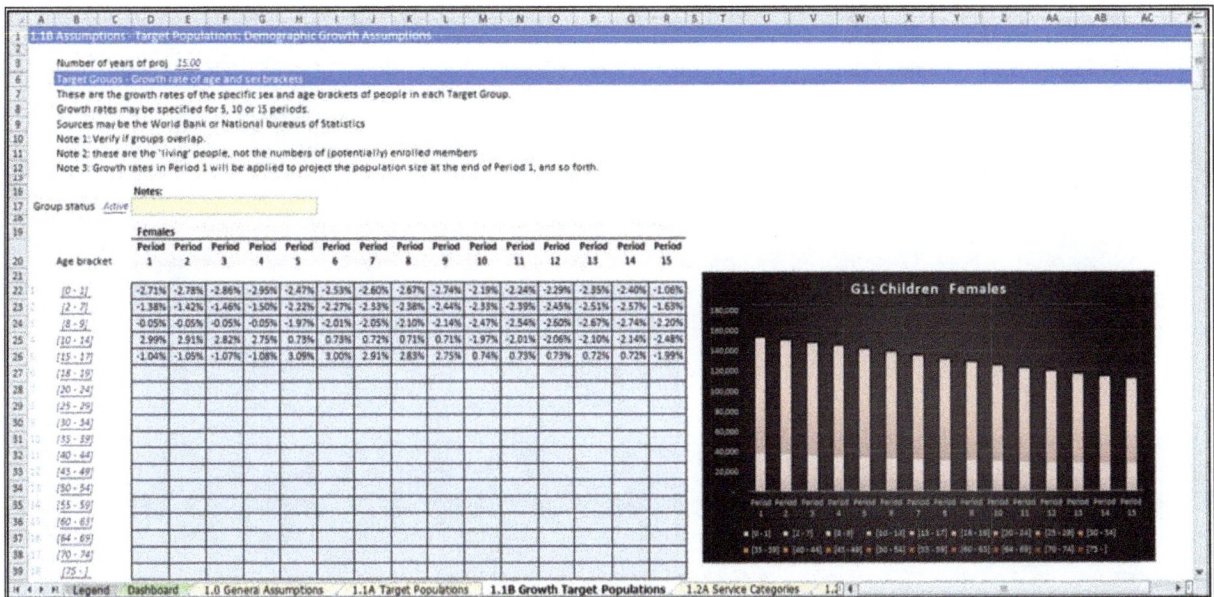

FOR YOUR INFORMATION

Cells found in this worksheet include:

Input Cells

| 100.00 | Input cell, restricted input (e.g., only positive values/only integers/dates/etc.) |

Free Text Cells

| Note | Input cell to write comments |

Calculation Cells

| _200.00_ | Linked and/or Calculation cell (locked); input to cell from another tab |

- Restricted input cells for encoding only positive numeric values;
- Free text cells for adding corresponding explanations, comments, sources, or other helpful texts pertaining to the encoded information; and
- Linked calculation cells (i.e., age bracket) that are locked and entries came from another tab.

The *Number of years of projections* in **cell E3** is automatically picked up from the *Number of Period* defined in the 1.0 General Assumptions worksheet (Figure 73).

**Figure 73: Input Cell for Number of Years of Projections
in the 1.1B Growth Target Populations Worksheet**

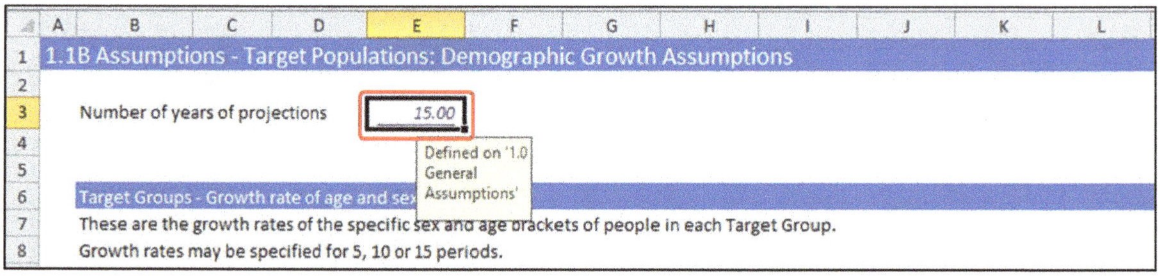

The worksheet is then divided into the following six sections representing the six *target groups*:

- **Rows 14–63** for Target Group 1 (Figure 74);
- **Rows 64–113** for Target Group 2 (Figure 75);
- **Rows 114–163** for Target Group 3 (Figure 76);
- **Rows 164–213** for Target Group 4 (Figure 77);
- **Rows 214–263** for Target Group 5 (Figure 78); and
- **Rows 264–313** for Target Group 6 (Figure 79).

Figure 74: Section for Target Group 1 in the 1.1B Target Growth Populations Worksheet

G1: Children

Group status *Active*   Notes:

Females

Age bracket	Period 1	Period 2	Period 3	Period 4	Period 5	Period 11	Period 12	Period 13	Period 14	Period 15
[0 - 1]	-2.71%	-2.78%	-2.86%	-2.95%	-2.47%	-2.24%	-2.29%	-2.35%	-2.40%	-1.06%
[2 - 7]	-1.38%	-1.42%	-1.46%	-1.50%	-2.22%	-2.39%	-2.45%	-2.51%	-2.57%	-1.63%
[8 - 9]	-0.05%	-0.05%	-0.05%	-0.05%	-1.97%	-2.54%	-2.60%	-2.67%	-2.74%	-2.20%
[10 - 14]	2.99%	2.91%	2.82%	2.75%	0.73%	-2.01%	-2.06%	-2.10%	-2.14%	-2.48%
[15 - 17]	-1.04%	-1.05%	-1.07%	-1.08%	3.09%	0.73%	0.73%	0.72%	0.72%	-1.99%
[18 - 19]										
[20 - 24]										
[25 - 29]										
[30 - 34]										
[35 - 39]										

Males

Age bracket	Period 1	Period 2	Period 3	Period 4	Period 5	Period 11	Period 12	Period 13	Period 14	Period 15
[0 - 1]	-2.83%	-2.91%	-3.00%	-3.09%	-2.62%	-2.41%	-2.47%	-2.53%	-2.59%	-1.23%
[2 - 7]	-1.50%	-1.54%	-1.58%	-1.63%	-2.36%	-2.55%	-2.62%	-2.69%	-2.76%	-1.79%
[8 - 9]	-0.16%	-0.16%	-0.16%	-0.16%	-2.09%	-2.70%	-2.77%	-2.85%	-2.93%	-2.35%
[10 - 14]	2.81%	2.73%	2.66%	2.59%	0.58%	-2.14%	-2.19%	-2.24%	-2.29%	-2.63%
[15 - 17]	-0.36%	-0.36%	-0.36%	-0.36%	2.76%	0.54%	0.53%	0.53%	0.53%	-2.13%
[18 - 19]										
[20 - 24]										
[25 - 29]										
[30 - 34]										
[35 - 39]										

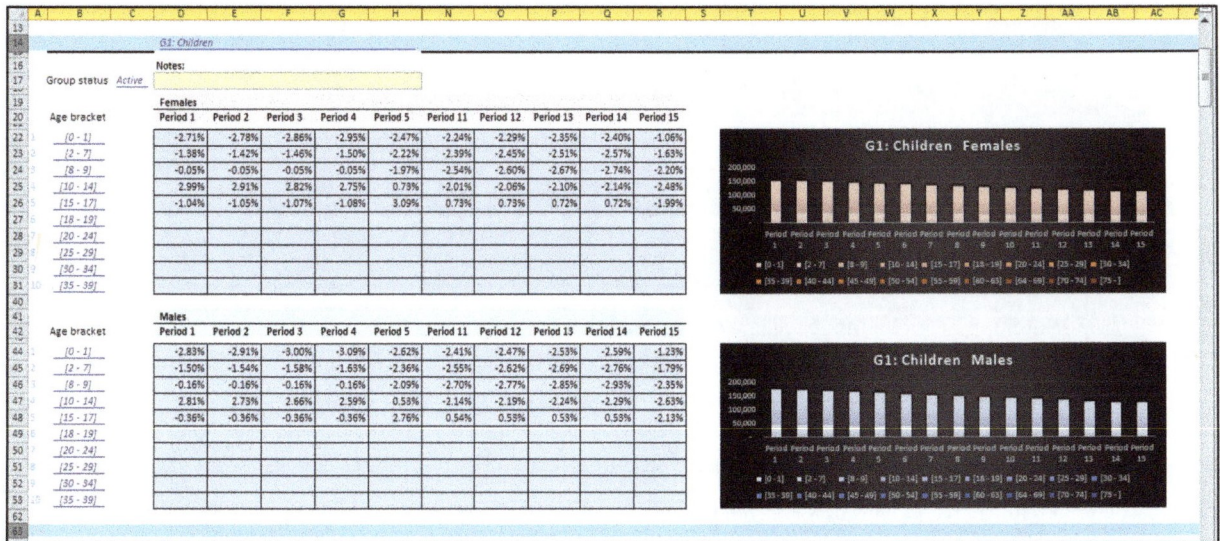

Note: Screenshot contains hidden rows and columns for illustration purposes only.

Figure 75: Section for Target Group 2 in the 1.1B Target Growth Populations Worksheet

G2: Formal Sector

Group status *Active*   Notes:

Females

Age bracket	Period 1	Period 2	Period 3	Period 4	Period 5	Period 11	Period 12	Period 13	Period 14	Period 15
[18 - 19]	-1.04%	-1.05%	-1.07%	-1.08%	3.09%	0.73%	0.73%	0.72%	0.72%	-1.99%
[20 - 24]	-6.47%	-6.92%	-7.43%	-8.03%	-1.47%	3.06%	2.97%	2.89%	2.81%	0.76%
[25 - 29]	-3.76%	-3.90%	-4.06%	-4.23%	-6.49%	-1.53%	-1.55%	-1.57%	-1.60%	3.23%
[30 - 34]	1.13%	1.11%	1.10%	1.09%	-3.00%	-7.01%	-7.54%	-8.16%	-8.88%	-1.52%
[35 - 39]	3.99%	3.83%	3.69%	3.56%	1.77%	-3.11%	-3.21%	-3.32%	-3.43%	-6.59%
[40 - 44]	2.18%	2.15%	2.09%	2.05%	4.52%	1.75%	1.72%	1.69%	1.66%	-3.02%
[45 - 49]	-0.66%	-0.67%	-0.67%	-0.67%	3.01%	4.35%	4.17%	4.00%	3.85%	1.80%
[50 - 54]	-4.00%	-4.16%	-4.35%	-4.54%	-1.08%	2.95%	2.86%	2.78%	2.71%	4.57%
[55 - 59]	-1.10%	-1.12%	-1.13%	-1.14%	-4.08%	-1.07%	-1.08%	-1.09%	-1.10%	3.07%
[60 - 63]	5.93%	5.60%	5.30%	5.03%	-0.46%	-4.21%	-4.40%	-4.60%	-4.82%	-1.02%

Males

Age bracket	Period 1	Period 2	Period 3	Period 4	Period 5	Period 11	Period 12	Period 13	Period 14	Period 15
[18 - 19]	-0.36%	-0.36%	-0.36%	-0.36%	2.76%	0.54%	0.53%	0.53%	0.53%	-2.13%
[20 - 24]	-3.76%	-3.91%	-4.06%	-4.24%	-1.14%	2.79%	2.72%	2.64%	2.58%	0.56%
[25 - 29]	-4.01%	-4.18%	-4.36%	-4.56%	-3.90%	-1.19%	-1.21%	-1.22%	-1.24%	2.99%
[30 - 34]	0.62%	0.61%	0.61%	0.61%	-2.83%	-4.15%	-4.32%	-4.52%	-4.73%	-1.20%
[35 - 39]	1.84%	1.81%	1.77%	1.74%	2.84%	-2.94%	-3.03%	-3.13%	-3.23%	-4.03%
[40 - 44]	1.17%	1.16%	1.14%	1.13%	4.35%	2.81%	2.73%	2.66%	2.59%	-2.87%
[45 - 49]	-1.14%	-1.15%	-1.17%	-1.18%	3.04%	4.24%	4.07%	3.91%	3.76%	2.95%
[50 - 54]	-5.53%	-5.85%	-6.21%	-6.62%	-0.10%	3.02%	2.93%	2.85%	2.77%	4.52%
[55 - 59]	-3.15%	-3.25%	-3.36%	-3.47%	-4.41%	-0.03%	-0.03%	-0.03%	-0.03%	3.21%
[60 - 63]	4.73%	4.52%	4.32%	4.14%	-1.32%	-4.52%	-4.74%	-4.97%	-5.23%	0.09%

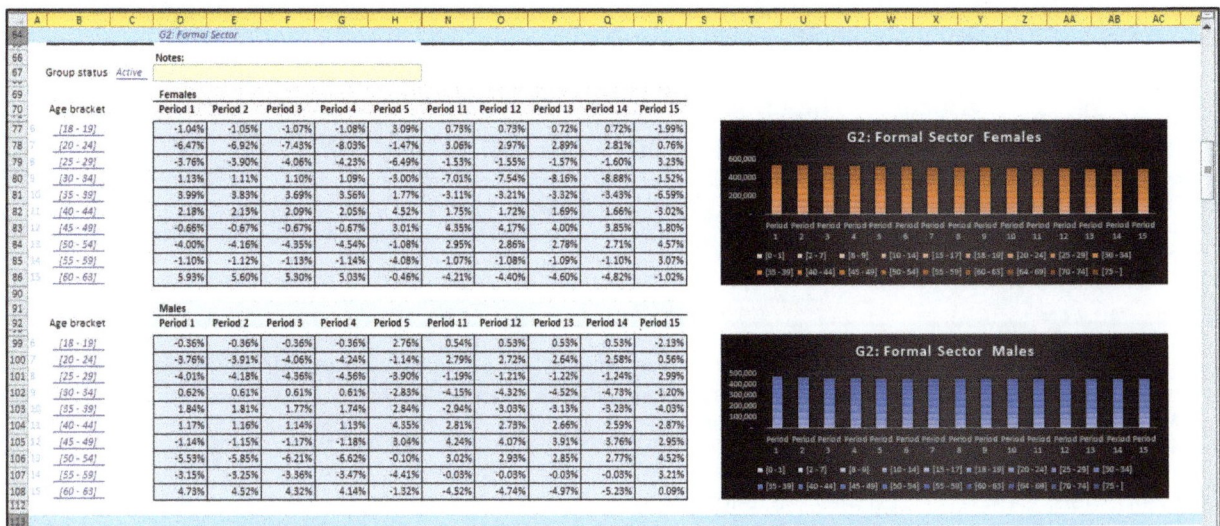

Note: Screenshot contains hidden rows and columns for illustration purposes only.

Figure 76: Section for Target Group 3 in the 1.1B Target Growth Populations Worksheet

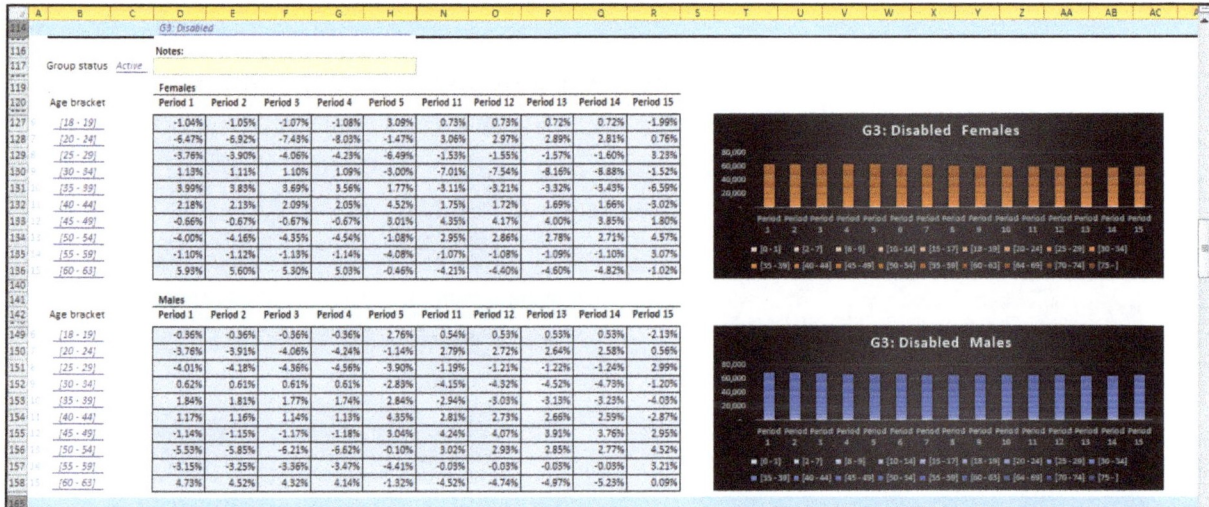

Age bracket	Period 1	Period 2	Period 3	Period 4	Period 5	Period 11	Period 12	Period 13	Period 14	Period 15
Females										
[18 - 19]	-1.04%	-1.05%	-1.07%	-1.08%	3.09%	0.73%	0.73%	0.72%	0.72%	-1.99%
[20 - 24]	-6.47%	-6.92%	-7.43%	-8.03%	-1.47%	3.06%	2.97%	2.89%	2.81%	0.76%
[25 - 29]	-3.76%	-3.90%	-4.06%	-4.23%	-6.49%	-1.53%	-1.55%	-1.57%	-1.60%	3.23%
[30 - 34]	1.13%	1.11%	1.10%	1.09%	-3.00%	-7.01%	-7.54%	-8.16%	-8.88%	-1.52%
[35 - 39]	3.99%	3.85%	3.69%	3.56%	1.77%	-3.11%	-3.21%	-3.32%	-5.43%	-6.59%
[40 - 44]	2.18%	2.13%	2.09%	2.05%	4.52%	1.75%	1.72%	1.69%	1.66%	-3.02%
[45 - 49]	-0.66%	-0.67%	-0.67%	-0.67%	3.01%	4.35%	4.17%	4.00%	3.85%	1.80%
[50 - 54]	-4.00%	-4.16%	-4.35%	-4.54%	-1.08%	2.95%	2.86%	2.78%	2.71%	4.57%
[55 - 59]	-1.10%	-1.12%	-1.13%	-1.14%	-4.08%	-1.07%	-1.08%	-1.09%	-1.10%	3.07%
[60 - 63]	5.93%	5.60%	5.30%	5.03%	-0.46%	-4.21%	-4.40%	-4.60%	-4.82%	-1.02%
Males										
[18 - 19]	-0.36%	-0.36%	-0.36%	-0.36%	2.76%	0.54%	0.53%	0.53%	0.53%	-2.13%
[20 - 24]	-3.76%	-3.91%	-4.06%	-4.24%	-1.14%	2.79%	2.72%	2.64%	2.58%	0.56%
[25 - 29]	-4.01%	-4.18%	-4.36%	-4.56%	-3.90%	-1.19%	-1.21%	-1.22%	-1.24%	2.99%
[30 - 34]	0.62%	0.61%	0.61%	0.61%	-2.83%	-4.15%	-4.32%	-4.52%	-4.73%	-1.20%
[35 - 39]	1.84%	1.81%	1.77%	1.74%	2.84%	-2.94%	-3.03%	-3.13%	-3.23%	-4.03%
[40 - 44]	1.17%	1.16%	1.14%	1.13%	4.35%	2.81%	2.73%	2.66%	2.59%	-2.87%
[45 - 49]	-1.14%	-1.15%	-1.17%	-1.18%	3.04%	4.24%	4.07%	3.91%	3.76%	2.95%
[50 - 54]	-5.53%	-5.85%	-6.21%	-6.62%	-0.10%	3.02%	2.93%	2.85%	2.77%	4.52%
[55 - 59]	-3.15%	-3.25%	-3.36%	-3.47%	-4.41%	-0.03%	-0.03%	-0.03%	-0.03%	3.21%
[60 - 63]	4.73%	4.52%	4.32%	4.14%	-1.32%	-4.52%	-4.74%	-4.97%	-5.23%	0.09%

Note: Screenshot contains hidden rows and columns for illustration purposes only.

Figure 77: Section for Target Group 4 in the 1.1B Target Growth Populations Worksheet

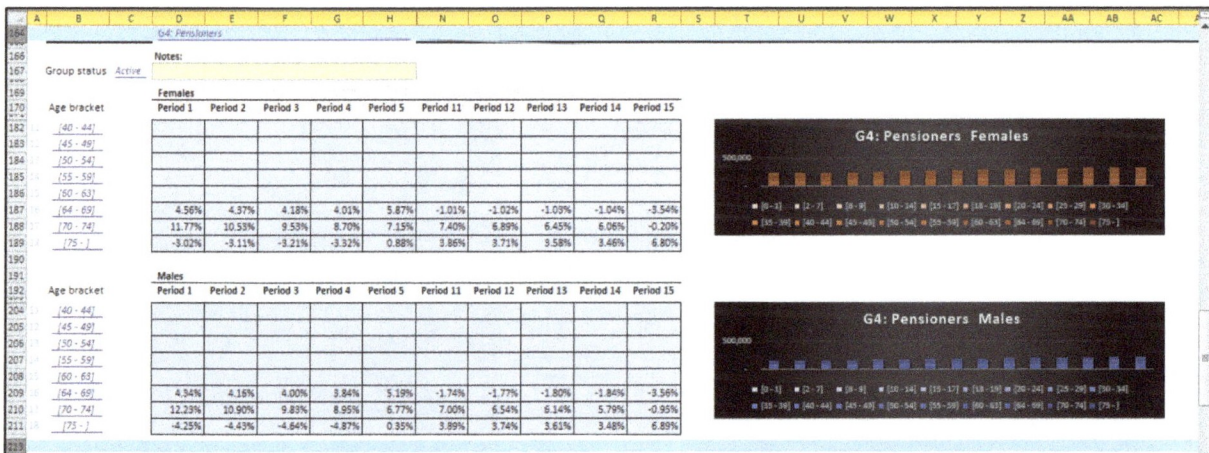

Age bracket	Period 1	Period 2	Period 3	Period 4	Period 5	Period 11	Period 12	Period 13	Period 14	Period 15
Females										
[40 - 44]										
[45 - 49]										
[50 - 54]										
[55 - 59]										
[60 - 63]										
[64 - 69]	4.56%	4.37%	4.18%	4.01%	5.87%	-1.01%	-1.02%	-1.03%	-1.04%	-3.54%
[70 - 74]	11.77%	10.53%	9.53%	8.70%	7.15%	7.40%	6.89%	6.45%	6.06%	-0.20%
[75 -]	-3.02%	-3.11%	-3.21%	-3.32%	0.88%	3.86%	3.71%	3.58%	3.46%	6.80%
Males										
[40 - 44]										
[45 - 49]										
[50 - 54]										
[55 - 59]										
[60 - 63]										
[64 - 69]	4.34%	4.16%	4.00%	3.84%	5.19%	-1.74%	-1.77%	-1.80%	-1.84%	-3.56%
[70 - 74]	12.23%	10.90%	9.83%	8.95%	6.77%	7.00%	6.54%	6.14%	5.79%	-0.95%
[75 -]	-4.25%	-4.43%	-4.64%	-4.87%	0.35%	3.89%	3.74%	3.61%	3.48%	6.89%

Note: Screenshot contains hidden rows and columns for illustration purposes only.

Figure 78: Section for Target Group 5 in the 1.1B Target Growth Populations Worksheet

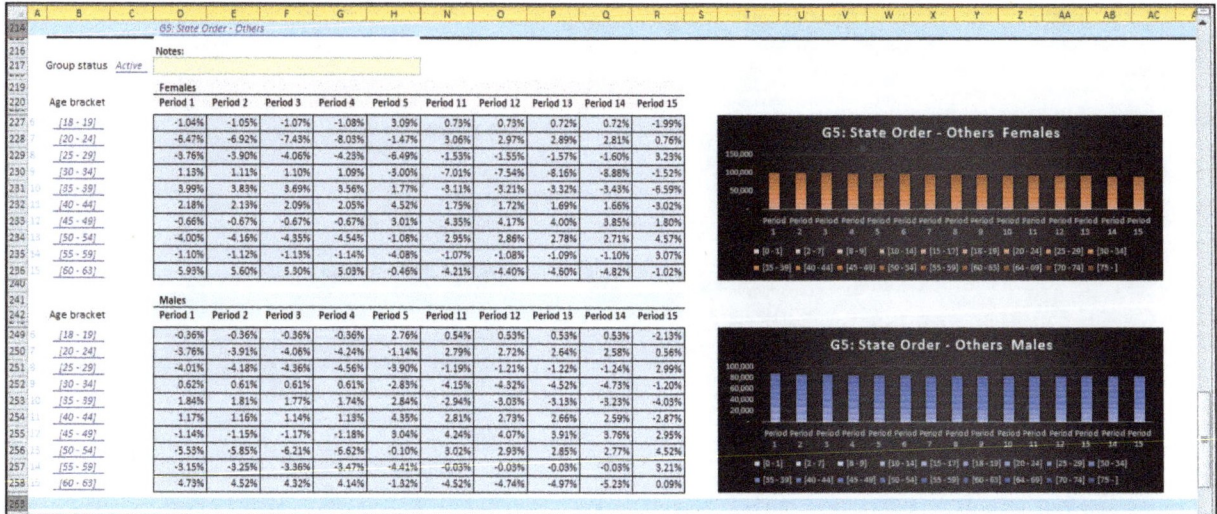

G5: State Order - Others

Group status *Active*

Notes:

Females

Age bracket	Period 1	Period 2	Period 3	Period 4	Period 5	Period 11	Period 12	Period 13	Period 14	Period 15
[18 - 19]	-1.04%	-1.05%	-1.07%	-1.08%	3.09%	0.73%	0.73%	0.72%	0.72%	-1.99%
[20 - 24]	-6.47%	-6.92%	-7.43%	-8.03%	-1.47%	3.06%	2.97%	2.89%	2.81%	0.76%
[25 - 29]	-3.76%	-3.90%	-4.06%	-4.23%	-6.49%	-1.53%	-1.55%	-1.57%	-1.60%	3.23%
[30 - 34]	1.13%	1.11%	1.10%	1.09%	-3.00%	-7.01%	-7.54%	-8.16%	-8.88%	-1.52%
[35 - 39]	3.99%	3.83%	3.69%	3.56%	1.77%	-3.11%	-3.21%	-3.32%	-3.43%	-6.59%
[40 - 44]	2.18%	2.13%	2.09%	2.05%	4.52%	1.75%	1.72%	1.69%	1.66%	-3.02%
[45 - 49]	-0.66%	-0.67%	-0.67%	-0.67%	3.01%	4.35%	4.17%	4.00%	3.85%	1.80%
[50 - 54]	-4.00%	-4.16%	-4.35%	-4.54%	-1.08%	2.95%	2.86%	2.78%	2.71%	4.57%
[55 - 59]	-1.10%	-1.12%	-1.13%	-1.14%	-4.08%	-1.07%	-1.08%	-1.09%	-1.10%	3.07%
[60 - 63]	5.93%	5.60%	5.30%	5.03%	-0.46%	-4.21%	-4.40%	-4.60%	-4.82%	-1.02%

G5: State Order - Others Females

Males

Age bracket	Period 1	Period 2	Period 3	Period 4	Period 5	Period 11	Period 12	Period 13	Period 14	Period 15
[18 - 19]	-0.36%	-0.36%	-0.36%	-0.36%	2.76%	0.54%	0.53%	0.53%	0.53%	-2.13%
[20 - 24]	-3.76%	-3.91%	-4.06%	-4.24%	-1.14%	2.79%	2.72%	2.64%	2.58%	0.56%
[25 - 29]	-4.01%	-4.18%	-4.36%	-4.56%	-3.90%	-1.19%	-1.21%	-1.22%	-1.24%	2.99%
[30 - 34]	0.62%	0.61%	0.61%	0.61%	-2.83%	-4.15%	-4.32%	-4.52%	-4.73%	-1.20%
[35 - 39]	1.84%	1.81%	1.77%	1.74%	2.84%	-2.94%	-3.03%	-3.13%	-3.23%	-4.03%
[40 - 44]	1.17%	1.16%	1.14%	1.13%	4.35%	2.81%	2.73%	2.66%	2.59%	-2.87%
[45 - 49]	-1.14%	-1.15%	-1.17%	-1.18%	3.04%	4.24%	4.07%	3.91%	3.76%	2.95%
[50 - 54]	-5.53%	-5.85%	-6.21%	-6.62%	-0.10%	3.02%	2.93%	2.85%	2.77%	4.52%
[55 - 59]	-3.15%	-3.25%	-3.36%	-3.47%	-4.41%	-0.03%	-0.03%	-0.03%	-0.03%	3.21%
[60 - 63]	4.73%	4.52%	4.32%	4.14%	-1.32%	-4.52%	-4.74%	-4.97%	-5.23%	0.09%

G5: State Order - Others Males

Note: Screenshot contains hidden rows and columns for illustration purposes only.

Figure 79: Section for Target Group 6 in the 1.1B Target Growth Populations Worksheet

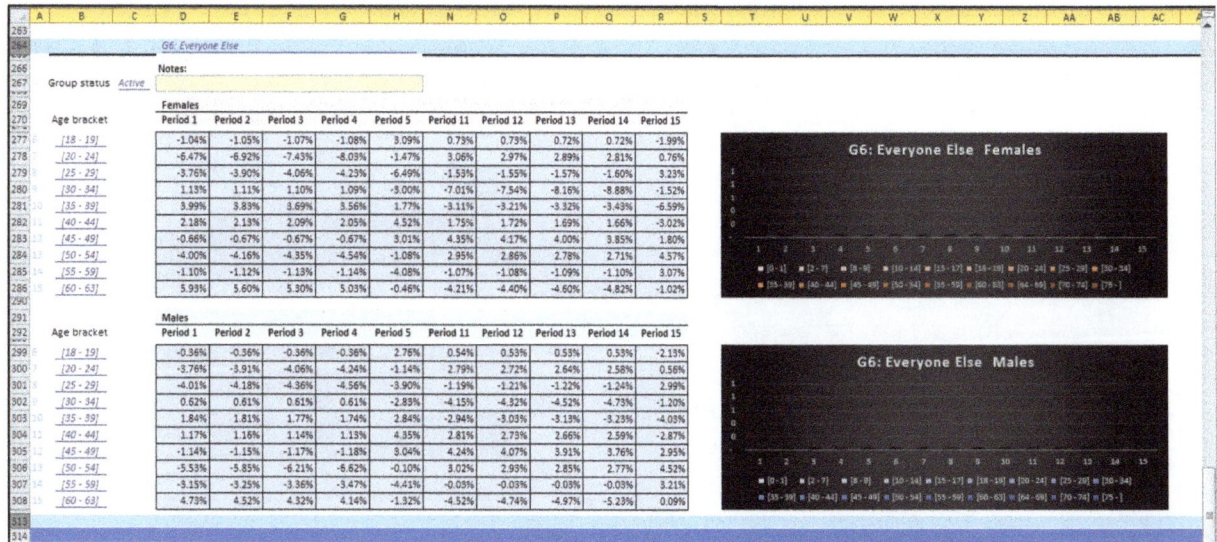

G6: Everyone Else

Group status *Active*

Notes:

Females

Age bracket	Period 1	Period 2	Period 3	Period 4	Period 5	Period 11	Period 12	Period 13	Period 14	Period 15
[18 - 19]	-1.04%	-1.05%	-1.07%	-1.08%	3.09%	0.73%	0.73%	0.72%	0.72%	-1.99%
[20 - 24]	-6.47%	-6.92%	-7.43%	-8.03%	-1.47%	3.06%	2.97%	2.89%	2.81%	0.76%
[25 - 29]	-3.76%	-3.90%	-4.06%	-4.23%	-6.49%	-1.53%	-1.55%	-1.57%	-1.60%	3.23%
[30 - 34]	1.13%	1.11%	1.10%	1.09%	-3.00%	-7.01%	-7.54%	-8.16%	-8.88%	-1.52%
[35 - 39]	3.99%	3.83%	3.69%	3.56%	1.77%	-3.11%	-3.21%	-3.32%	-3.43%	-6.59%
[40 - 44]	2.18%	2.13%	2.09%	2.05%	4.52%	1.75%	1.72%	1.69%	1.66%	-3.02%
[45 - 49]	-0.66%	-0.67%	-0.67%	-0.67%	3.01%	4.35%	4.17%	4.00%	3.85%	1.80%
[50 - 54]	-4.00%	-4.16%	-4.35%	-4.54%	-1.08%	2.95%	2.86%	2.78%	2.71%	4.57%
[55 - 59]	-1.10%	-1.12%	-1.13%	-1.14%	-4.08%	-1.07%	-1.08%	-1.09%	-1.10%	3.07%
[60 - 63]	5.93%	5.60%	5.30%	5.03%	-0.46%	-4.21%	-4.40%	-4.60%	-4.82%	-1.02%

G6: Everyone Else Females

Males

Age bracket	Period 1	Period 2	Period 3	Period 4	Period 5	Period 11	Period 12	Period 13	Period 14	Period 15
[18 - 19]	-0.36%	-0.36%	-0.36%	-0.36%	2.76%	0.54%	0.53%	0.53%	0.53%	-2.13%
[20 - 24]	-3.76%	-3.91%	-4.06%	-4.24%	-1.14%	2.79%	2.72%	2.64%	2.58%	0.56%
[25 - 29]	-4.01%	-4.18%	-4.36%	-4.56%	-3.90%	-1.19%	-1.21%	-1.22%	-1.24%	2.99%
[30 - 34]	0.62%	0.61%	0.61%	0.61%	-2.83%	-4.15%	-4.32%	-4.52%	-4.73%	-1.20%
[35 - 39]	1.84%	1.81%	1.77%	1.74%	2.84%	-2.94%	-3.03%	-3.13%	-3.23%	-4.03%
[40 - 44]	1.17%	1.16%	1.14%	1.13%	4.35%	2.81%	2.73%	2.66%	2.59%	-2.87%
[45 - 49]	-1.14%	-1.15%	-1.17%	-1.18%	3.04%	4.24%	4.07%	3.91%	3.76%	2.95%
[50 - 54]	-5.53%	-5.85%	-6.21%	-6.62%	-0.10%	3.02%	2.93%	2.85%	2.77%	4.52%
[55 - 59]	-3.15%	-3.25%	-3.36%	-3.47%	-4.41%	-0.03%	-0.03%	-0.03%	-0.03%	3.21%
[60 - 63]	4.73%	4.52%	4.32%	4.14%	-1.32%	-4.52%	-4.74%	-4.97%	-5.23%	0.09%

G6: Everyone Else Males

Note: Screenshot contains hidden rows and columns for illustration purposes only.

The title of each section (**rows 14, 64, 114, 164, 214, and 264**) represents the name of *target groups* automatically up picked from the 1.1A Target Populations" worksheet (Figure 80).

Figure 80: Name of Target Group 1.1B Target Growth Populations Worksheet

	A	B	C	D	E	F	G	H	N	O	P	Q	R
5													
6		Target Groups - Growth rate of age and sex brackets											
7		These are the growth rates of the specific sex and age brackets of people in each Target Group.											
8		Growth rates may be specified for 5, 10 or 15 periods.											
9		Sources may be the World Bank or National bureaus of Statistics											
10		Note 1: Verify if groups overlap.											
11		Note 2: these are the 'living' people, not the numbers of (potentially) enrolled members											
12		Note 3: Growth rates in Period 1 will be applied to project the population size at the end of Period 1, and so forth.											
13													
14				G1: Children									
16				Notes:									
17		Group status	Active			Defined on '1.1A Target Populations'							
19				Females									

The *Group Status* (**cells C17, C67, C117, C167, C217, and C267**) of each *target group* is also derived from the 1.1A Target Populations worksheet (Figure 81). If the user defined the group as part of the projections, it is labeled as active. Otherwise, it will be noted as inactive.

Figure 81: Linked Cell for Group Status in the 1.1B Target Growth Population Worksheet

	A	B	C	D	E	F	G	H	N	O	P	Q	R
13													
14				G1: Children									
16				Notes:									
17		Group status	Active										
19				Defined on '1.1A Target Populations'									
20		Age bracket			Period 2	Period 3	Period 4	Period 5	Period 11	Period 12	Period 13	Period 14	Period 15
22	1	[0 - 1]			-2.78%	-2.86%	-2.95%	-2.47%	-2.24%	-2.29%	-2.35%	-2.40%	-1.06%
23	2	[2 - 7]		-1.38%	-1.42%	-1.46%	-1.50%	-2.22%	-2.39%	-2.45%	-2.51%	-2.57%	-1.63%

A *Notes* cell next to the activation cell is provided for the user to input any remarks (Figure 82).

Figure 82: Notes on Group Status in the 1.1B Target Growth Population Worksheet

	A	B	C	D	E	F	G	H	N	O	P	Q	R
13													
14				G1: Children									
16				Notes:									
17		Group status	Active										
19				Females									
20		Age bracket		Period 1	Period 2	Period 3	Period 4	Period 5	Period 11	Period 12	Period 13	Period 14	Period 15
22	1	[0 - 1]		-2.71%	-2.78%	-2.86%	-2.95%	-2.47%	-2.24%	-2.29%	-2.35%	-2.40%	-1.06%
23	2	[2 - 7]		-1.38%	-1.42%	-1.46%	-1.50%	-2.22%	-2.39%	-2.45%	-2.51%	-2.57%	-1.63%
24	3	[8 - 9]		-0.05%	-0.05%	-0.05%	-0.05%	-1.97%	-2.54%	-2.60%	-2.67%	-2.74%	-2.20%
25	4	[10 - 14]		2.99%	2.91%	2.82%	2.75%	0.73%	-2.01%	-2.06%	-2.10%	-2.14%	-2.48%
26	5	[15 - 17]		-1.04%	-1.05%	-1.07%	-1.08%	3.09%	0.73%	0.73%	0.72%	0.72%	-1.99%

Age Bracket defined in the 1.1A Target Populations worksheet is automatically provided in **column B** for all target groups (Figure 83).

Figure 83: Age Bracket in the 1.1B Target Growth Population Worksheet

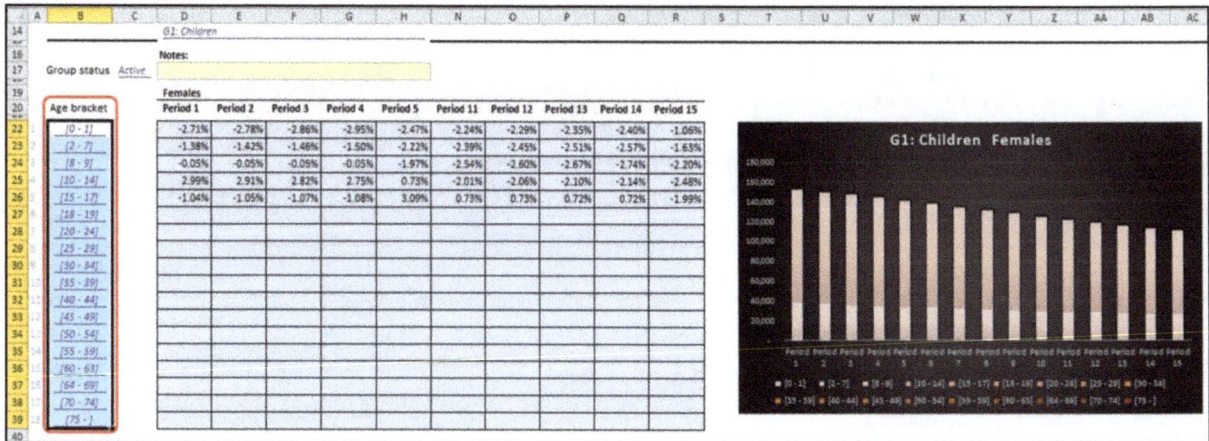

Age bracket	Period 1	Period 2	Period 3	Period 4	Period 5	Period 11	Period 12	Period 13	Period 14	Period 15
[0 - 1]	-2.71%	-2.78%	-2.86%	-2.95%	-2.47%	-2.24%	-2.29%	-2.35%	-2.40%	-1.06%
[2 - 7]	-1.38%	-1.42%	-1.46%	-1.50%	-2.22%	-2.39%	-2.45%	-2.51%	-2.57%	-1.63%
[8 - 9]	-0.05%	-0.05%	-0.05%	-0.05%	-1.97%	-2.54%	-2.60%	-2.67%	-2.74%	-2.20%
[10 - 14]	2.99%	2.91%	2.82%	2.75%	0.73%	-2.01%	-2.06%	-2.10%	-2.14%	-2.48%
[15 - 17]	-1.04%	-1.05%	-1.07%	-1.08%	3.09%	0.73%	0.73%	0.72%	0.72%	-1.99%
[18 - 19]										
[20 - 24]										
[25 - 29]										
[30 - 34]										
[35 - 39]										
[40 - 44]										
[45 - 49]										
[50 - 54]										
[55 - 59]										
[60 - 63]										
[64 - 69]										
[70 - 74]										
[75 -]										

Separate panels for growth rates of females (**upper panel**) and males (**lower panel**) for all periods of projections are encoded under **column D** for Period 1, **column E** for Period 2, and so on, up to **column R** for Period 15 (Figure 84). The input cells for growth rates are restricted to accept only numeric entries.

Figure 84: Panels for Growth Rates per Sex for Females (Upper) and Males (Lower) by Age Bracket in the 1.1B Target Growth Populations Worksheet

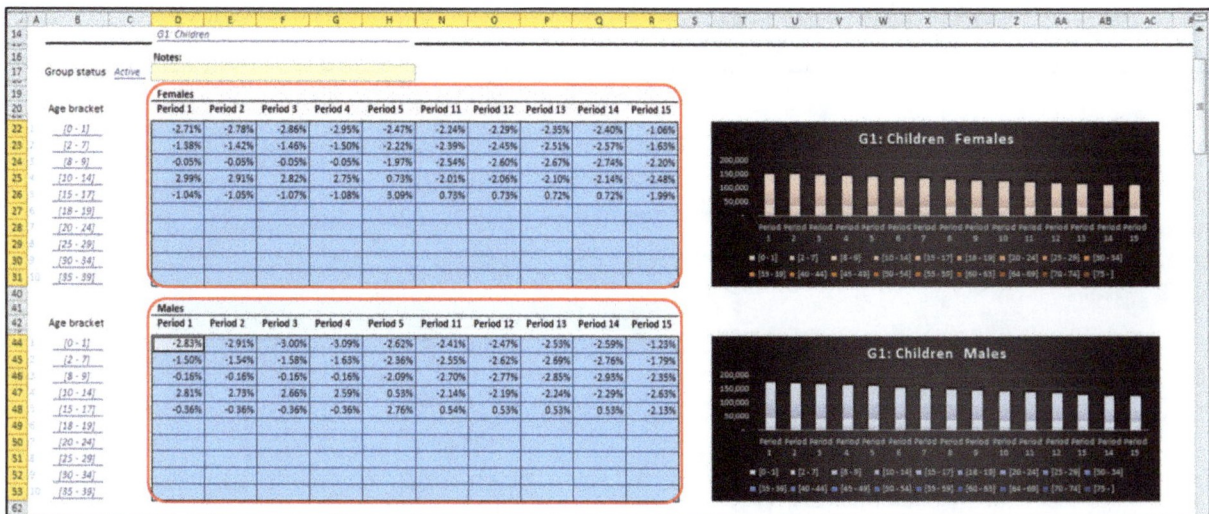

Females

Age bracket	Period 1	Period 2	Period 3	Period 4	Period 5	Period 11	Period 12	Period 13	Period 14	Period 15
[0 - 1]	-2.71%	-2.78%	-2.86%	-2.95%	-2.47%	-2.24%	-2.29%	-2.35%	-2.40%	-1.06%
[2 - 7]	-1.38%	-1.42%	-1.46%	-1.50%	-2.22%	-2.39%	-2.45%	-2.51%	-2.57%	-1.63%
[8 - 9]	-0.05%	-0.05%	-0.05%	-0.05%	-1.97%	-2.54%	-2.60%	-2.67%	-2.74%	-2.20%
[10 - 14]	2.99%	2.91%	2.82%	2.75%	0.73%	-2.01%	-2.06%	-2.10%	-2.14%	-2.48%
[15 - 17]	-1.04%	-1.05%	-1.07%	-1.08%	3.09%	0.73%	0.73%	0.72%	0.72%	-1.99%
[18 - 19]										
[20 - 24]										
[25 - 29]										
[30 - 34]										
[35 - 39]										

Males

Age bracket	Period 1	Period 2	Period 3	Period 4	Period 5	Period 11	Period 12	Period 13	Period 14	Period 15
[0 - 1]	-2.83%	-2.91%	-3.00%	-3.09%	-2.62%	-2.41%	-2.47%	-2.53%	-2.59%	-1.23%
[2 - 7]	-1.50%	-1.54%	-1.58%	-1.63%	-2.36%	-2.55%	-2.62%	-2.69%	-2.76%	-1.79%
[8 - 9]	-0.16%	-0.16%	-0.16%	-0.16%	-2.09%	-2.70%	-2.77%	-2.85%	-2.93%	-2.35%
[10 - 14]	2.81%	2.73%	2.66%	2.59%	0.53%	-2.14%	-2.19%	-2.24%	-2.29%	-2.63%
[15 - 17]	-0.36%	-0.36%	-0.36%	-0.36%	2.76%	0.54%	0.53%	0.53%	0.53%	-2.13%
[18 - 19]										
[20 - 24]										
[25 - 29]										
[30 - 34]										
[35 - 39]										

Note: Screenshot contains hidden rows and columns for illustration purposes only.

Column bars (Figure 85) showing the projected target population for the defined periods by *Sex* and *Age Bracket* are provided in the right side of the panels for growth rates.

Figure 85: Column Bars on Projected Target Population for Defined Periods by Sex and Age Bracket in the 1.1B Target Growth Populations Worksheet

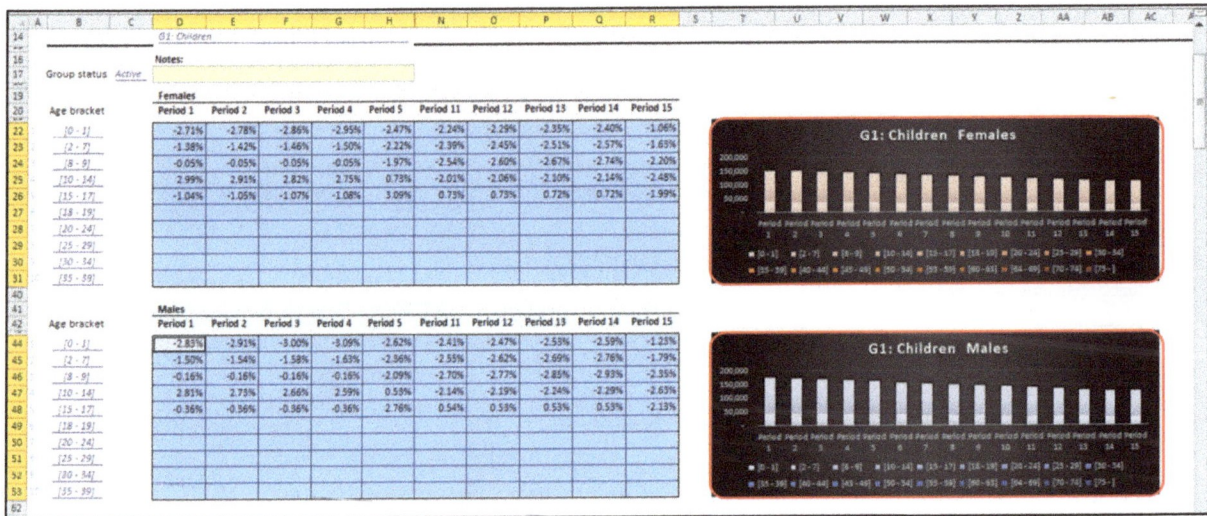

G1: Children

Notes:

Group status *Active*

Females

Age bracket	Period 1	Period 2	Period 3	Period 4	Period 5	Period 11	Period 12	Period 13	Period 14	Period 15
[0 - 1]	-2.71%	-2.78%	-2.86%	-2.95%	-2.47%	-2.24%	-2.29%	-2.35%	-2.40%	-1.06%
[2 - 7]	-1.38%	-1.42%	-1.46%	-1.50%	-2.22%	-2.39%	-2.45%	-2.51%	-2.57%	-1.63%
[8 - 9]	-0.05%	-0.05%	-0.05%	-0.05%	-1.97%	-2.54%	-2.60%	-2.67%	-2.74%	-2.20%
[10 - 14]	2.99%	2.91%	2.82%	2.75%	0.73%	-2.01%	-2.06%	-2.10%	-2.14%	-2.48%
[15 - 17]	-1.04%	-1.05%	-1.07%	-1.08%	3.09%	0.73%	0.73%	0.72%	0.72%	-1.99%
[18 - 19]										
[20 - 24]										
[25 - 29]										
[30 - 34]										
[35 - 39]										

Males

Age bracket	Period 1	Period 2	Period 3	Period 4	Period 5	Period 11	Period 12	Period 13	Period 14	Period 15
[0 - 1]	-2.83%	-2.91%	-3.00%	-3.09%	-2.62%	-2.41%	-2.47%	-2.53%	-2.59%	-1.25%
[2 - 7]	-1.50%	-1.54%	-1.58%	-1.63%	-2.36%	-2.55%	-2.62%	-2.69%	-2.76%	-1.79%
[8 - 9]	-0.16%	-0.16%	-0.16%	-0.16%	-2.09%	-2.70%	-2.77%	-2.85%	-2.93%	-2.35%
[10 - 14]	2.81%	2.75%	2.66%	2.59%	0.55%	-2.14%	-2.19%	-2.24%	-2.29%	-2.63%
[15 - 17]	-0.36%	-0.36%	-0.36%	-0.36%	2.76%	0.54%	0.53%	0.53%	0.53%	-2.13%
[18 - 19]										
[20 - 24]										
[25 - 29]										
[30 - 34]										
[35 - 39]										

Note: Screenshot contains hidden rows and columns for illustration purposes only.

If a group is declared as inactive in worksheet 1.1A Target Populations, the previous entries in the 1.1B Growth Target Populations worksheet for the same group will be automatically hidden and the projected entries in the graph will not be shown (Figure 86).

Figure 86: Sample Inactivated Data for Target Group 1 in the 1.1B Target Growth Populations Worksheet

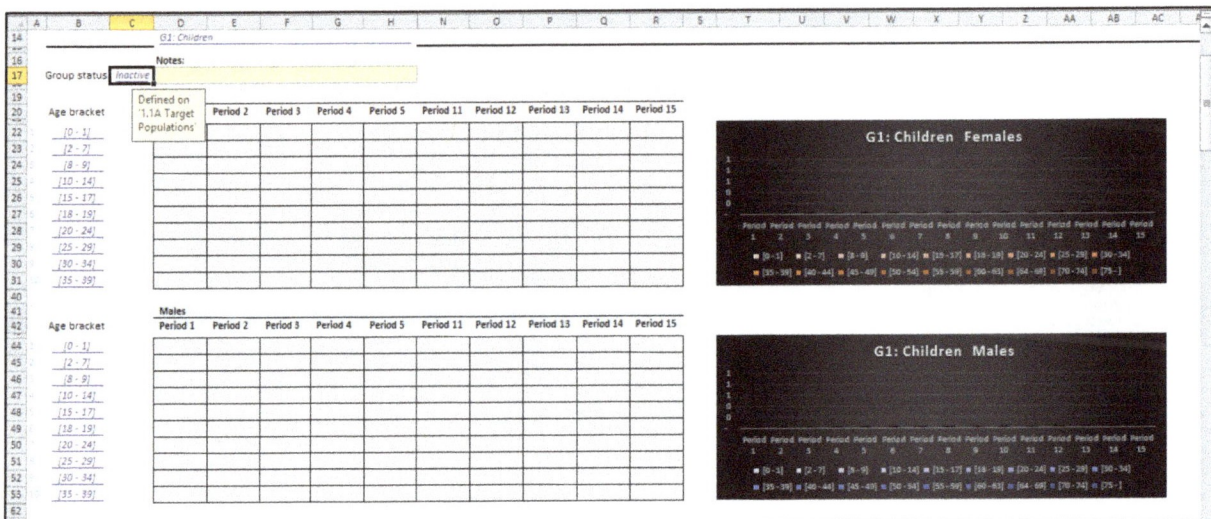

Note: Screenshot contains hidden rows and columns for illustration purposes only.

C.   The 1.2A Service Categories Input Sheet

This worksheet (Figure 87) allows for adding, defining, and deleting *Service Categories* (e.g., general surgery, cardiology, gynecology) and *Services* (e.g., appendectomy, burn treatment). It shows the list of services provided to the members of the health insurance program, and all health services are classified by health category. Specifically, this worksheet provides for inputting *Assumption 18 (Health Categories)* described in Chapter II-D.

Figure 87: Preview of the 1.2A Service Categories Worksheet

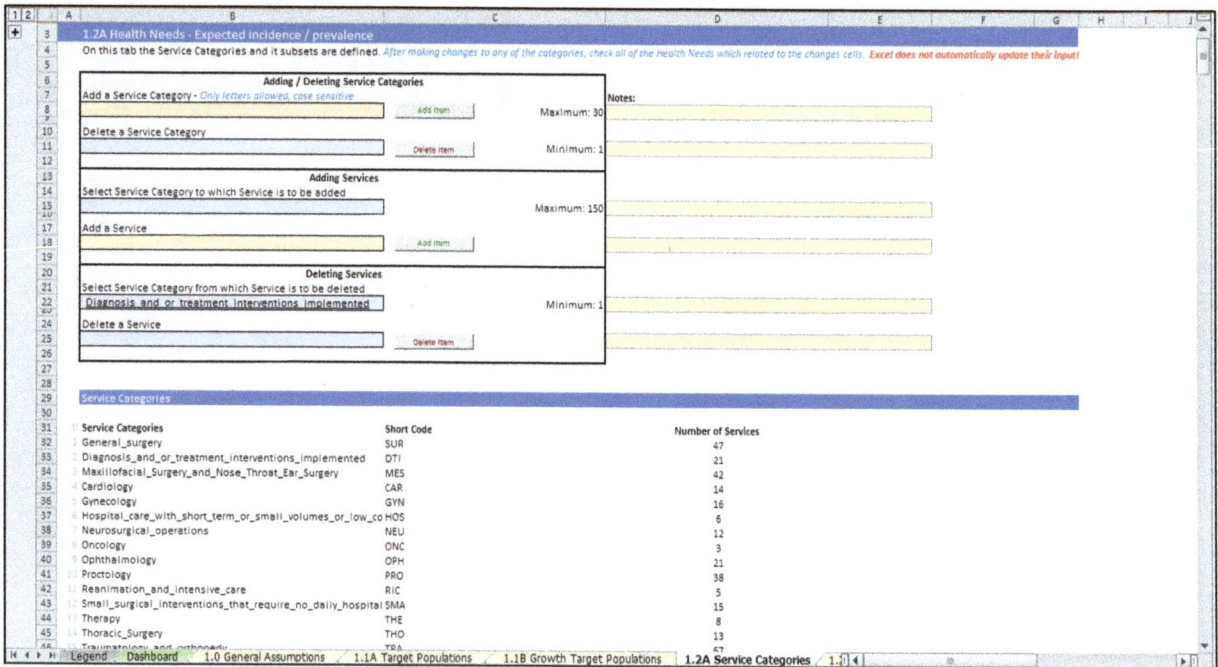

The drop-down lists in this worksheet are automatically updated once data lists are edited. For instance, when a *"Sample Category"* was added using the **Add Item** button in the *Add a Service Category*, the *Delete a Service Category* automatically included *"Sample_Category"* in the list (Figure 88).

Figure 88: Drop-Down Lists Automatically Updated with Sample Category

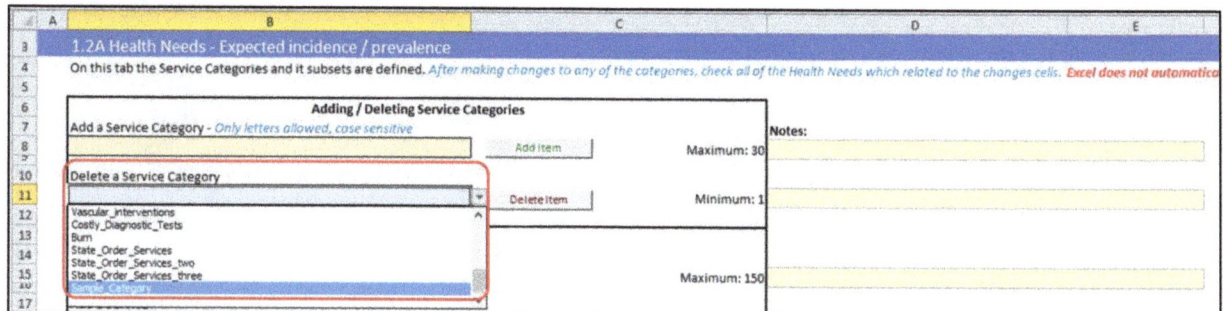

TAKE NOTE

In case the user is editing a SLAM Excel file version that already had filled entries in the 1.2B Health Needs, the user must review the Health Needs entries that are related to the edited health services in the 1.2A Service Categories worksheet.

FOR YOUR INFORMATION

Cells found in this worksheet include:

Input Cells	
100.00	Input cell, unrestricted
100.00	Input cell, select option from list
Free Text Cells	
Note	Input cell to write comments
Buttons	
Add Item	Button to perform action such as adding or deleting rows and/or columns, selecting an option or performing an action
	Green text on a button means an item is added, red text means an item is deleted

- Unrestricted input cells that accept alphanumeric keys;
- Restricted input cells for selection from a drop-down list;
- Free text cells for adding corresponding explanations, comments, sources, or other helpful texts pertaining to encoded information; and
- Buttons with green text for adding an item, and buttons with red text for deleting an item.

SUMMARY REMINDERS FOR OPENING THE SLAM EXCEL FILE

Microsoft Excel Visual Basic for Applications (VBA) operates via buttons add and delete in this worksheet to prevent users from making mistakes if they try to add or remove variables. The model that has been programmed in Excel is fairly complex and inadvertently adding or removing a row or column manually (without using VBA buttons) on one sheet has consequences on the formulas written on multiple other sheets.

Service Categories

The SLAM Excel file has 22 default *Service Categories* summarized in the **Service Categories** section of the worksheet, specifically **row 29** (Section Header) to **row 55** (Total Services) (Figure 89). A line number in blue font color next to the service categories is in place for reference.

Figure 89: Service Categories Summary List Section in the 1.2A Service Categories Worksheet

	A	B	C	D	E
29		Service Categories			
30					
31		Service Categories	Short Code	Number of Services	
32		1 General_surgery	SUR	47	
33		2 Diagnosis_and_or_treatment_interventions_implemented	DTI	21	
34		3 Maxillofacial_Surgery_and_Nose_Throat_Ear_Surgery	MES	42	
35		4 Cardiology	CAR	14	
36		5 Gynecology	GYN	16	
37		6 Hospital_care_with_short_term_or_small_volumes_or_low_cost	HOS	6	
38		7 Neurosurgical_operations	NEU	12	
39		8 Oncology	ONC	3	
40		9 Ophthalmology	OPH	21	
41		10 Proctology	PRO	38	
42		11 Reanimation_and_intensive_care	RIC	5	
43		12 Small_surgical_interventions_that_require_no_daily_hospital_care	SMA	15	
44		13 Therapy	THE	8	
45		14 Thoracic_Surgery	THO	13	
46		15 Traumatology_and_orthopedy	TRA	67	
47		16 Urology	URO	49	
48		17 Vascular_interventions	VAS	17	
49		18 Costly_Diagnostic_Tests	CDT	12	
50		19 Burn	BUR	1	
51		20 State_Order_Services	XXX	56	
52		21 State_Order_Services_two	XX2	143	
53		22 State_Order_Services_three	XX3	1	
55		Total services		607	

Users may add or delete more service categories in the **Adding/Deleting Service Categories** section of the worksheet (Figure 90). Up to 30 service categories may be inputted while minimum requirement is one category. For each category, at least one health service must be defined.

Figure 90: The Adding/Deleting Service Categories Section in the 1.2A Service Categories Worksheet

	A	B	C	D	E
3		1.2A Health Needs - Expected incidence / prevalence			
4		On this tab the Service Categories and it subsets are defined. *After making changes to any of the categories, check all of the Health Needs which related to the changes cells.* **Excel does not automatica**			
5					
6		Adding / Deleting Service Categories			
7		Add a Service Category - *Only letters allowed, case sensitive*		Notes:	
8			Add Item	Maximum: 30	
10		Delete a Service Category			
11			Delete Item	Minimum: 1	
12					

> **! TAKE NOTE**
>
> Users must be careful in using the add and delete VBA buttons since "Undo" or "CTRL+Z" does not work with these macros.

To add a new service category: (i) the user must input the name of the category in **cell B8** (e.g., Emergency Services) and then (ii) click the <u>Add Item</u> button beside it (Figure 91).

Figure 91: Steps in Adding a New Service Category in the 1.2A Service Categories Worksheet

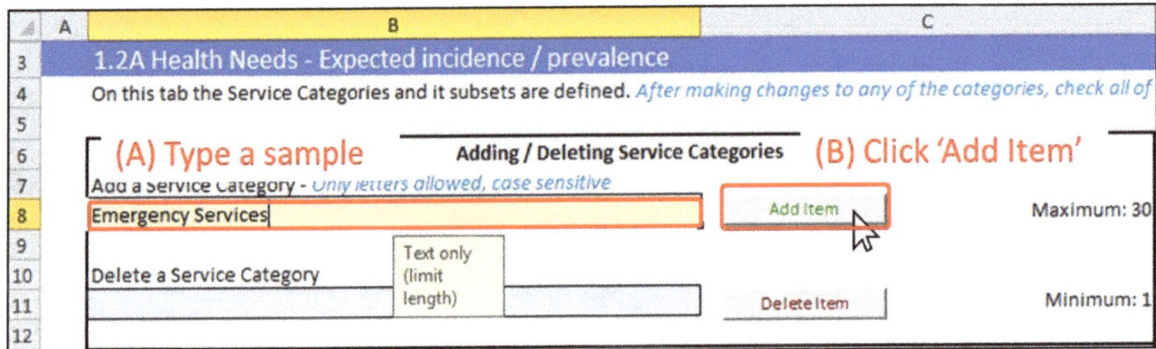

A dialog box will then be displayed and the user should click <u>OK</u> (Figure 92).

Figure 92: Message Box after Adding a New Service Category in the 1.2A Service Categories Worksheet

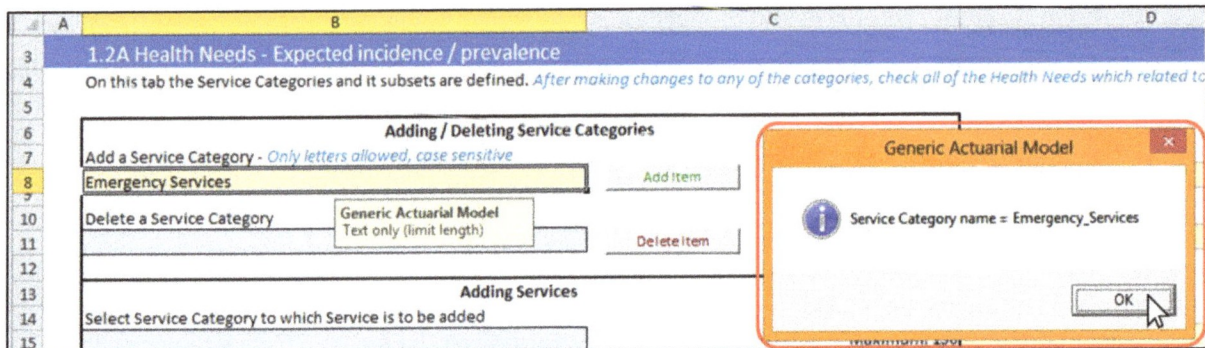

The user will then be instructed to assign a 3-character code (e.g., EMR) in the next dialog box and click <u>OK</u> (Figure 93).

Figure 93: Assigning a 3-Character Code for the Added Service Category in the 1.2A Service Categories Worksheet

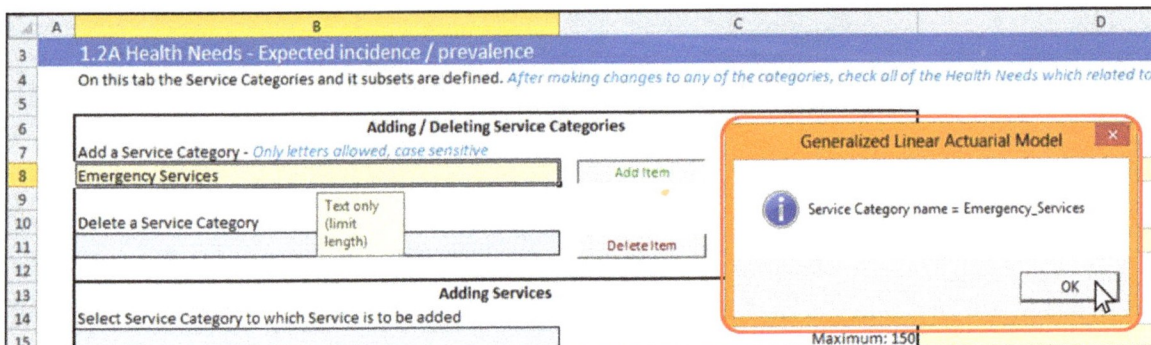

The number of service categories increased from 22 to 23, and the new category will now be displayed in the **Service Categories** section (Figure 94). Note that the SLAM program will automatically provide one healthcare service under the newly added service category. Also notice that there will be movement of rows as more service categories are added (i.e., the row for Total Services became **row 56** instead of the default row 55).

Figure 94: New Service Category Added in the Service Categories Summary List of the 1.2A Service Categories Worksheet

	A	B	C	D
29		Service Categories		
30				
31	0	Service Categories	Short Code	Number of Services
32	1	General_surgery	SUR	47
33	2	Diagnosis_and_or_treatment_interventions_implemented	DTI	21
34	3	Maxillofacial_Surgery_and_Nose_Throat_Ear_Surgery	MES	42
35	4	Cardiology	CAR	14
36	5	Gynecology	GYN	16
37	6	Hospital_care_with_short_term_or_small_volumes_or_low_cost	HOS	6
38	7	Neurosurgical_operations	NEU	12
39	8	Oncology	ONC	3
40	9	Ophthalmology	OPH	21
41	10	Proctology	PRO	38
42	11	Reanimation_and_intensive_care	RIC	5
43	12	Small_surgical_interventions_that_require_no_daily_hospital_care	SMA	15
44	13	Therapy	THE	8
45	14	Thoracic_Surgery	THO	13
46	15	Traumatology_and_orthopedy	TRA	67
47	16	Urology	URO	49
48	17	Vascular_interventions	VAS	17
49	18	Costly_Diagnostic_Tests	CDT	12
50	19	Burn	BUR	1
51	20	State_Order_Services	XXX	56
52	21	State_Order_Services_two	XX2	143
53	22	State_Order_Services_three	XX3	1
54	23	Emergency_Services	EMR	1
56		Total services		608

The new healthcare service (e.g., short code "EMR_1") will be displayed at the end of existing rows (e.g., **row 666**, or **line number 608**) in the "**List of services**" section. Since the user has yet to define a specific health service under the new category, it is automatically labeled as "Please replace with Service name." See Figure 95 for illustration.

Figure 95: New Health Service Under the List of Services Section of the 1.2A Service Categories Worksheet

	A	B	C	D	E	F
650	592	XX2_130	State_Order_Services_two	Tonsillectomy, adenoidectomy General anesthesia		
651	593	XX2_131	State_Order_Services_two	Tonsillectomy, adenoidectomy general anesthesia / adult /		
652	594	XX2_132	State_Order_Services_two	Tonsillectomy, adenoidectomy local anesthetic		
653	595	XX2_133	State_Order_Services_two	Tonsillectomy, adenoidectomy local anesthesia / adult /		
654	596	XX2_134	State_Order_Services_two	Small metal constructions, cloves platform, platform forearm, collarbone platform (for everyone)		
655	597	XX2_135	State_Order_Services_two	Minor surgical interventions / adult /		
656	598	XX2_136	State_Order_Services_two	Kidney stone lithotripsy through (up to 4,000 stroke)		
657	599	XX2_137	State_Order_Services_two	Otolaryngological		
658	600	XX2_138	State_Order_Services_two	Otolaryngological /adult/		
659	601	XX2_139	State_Order_Services_two	Otolaryngological day cre / adult /		
660	602	XX2_140	State_Order_Services_two	Orthopedic		
661	603	XX2_141	State_Order_Services_two	Orthopedic / adult /		
662	604	XX2_142	State_Order_Services_two	Orthopedic, surgical intervention		
663	605	XX2_143	State_Order_Services_two	Orthopedic day care /adult/		
664	606	XX2_144	State_Order_Services_two	Pustular surgery (including blood sowing established sepsis) / adult /		
665	607	XX3_2	State_Order_Services_three	General Surgical /adult/1_08/		
666	608	EMR_1	Emergency_Services	Please replace with Service name		
667						

Note: The screenshot above contains hidden rows for illustration purposes only.

To assign a new name for the corresponding health service under the new service category, the user may directly edit the cell by replacing the "Please replace with Service name" with for instance, "Accident/Trauma." See Figure 96 for illustration.

Figure 96: Assigning Name for New Health Service in 1.2A Service Categories Worksheet

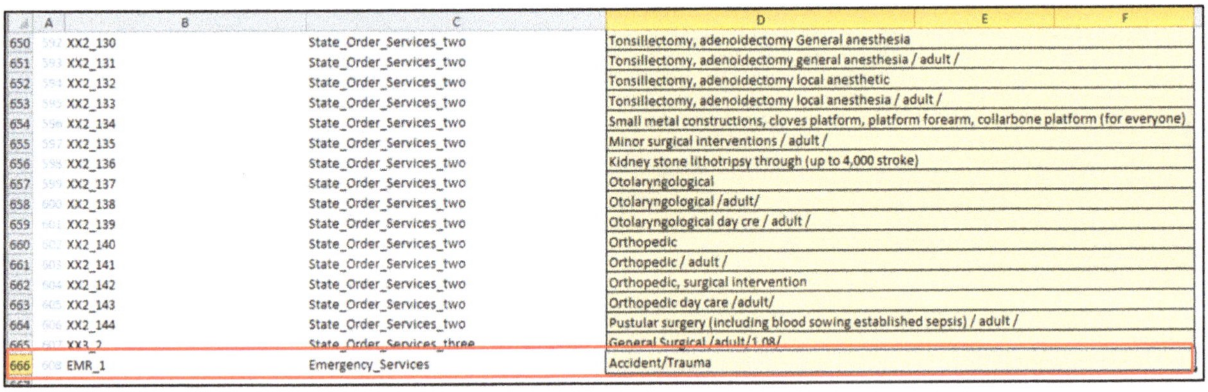

Note: Screenshot contains hidden rows for illustration purposes only.

To delete a service category: (i) the user must select the name of the category (e.g., "Emergency Services") from the drop-down menu of **cell B11** and then (ii) click the Delete Item button beside it (Figure 97).

Figure 97: Deleting a Service Category in the 1.2A Service Categories Worksheet

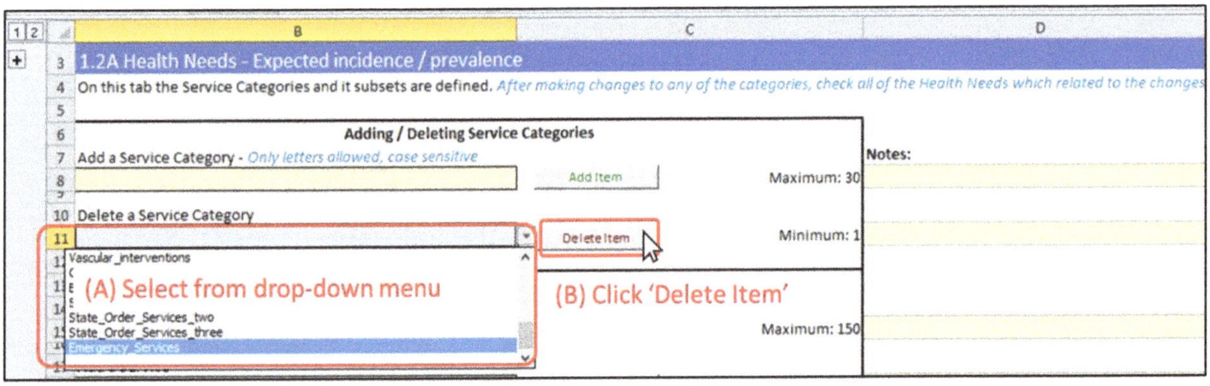

A dialog box will then be displayed and the user should click <u>OK</u> (Figure 98). Clicking the exit (X) button in the upper left corner of the dialog box **will still delete** the selected service category.

Figure 98: Message Box After Deleting a Service Category in the 1.2A Service Categories Worksheet

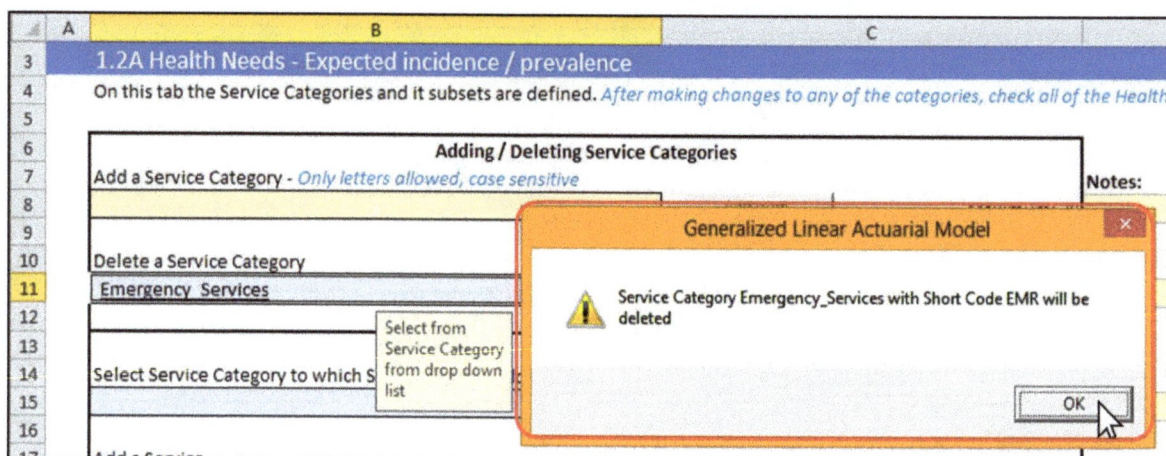

The deleted category will no longer be found in the "Delete a Service Category" drop-down menu of **"Adding/Deleting Service Categories"** section or displayed in the **"Service Categories"** section; corresponding health services under the deleted category will no longer be seen in the **"List of Services"** section (Figure 99).

Figure 99: Emergency Services Category Removed in the 1.2A Service Categories Worksheet

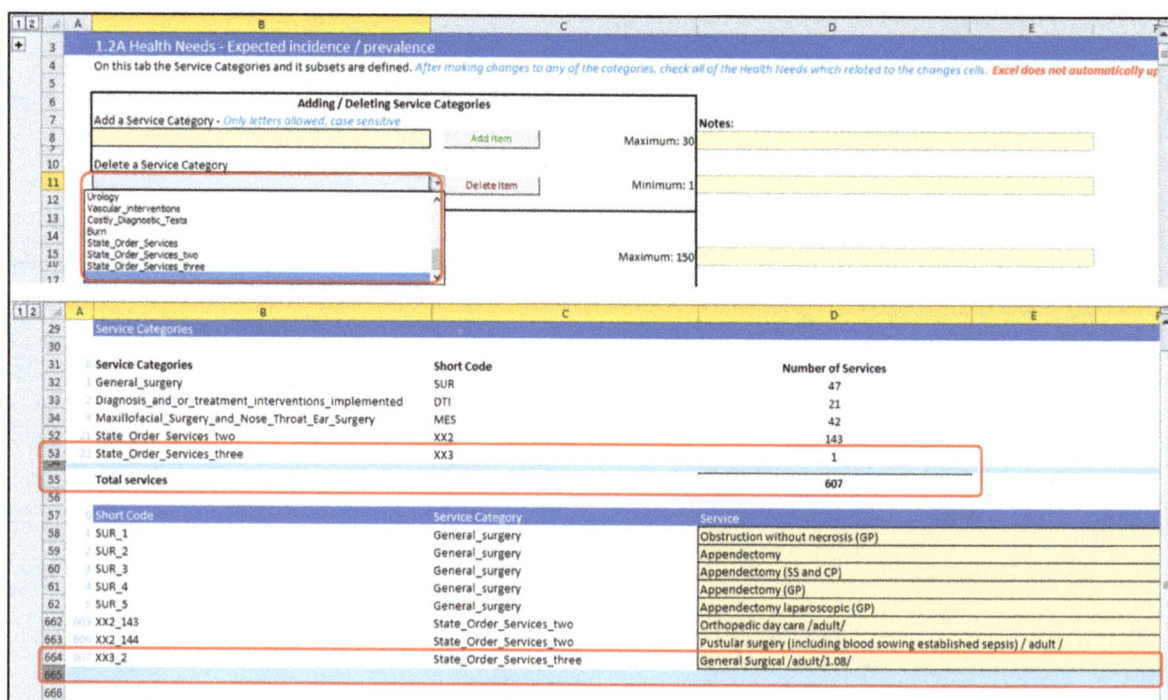

Note: Screenshot contains hidden rows for illustration purposes only.

> **TAKE NOTE**
>
> It is very important to note that "Undo" or "CTRL+Z" does not work in <u>add</u> and <u>delete</u> VBA buttons. Deleting an existing service category deletes ALL health services under that category, thus, make sure the category is no longer needed.

Services

All health *Services* are classified by health category. By default, a total of 607 health services are preset in the SLAM file for the 22 default health categories (Figure 100).

Figure 100: Number of Services in the Service Category Summary List of the 1.2A Service Categories Worksheet

Service Categories	Short Code	Number of Services
General_surgery	SUR	47
Diagnosis_and_or_treatment_interventions_implemented	DTI	21
Maxillofacial_Surgery_and_Nose_Throat_Ear_Surgery	MES	42
Cardiology	CAR	14
Gynecology	GYN	16
Hospital_care_with_short_term_or_small_volumes_or_low_cost	HOS	6
Neurosurgical_operations	NEU	12
Oncology	ONC	3
Ophthalmology	OPH	21
Proctology	PRO	38
Reanimation_and_intensive_care	RIC	5
Small_surgical_interventions_that_require_no_daily_hospital_c	SMA	15
Therapy	THE	8
Thoracic_Surgery	THO	13
Traumatology_and_orthopedy	TRA	67
Urology	URO	49
Vascular_interventions	VAS	17
Costly_Diagnostic_Tests	CDT	12
Burn	BUR	1
State_Order_Services	XXX	56
State_Order_Services_two	XX2	143
State_Order_Services_three	XX3	1
Total services		607

Users may add health services in the **Adding Services** section of the worksheet (Figure 101) and delete health services in the **Deleting Services** section of the worksheet (Figure 102). Up to 150 services may be added per health category, while at least one health service must remain for each health category.

Figure 101: The Adding Services Section in the 1.2A Service Categories Worksheet

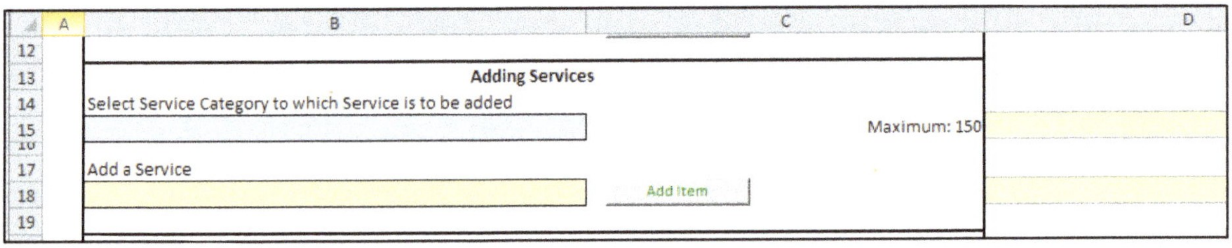

Figure 102: The Deleting Services Section in the 1.2A Service Categories Worksheet

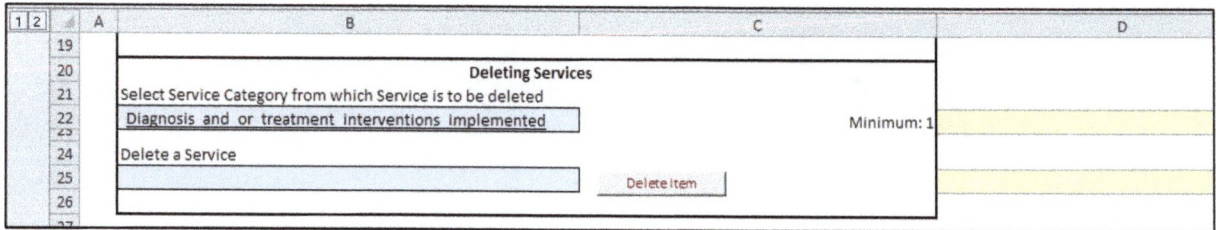

> **TAKE NOTE**
>
> Users must be careful in using add and delete VBA buttons since "Undo" or "CTRL+Z" does not work with these macros.

To add a new health service under an existing service category: (i) select the existing service category of interest (e.g., "Inpatient Services") in the drop-down menu of **cell B15**; (ii) encode the name of the health service (e.g., "Accident/Trauma") in **cell B18**; and (iii) click the Add Item button beside it. See illustration in Figure 103.

Figure 103: Adding Services in the 1.2A Service Categories Worksheet

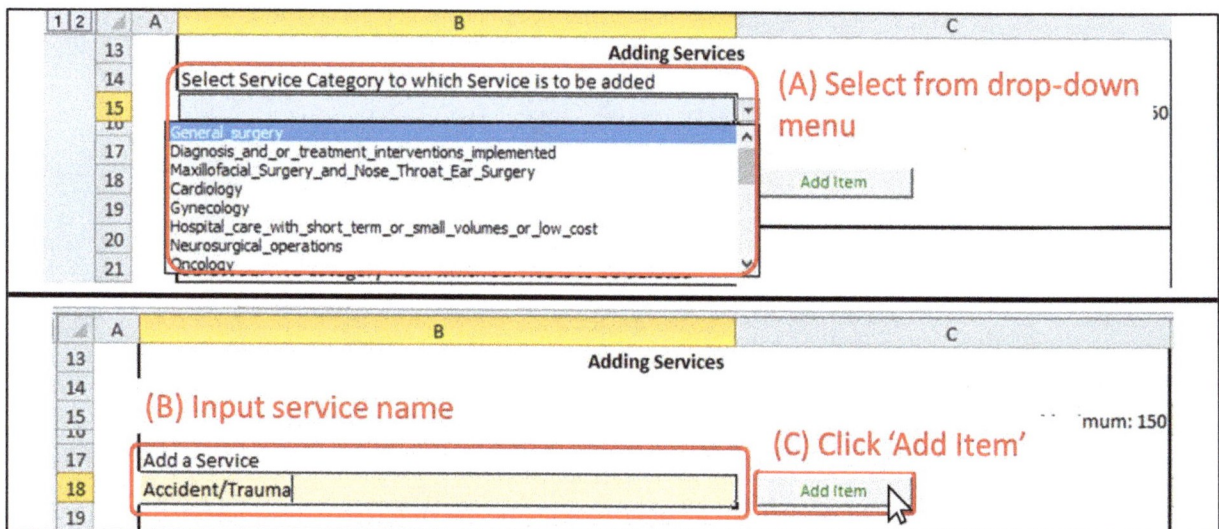

The new healthcare service will now be added to the "Number of Services" corresponding to the "Service Category" in the **"Service Categories"** section. For example, the number of services for category "General_surgery" increased from the default 47 to 48. See illustration in Figure 104.

Figure 104: Number of Services Updated in the Service Categories
Summary List in the 1.2A Service Categories Worksheet

	A	B	C	D
29		Service Categories		
30				
31		Service Categories	Short Code	Number of Services
32		General_surgery	SUR	48
33		Diagnosis_and_or_treatment_interventions_implemented	DTI	21
34		Maxillofacial_Surgery_and_Nose_Throat_Ear_Surgery	MES	42
35		Cardiology	CAR	14
36		Gynecology	GYN	16
37		Hospital_care_with_short_term_or_small_volumes_or_low_cost	HOS	6
38		Neurosurgical_operations	NEU	12
39		Oncology	ONC	3
40		Ophthalmology	OPH	21
41		Proctology	PRO	38
42		Reanimation_and_intensive_care	RIC	5
43		Small_surgical_interventions_that_require_no_daily_hospital_c	SMA	15
44		Therapy	THE	8
45		Thoracic_Surgery	THO	13
46		Traumatology_and_orthopedy	TRA	67
47		Urology	URO	49
48		Vascular_interventions	VAS	17
49		Costly_Diagnostic_Tests	CDT	12
50		Burn	BUR	1
51		State_Order_Services	XXX	56
52		State_Order_Services_two	XX2	143
53		State_Order_Services_three	XX3	1
55		Total services		608

The new healthcare service (e.g., "Accident/Trauma") will be displayed at the end of existing rows (e.g., **row 105**, or **line number 48**) under the "General_surgery" category in the **List of services** section. See Figure 105 for illustration.

Figure 105: New Service Added in the List of Services
Section of the 1.2A Service Categories Worksheet

	A	B	C	D	E	F
87		SUR_30	General_surgery	strumectomy average volume (GP)		
88		SUR_31	General_surgery	Strumectomy radical lymph dissection volume		
89		SUR_32	General_surgery	strumectomy radical lymph dissection volume (GP)		
90		SUR_33	General_surgery	strumectomy small volume (GP)		
91		SUR_34	General_surgery	Ventral hernia great (without a net value) (GP)		
92		SUR_35	General_surgery	Ventral hernia great (without a net value) (SS and CP)		
93		SUR_36	General_surgery	Focal surgery for intestinal pathologies (SS and CP)		
94		SUR_37	General_surgery	Operations obstruction case (GP)		
95		SUR_38	General_surgery	Operations on choledochus (SS and CP)		
96		SUR_39	General_surgery	Operations on choledochus (GP)		
97		SUR_40	General_surgery	Operations of ulcerative disease (GP)		
98		SUR_41	General_surgery	In case of gastric cancer surgery pathologies (SS and CP)		
99		SUR_42	General_surgery	Removal of the spleen (GP)		
100		SUR_43	General_surgery	Removal of small tumors (general anesthesia) (SS and CP)		
101		SUR_44	General_surgery	Removal of small tumors (general anesthesia) (GP)		
102		SUR_45	General_surgery	Removal of small tumors (local anesthesia) (SS and CP)		
103		SUR_46	General_surgery	Removal of small tumors (local anesthesia) (GP)		
104		SUR_47	General_surgery	Circular resection for rectal use device		
105		SUR_48	General_surgery	Accident/Trauma		
106		DTI_1	Diagnosis_and_or_treatment_interventions_imple	Diagnostic thoracotomy (SS and CP)		

Note: Screenshot contains hidden rows for illustration purposes only.

To delete a single service (e.g., "Accident/Trauma") under an existing service category, select first the existing service category of interest (e.g., "General surgery") in the drop-down menu of **cell B22** (Figure 106).

Figure 106: Selecting an Existing Service Category in the 1.2A Service Categories Worksheet

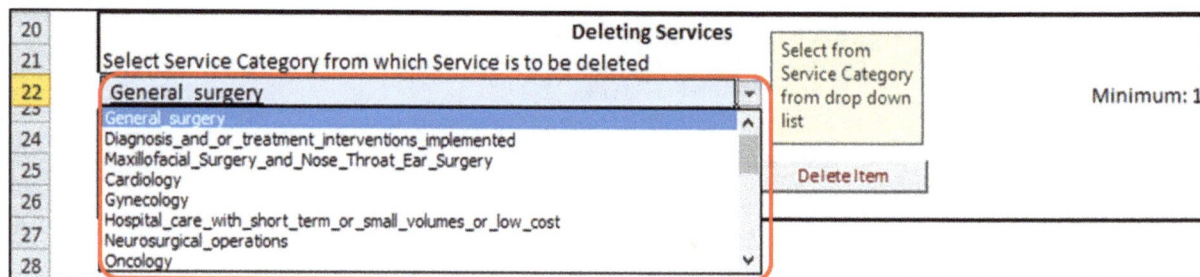

The list of short codes for health services under the chosen category will be displayed in the drop-down menu of **cell B25**. To continue deletion, (i) select the name service to be deleted (e.g., "Accident/Trauma" under "General surgery" health category) and then (ii) click the **Delete Item** button, as illustrated in Figure 107.

Figure 107: Deleting a Single Health Service Under a Service Category in the 1.2A Service Categories Worksheet

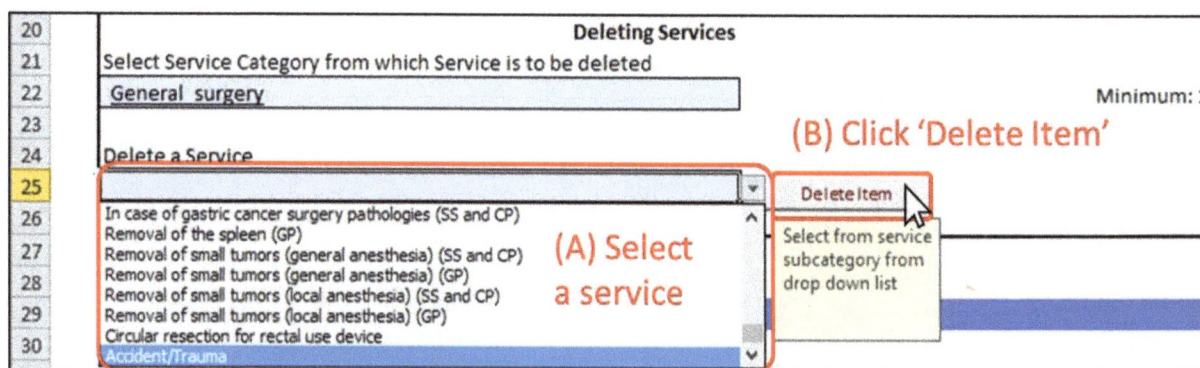

> **TAKE NOTE**
>
> Users must be careful to select the correct code to be deleted since "Undo" or "CTRL+Z" does not work with the **Delete Item** VBA-button.

A dialog box will then be displayed, verifying removal of the selected healthcare service. Selecting Yes in the message box will delete the chosen health service, while selecting No will abort the deletion process and will retain the identified health service (Figure 108).

Figure 108: Message Box Verifying Deletion of a Health Service in the 1.2A Service Categories Worksheet

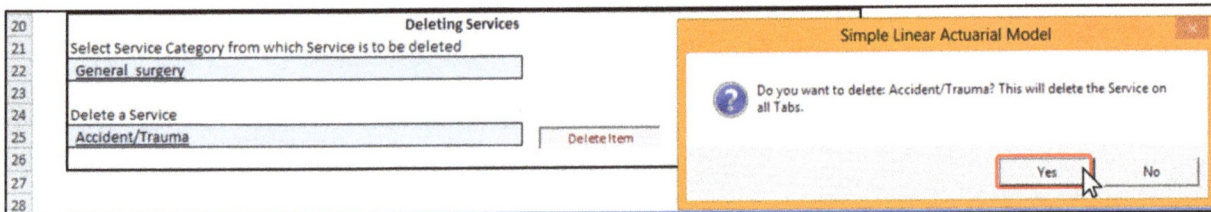

The deleted health service category will no longer be found in the "Delete a Service" drop-down menu of the "**Deleting Services**" section; will not be counted in the "**Service Categories**" section (i.e., 47 services for "General surgery" category from earlier 48); and will not be displayed in the "**List of Services**" section for the specified service category (Figure 109).

Figure 109: Sample Accident/Trauma Service Under General Surgery Category Removed in the 1.2A Service Categories Worksheet

Note: Screenshot contains hidden rows for illustration purposes only.

On the other hand, deleting ALL services under an existing service category is similar to deleting a service category, as discussed earlier. Simply (i) select the name of the category (e.g., "Inpatient Services") from the drop-down menu of **cell B11**, (ii) click the **Delete Item** button beside it, and (iii) click **OK** in the displayed dialog box (Figure 110). Clicking the exit (X) button in the upper left corner of the dialog box **will still delete** the selected service category, thereby deleting ALL services in that category.

Figure 110: Deleting All Health Services Under an Existing Service Category in the 1.2A Service Categories the Worksheet

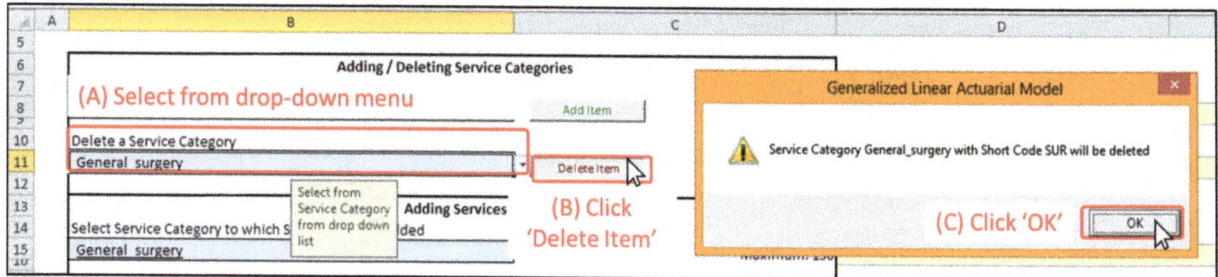

The deleted category will no longer be found in the "Delete a Service Category" drop-down menu of "**Adding/Deleting Service Categories**" section; not displayed in the "**Service Categories**" section; and all health services under the deleted category will no longer be seen in the "**List of Services**" section (Figure 111).

Figure 111: Example of Deleting All Health Services Under the Inpatient Services Category

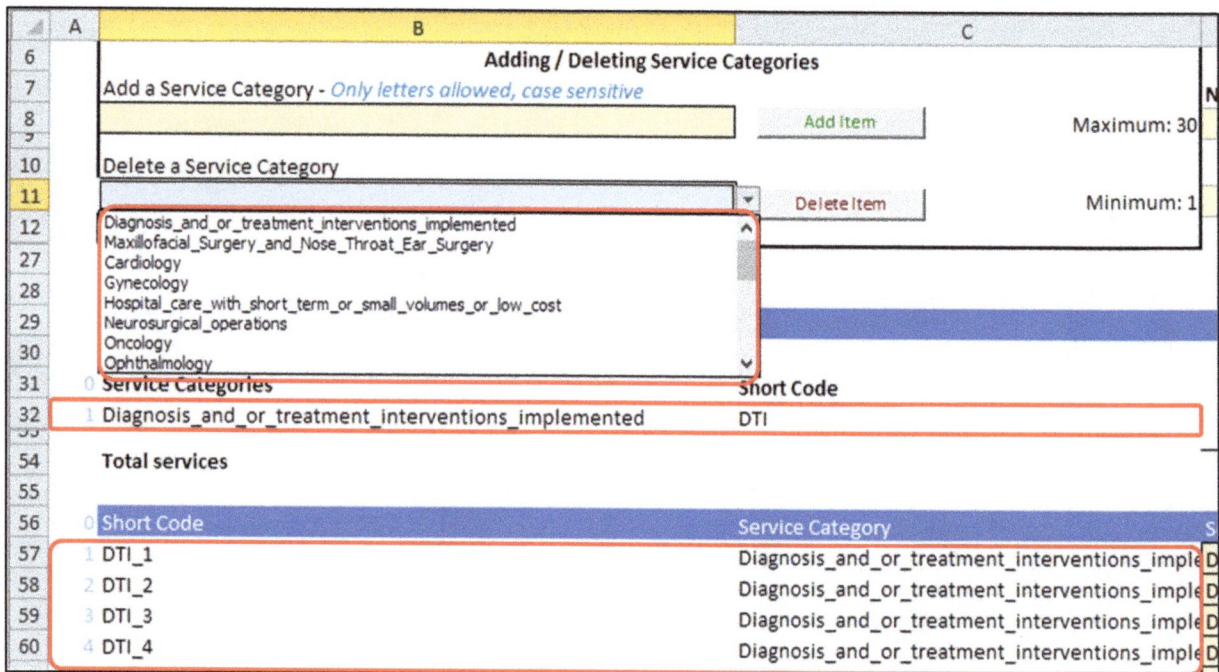

> **! TAKE NOTE**
>
> It is very important to note that "Undo" or "CTRL+Z" does not work in add and delete VBA buttons. Deleting an existing service category deletes ALL health services under that category, thus make sure the category is no longer needed.

D. The 1.2B Health Needs Input Sheet

This worksheet (Figure 112) provides space for recording the *health needs* of the target population. As discussed in Chapter III-D6 (Health needs, health services and health service costs), SLAM assumes that *health services* represent the health needs of the insured household members.

Mainly, this worksheet provides for inputting the following assumptions, described in Chapter II-D:

- Assumption 19: Predicting Future Health Needs
- Assumption 20: Stable Incidences and Prevalences under the Baseline Scenario

Specifically, this worksheet allows setting up per health service of the service *code*; standardization *per 1,000 / 10,000/100,00* population; *target population*; *sex*; lower bound age *(Age: LB)*; upper bound age *(Age:UB)*; *sensitivity factor*; *incidence/prevalence*; and *inpatient days of the service* (if applicable).

Figure 112: Preview of the 1.2B Health Needs Worksheet

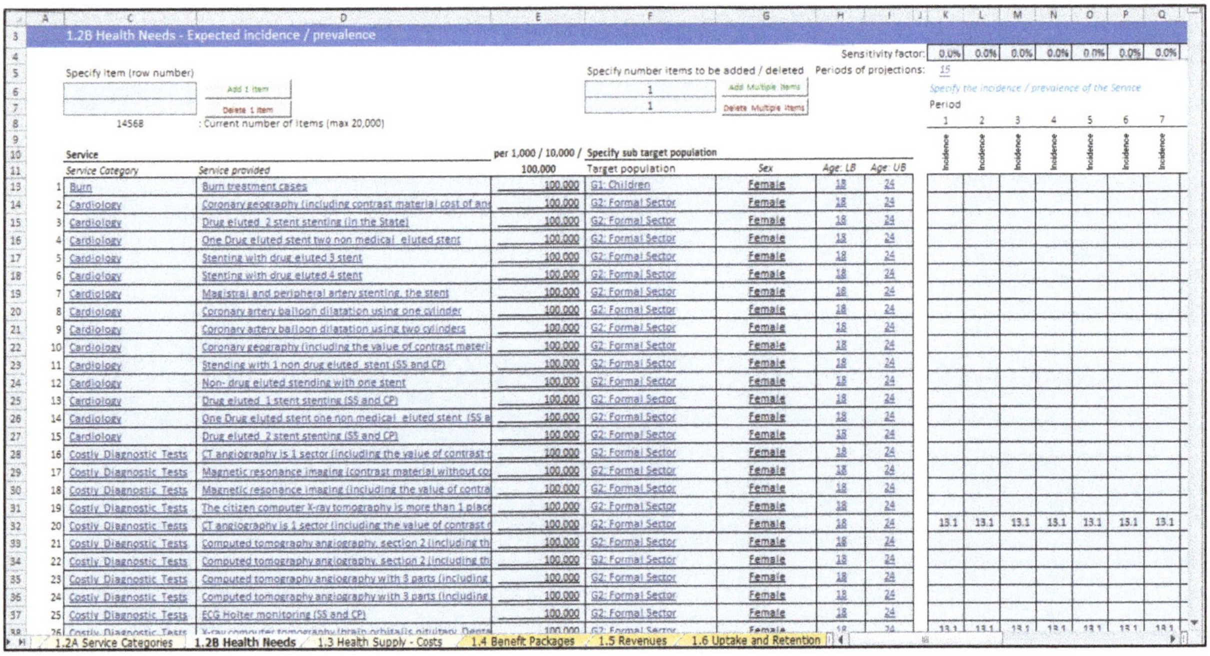

Notes: CT= computed tomography, ECG = electrocardiogram.

> ### (i) FOR YOUR INFORMATION
>
> Cells found in this worksheet include:
>
> **Input Cells**
>
> | 100.00 | Input cell, restricted input (e.g., only positive values/only integers/dates/etc.)
>
> | 100.00 | Input cell, select option from list
>
> | 100.00 | Input cell, select option from list, input defined on another sheet
>
> **Free Text Cells**
>
> | Note | Input cell to write comments
>
> **Calculation Cells**
>
> | 200.00 | Cell used to (visually) check results (locked)
>
> **Buttons**
>
> | Add Item | Button to perform action such as adding or deleting rows and/or columns, selecting an option or performing an action
> Green text on a button means an item is added, red text means an item is deleted
>
> - Restricted input cells for encoding only positive numeric values;
> - Restricted input cells for selection from a drop-down list;
> - Restricted input cells for selection from a drop-down list of inputs defined on another worksheet;
> - Free text cells for adding corresponding explanations, comments, sources, or other helpful texts pertaining to encoded information;
> - Calculation cells that are locked and used to visually check results; and
> - Buttons with green text for adding an item, and buttons with red text for deleting an item.

For discussion purposes, this worksheet will be divided into four sections:

- **Columns A–I** for service specifications, or *Assumption 19* (Figure 113);
- **Columns K–Y** for incidence/prevalence of service specifications, or *Assumption 20* (Figure 114);
- **Column AA–AO** for inpatient days of the service specifications (Figure 115); and
- **Column AQ–BD** for control, validation, and notes (Figure 116).

Figure 113: Service Specifications Section in the 1.2B Health Needs Worksheet

	A	C	D	E	F	G	H	I
3		1.2B Health Needs - Expected incidence / prevalence						
4								Sensitivity fact
5		Specify item (row number)			Specify number items to be added / deleted	Periods of projection		
6			Add 1 Item		1	Add Multiple Items		
7			Delete 1 Item		1	Delete Multiple Items		
8		14568	: Current number of items (max 20,000)					
9								
10		Service		per 1,000 / 10,000 /	Specify sub target population			
11		Service Category	Service provided	100,000	Target population	Sex	Age: LB	Age: UB
13	1	Burn	Burn treatment cases	100,000	G1: Children	Female	18	24
14	2	Cardiology	Coronary geography (including contrast material cost of anest	100,000	G2: Formal Sector	Female	18	24
15	3	Cardiology	Drug eluted 2 stent stenting (in the State)	100,000	G2: Formal Sector	Female	18	24
16	4	Cardiology	One Drug eluted stent two non medical eluted stent	100,000	G2: Formal Sector	Female	18	24
17	5	Cardiology	Stenting with drug eluted 3 stent	100,000	G2: Formal Sector	Female	18	24

Figure 114: Incidence/Prevalence of the Service Specifications Section in the 1.2B Health Needs Worksheet

	H	I	J	K	L	M	N	O	P	Q	R	S	T	U	V	W	X	Y
3																		
4	Sensitivity factor:			0.0%	0.0%	0.0%	0.0%	0.0%	0.0%	0.0%	0.0%	0.0%	0.0%	0.0%	0.0%	0.0%	0.0%	0.0%
5	Periods of projections:			15														
6				*Specify the incidence/prevalence of the service*														
7				Period														
8				1	2	3	4	5	6	7	8	9	10	11	12	13	14	15
9				Incidence	Incidence	Incidence	Incidence	Incidence	Incidence	Incidence	Incidence	Incidence	Incidence	Incidence	Incidence	Incidence	Incidence	Incidence
10																		
11	Age: LB	Age: UB																
13	18	24		**Simple Linear Actuarial Model** Number of expected services per rate as set in column E														
14	18	24																
15	18	24																
16	18	24																

Figure 115: Inpatient days of the Service Specifications Section in the 1.2B Health Needs Worksheet

	Z	AA	AB	AC	AD	AE	AF	AG	AH	AI	AJ	AK	AL	AM	AN	AO
3																
4																
5																
6		*Specify the estimated associated number of inpatient days of the Service (if applicable)*														
7		Period														
8		1	2	3	4	5	6	7	8	9	10	11	12	13	14	15
9		Nbr of days	Nbr of days	Nbr of days	Nbr of days	Nbr of days	Nbr of days	Nbr of days	Nbr of days	Nbr of days	Nbr of days	Nbr of days	Nbr of days	Nbr of days	Nbr of days	Nbr of days
10																
11																
13		**Simple Linear Actuarial Model** Number of inpatient days admitted per episode. Only applicable for service that have inpatient admission, else leave empty.														
14																
15																
16																
17																
18																

Figure 116: Control, Validation, and Notes Section in 1.2B Health Needs Worksheet

	AP	AQ	AR	AS	AT	BA	BB	BC	BD
8									
9						Expected	Expected # IPD		
10		Control cells (warning texts)				period events	days per period		Notes:
11									
13						-	-		
14						-	-		
15						-	-		
16						-	-		
17						-	-		
18						-	-		

Service

The default setting of this worksheet includes all *Service Category* (**column C**) and *Service provided* (**column D**) defined in the 1.2A Service Categories" worksheet (Figure 117).

Figure 117: Service Category and Service Provided Columns in the 1.2B Health Needs Worksheet Defined in 1.2A Service Categories Worksheet

	A	C	D	E	F	G	H	I
10		Service		per 1,000 / 10,000 /	Specify sub target population			
11		Service Category	Service provided	100,000	Target population	Sex	Age: LB	Age: UB
13	1	Burn	Burn treatment cases	100,000	G1: Children	Female	18	24
14	2	Cardiology	Coronary geography (including	100,000	G2: Formal Sector	Female	18	24
15	3	Cardiology	Drug eluted 2 stent stenting (	100,000	G2: Formal Sector	Female	18	24
16	4	Cardiology	One Drug eluted stent two nor	100,000	G2: Formal Sector	Female	18	24
17	5	Cardiology	Stenting with drug eluted 3 st	100,000	G2: Formal Sector	Female	18	24
18	6	Cardiology	Stenting with drug eluted 4 st	100,000	G2: Formal Sector	Female	18	24

(Note: Simple Linear Actuarial Model — Defined on '1.2A Service Categories'. Do not forget to update after changes are made to the Service Categories)

All incidence, prevalence, and inpatient days will be recorded for all target groups defined in the 1.1A Target Populations worksheet, which are the following:

- Group 1: Children
- Group 2: Formal Sector
- Group 3: Disabled
- Group 4: Pensioners
- Group 5: State Order - Others
- Group 6: Everyone Else

This means that the rows of service types defined in the 1.2A Service Categories worksheet should be repeated for all applicable target groups, sex, and age bracket. The current setting of the SLAM limits the number of items or rows into 20,000. In its default setting for 1.2B Health Needs, the worksheet includes all health services for applicable member groups and respective sex and age bracket totaling to 14,568 items for health needs definition (Figure 118).

Figure 118: Control, Validation, and Notes Section in 1.2B Health Needs Worksheet

	A	C	D	E	F	G	H	I
3		1.2B Health Needs - Expected incidence / prevalence						
4								Sensitivity facto
5		Specify item (row number)			Specify number items to be added / deleted		Periods of projection	
6			Add 1 Item		1	Add Multiple Items		
7			Delete 1 Item		1	Delete Multiple Items		
8		14568	: Current number of items (max 20,000)					
9								
10		Service		per 1,000 / 10,000 /	Specify sub target population			
11		Service Category	Service provided	100,000	Target population	Sex	Age: LB	Age: UB
14574	14562	Vascular interventions	Bilateral Venetectomy	100,000	G6: Everyone Else	Male	45	63
14575	14563	Vascular interventions	Bilateral Venetectomy (GP)	100,000	G6: Everyone Else	Male	45	63
14576	14564	Vascular interventions	Artery - venous hemodialysis for design fistula	100,000	G6: Everyone Else	Male	45	63
14577	14565	Vascular interventions	Major vascular surgery, thoracic and lumbar sympathectomy,	100,000	G6: Everyone Else	Male	45	63
14578	14566	Vascular interventions	Magistral and balloon dilatation of peripheral arteries using a	100,000	G6: Everyone Else	Male	45	63
14579	14567	Vascular interventions	Magistral and peripheral arterial stenting and balloon dilatati	100,000	G6: Everyone Else	Male	45	63
14580	14568	Vascular interventions	Magistral and peripheral artery stenting, 2 stent	100,000	G6: Everyone Else	Male	45	63

The modeling of future health needs is done per health service and standardized per 1,000, 10,000 or 100,000 members by target group. **Column E** (Figure 119) allows the user to select the standardization figure to use. The default setting provided is per 1,000 population but users may edit the selection using the drop-down list. If left empty, the SLAM will assume that per 100,000 population is required for analysis.

Figure 119: Input Cells for Standardization per 1,000/10,000/100,000 in the 1.2B Health Needs Worksheet

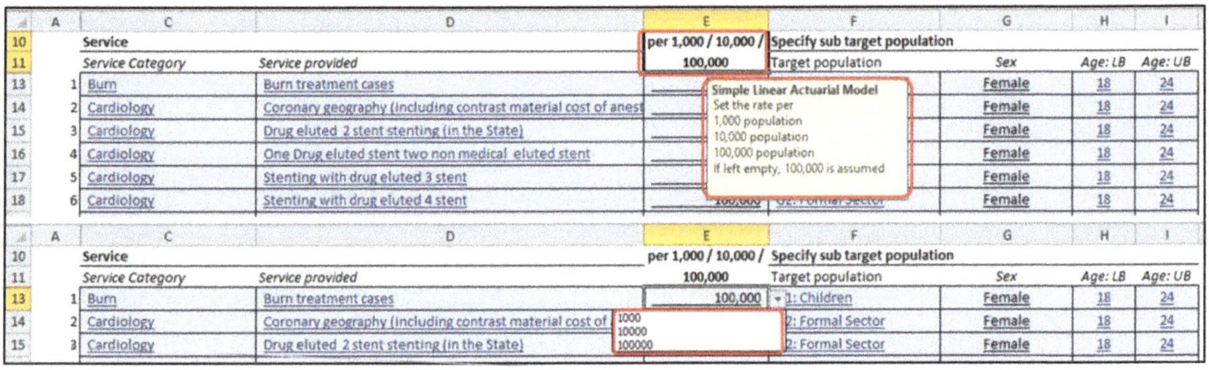

While an automated list is provided for each health service row in **Column E**, it is not necessary, and tedious as well, to use the drop-down menu when editing the target standardization figures. For convenience, users may edit the first entry (e.g., cell E13) then copy-paste-hard-values the selection to the rest of health services that will require changes (e.g., cells E14–E14580).

Column F meanwhile provides the space for defining the *Target Population* to which the health needs for the health service in column D will be specified (Figure 120). The options are automatically picked up by the program from the groups defined in the 1.1A Target Populations worksheet.

Figure 120: Input Cells for Target Population in the 1.2B Health Needs Worksheet

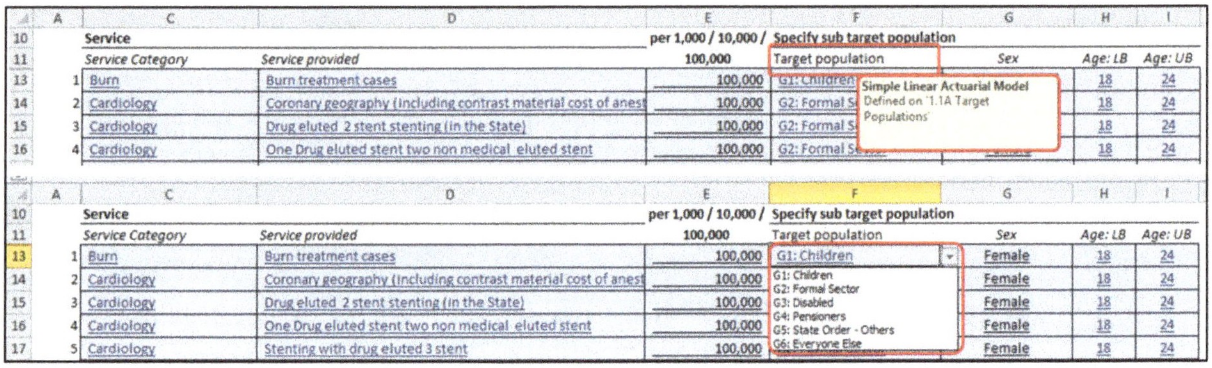

Similar with column E, it is not necessary, and tedious as well, to choose from the drop-down list for all cells in **column F**. A user may select a target group (e.g., G2: Formal Sector in cell F13) then copy the contents to the rest cells pertaining to where the selected target group is appropriate (e.g., F14 up to F14,580).

For each service and target populations defined in columns B to F, users are then required in **column G** (Figure 121) to identify corresponding *Sex* such that whether the calculations will be applied to "Female," "Male," or "Both." If left empty, the SLAM program will automatically compute for both females and males.

Figure 121: Input Cells for Sex in the 1.2B Health Needs Worksheet

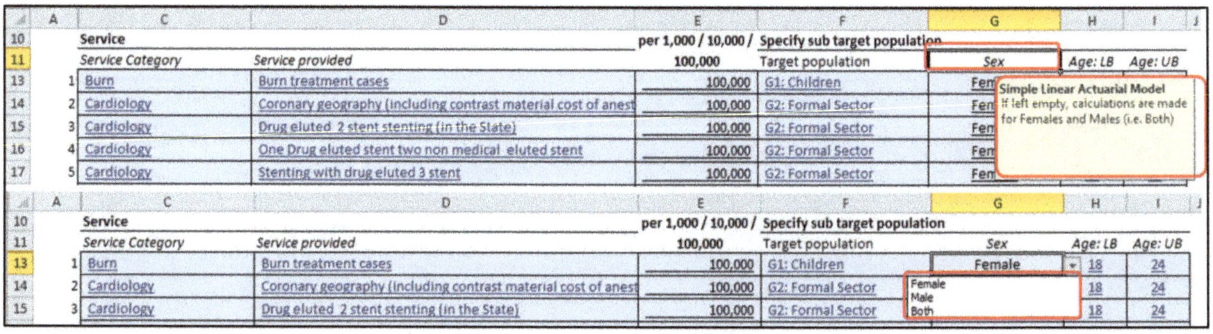

Column G (*Sex*) also allows for copying the contents of cells within this column. However, users must review carefully the services provided to determine whether appropriate sex entries are selected. While most healthcare services are for both males and females, breast removal and all gynecology services, for instance, apply only to females.

Column H (*Lower Bound Age*) and **column I** (*Upper Bound Age*) as shown in Figure 122, require the user to define the applicable age range for each of the health services defined in Column D. For instance, only women of reproductive health age (i.e., 15–49 years) are expected to obtain health services that are related to childbirth. The options in the drop-down list are those defined in the 1.1A Target Populations worksheet. If the cells are left empty in columns H and I the program will assume the lowest and highest possible age bound, respectively. These two columns also allow for copying of cells within the same column.

Figure 122: Input Cells for Age Bracket in the 1.2B Health Needs Worksheet

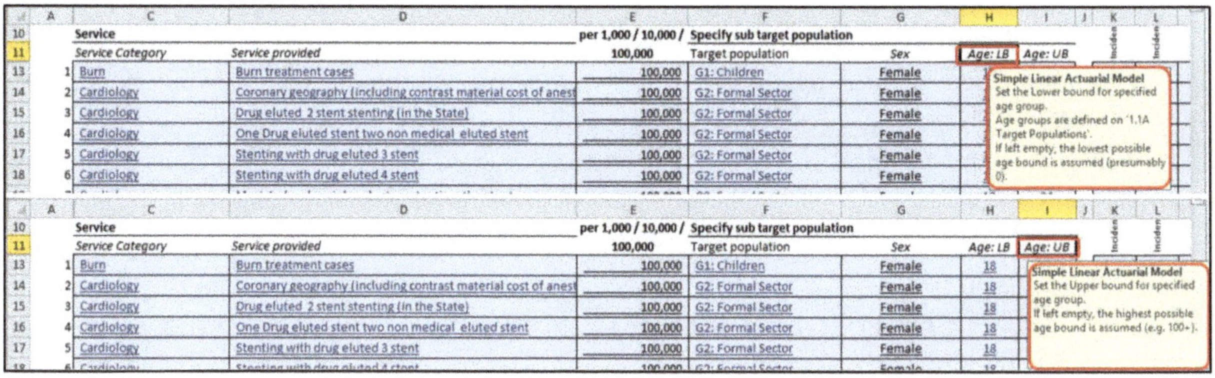

Adding and/or Deleting Services

In adding and/or deleting services (Figure 123), row number after which service(s) should be added (**cell C6**) or deleted (**cell C7**) must be specified first. After which, the number of rows corresponding to the number of items to be added (**cell F6**) or deleted (**cell F6**) can be specified.

Figure 123: Input Cells for Adding and/or Deleting Services in the 1.2B Health Needs Worksheet

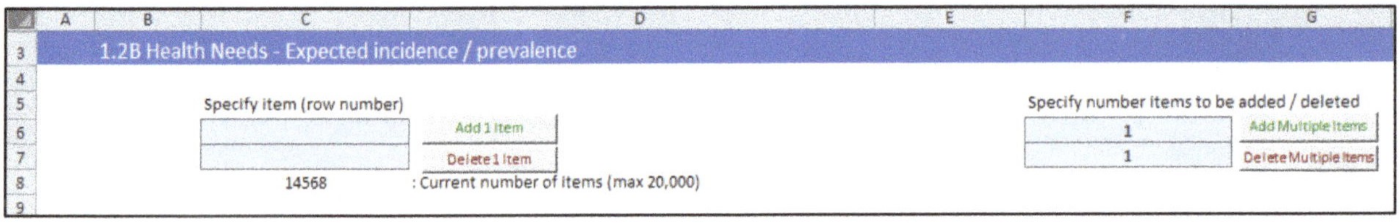

Suppose the user wants to add a new health service and it needs to be at or near the top of the list of services. The user should input "1" in **cell C6** (Figure 124) to indicate that the new item will be added AFTER the first health service. The default setting in the SLAM program allows for adding new entries in all rows except for the very first health service. Thus, the row number specified in C6 should be equal or greater than 1. If left empty, the new item(s) will be added at the end of the list.

Figure 124: Input Cells for Specifying Row Number in the 1.2B Health Needs Worksheet (Part 1)

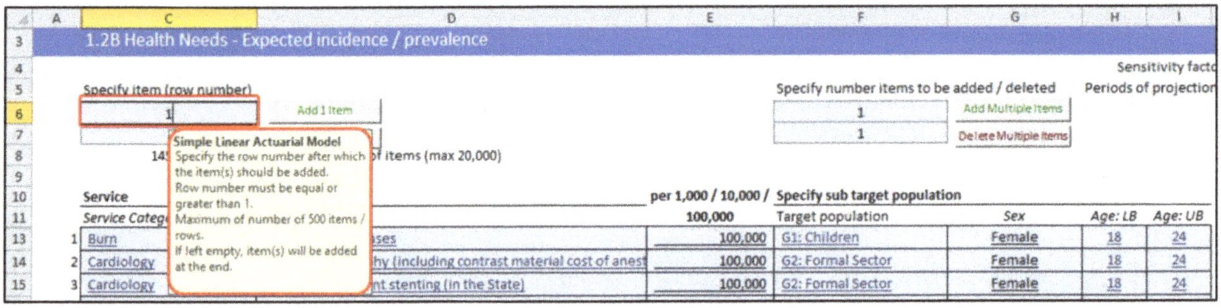

After indicating the row number in cell C6, the user must click on the **Add 1 item** button in **cell D6**. A new row (e.g., row 14 or line number 2 in column A) as shown in Figure 125, will then be displayed with undefined entries in columns B–I.

Figure 125: Input Cells for Specifying Row Number in the 1.2B Health Needs Worksheet (Part 2)

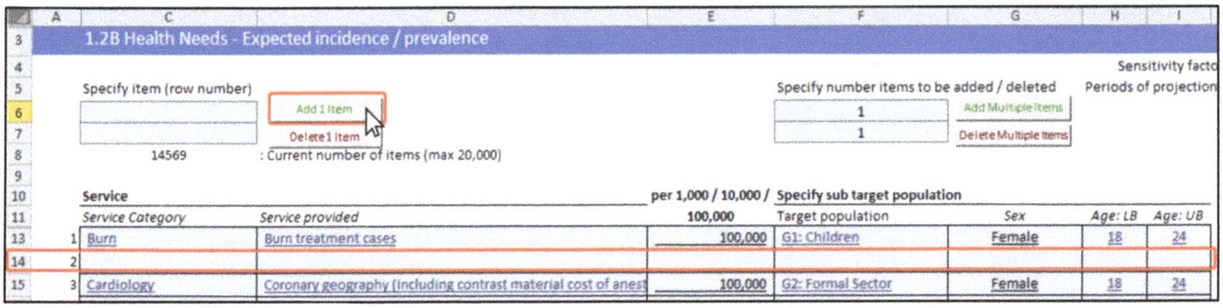

If the user prefers that a new entry be displayed at the top of the list of services (i.e., row 13 or line number 1), the entries in the current top of the list must be first replicated to the newly added row (e.g., row 14 or line number 2). Only then should the top of the list be updated with information of the new entry of services.

For example, the current top of the list pertains to "Burn treatment cases" under the category "Burn" and the new entry is the "Accident/Trauma" under the category "General surgery" defined earlier in the *Service Categories* section on *page 56*. The following is the stepwise guide so that the new entry will be displayed at the top of the list:

1. In **cell B14**, select a service category parameter using the drop-down menu (e.g., Burn) (Figure 126).

Figure 126: Selecting Service Category for New Row in the 1.2B Health Needs Worksheet

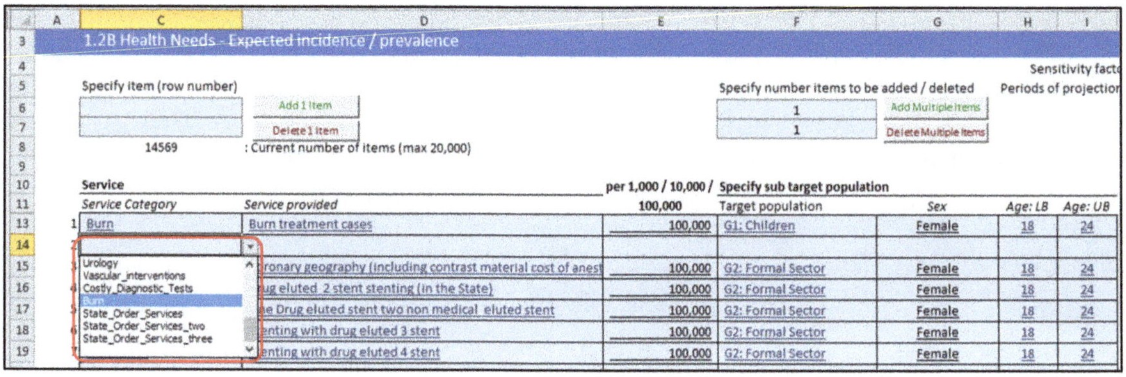

2. In **cell B14**, select a "service provided" parameter using the drop-down menu (e.g., "Burn treatment cases") (Figure 127).

Figure 127: Selecting Service Provided for New Row in the 1.2B Health Needs Worksheet

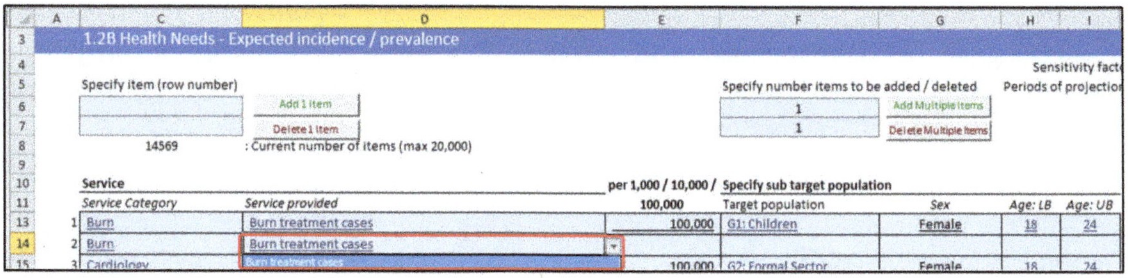

3. The user may then copy the entries in cells E13 to I13 into cells E14 to I14 (Figure 128).

Figure 128: Copying Entries of Current Top of the List to the Newly Added Row in the1.2B Health Needs Worksheet

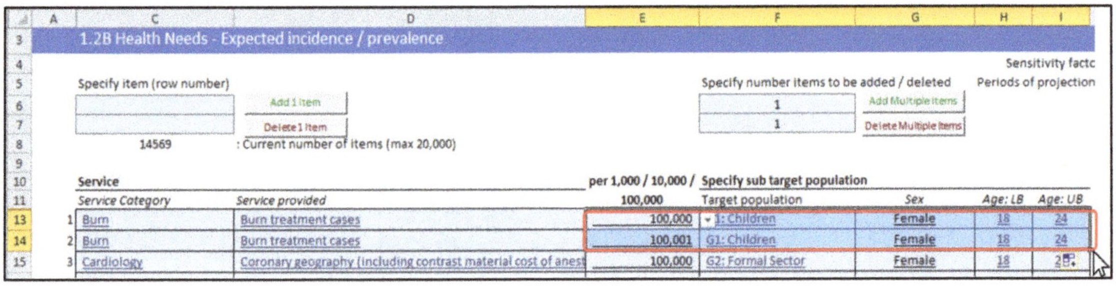

4. Once the current top of the list has been replicated to the newly added row (Figure 129), the user can now edit the top of the list into the new service item of interest (e.g., "Accident/Trauma" previously added in the 1.2A Service Catergory worksheet).

Figure 129: Current Top of the List Replicated to the Newly Added Row in the 1.2B Health Needs Worksheet

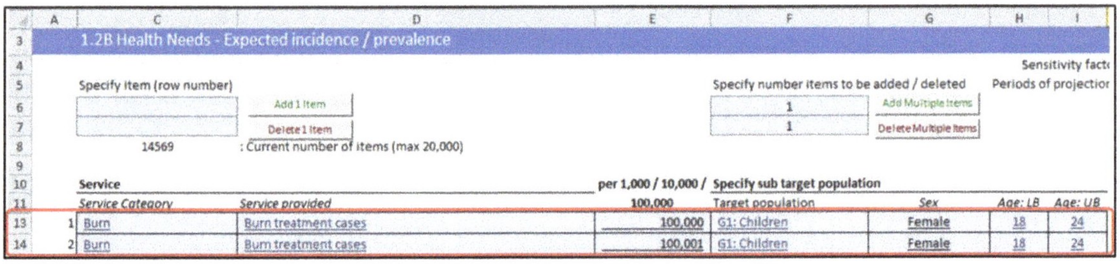

Entries in **column C** (Service Category) and **column D** (Service provided) can be redefined to General surgery and Accident/Trauma. **Column E** (Standardization figure), **column F** (Target population), **column G** (Sex), **column H** (Lower bound age), and **column I** (Upper bound age) can then be defined accordingly (Figure 130).

Figure 130: Top of the List Updated with New Entries in the 1.2B Health Needs Worksheet

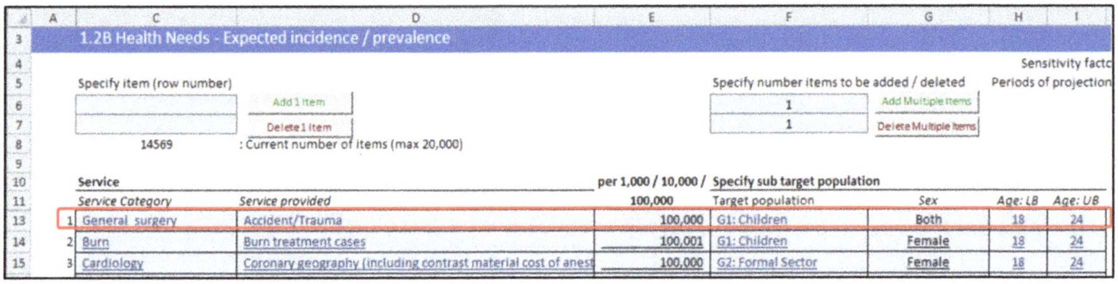

On the other hand, to add multiple new health services (e.g., Cesarean Section and Debridement of wound, burn, or infection) under the General surgery category, and then insert such after the service Accident/Trauma, the user must:

(i)   first check whether the health services "Cesarean Section" and "Debridement of wound, burn, or infection" are already defined in the 1.2A Service Categories worksheet. If not yet listed in the worksheet, see *page 56* for adding new health services under an existing service category.

> **TAKE NOTE**
>
> Only health services defined in the 1.2A Service Categories section can be added in the 1.2B Health Needs worksheet. Thus, after making changes to the 1.2A Service Category worksheet, check all of the health needs related to the changed cells because the SLAM program does not automatically update inputs.

(ii)   once health services of interest are defined in the 1.2A Service Categories worksheet, input "1" in **cell C6** of the 1.2B Health Needs worksheet to indicate that new entries will be added after the first row of health services (Figure 131);

(iii)   Input "2" in **cell F6** in the 1.2B Health Needs worksheet to note that two new items will be inserted after the first row (Figure 131);

Figure 131: Specifying Row Number and Number of Items to be Added/Deleted in 1.2B Health Needs Worksheet

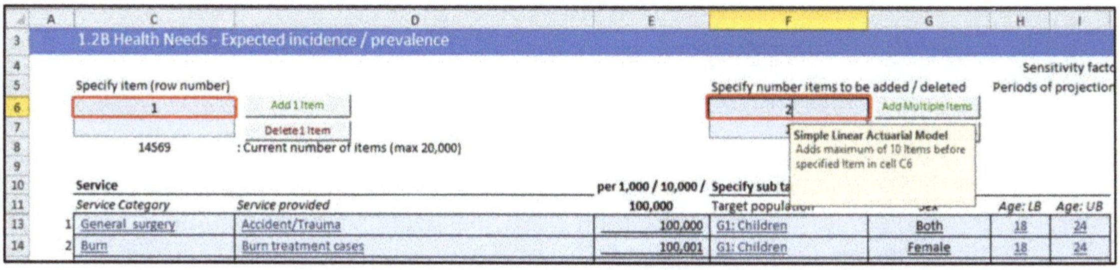

(iv)   click the Add Multiple Items button to add two new rows after line 1 (Figure 132).

Figure 132: Sample Two New Rows Added After Line Number 1 in the 1.2B Health Needs Worksheet

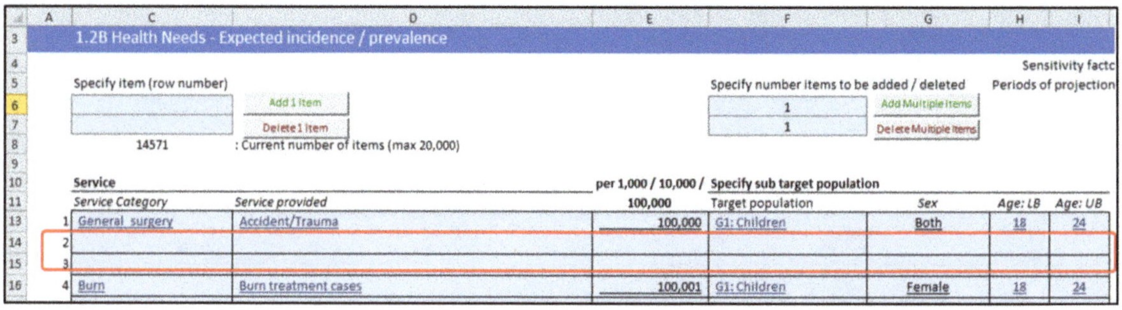

(v) select the service category and service provided parameters of interest in the drop-down list under **column C** and **column D** (Figure 133);

Figure 133: Defining Sample Service in the 1.2B Health Needs Worksheet

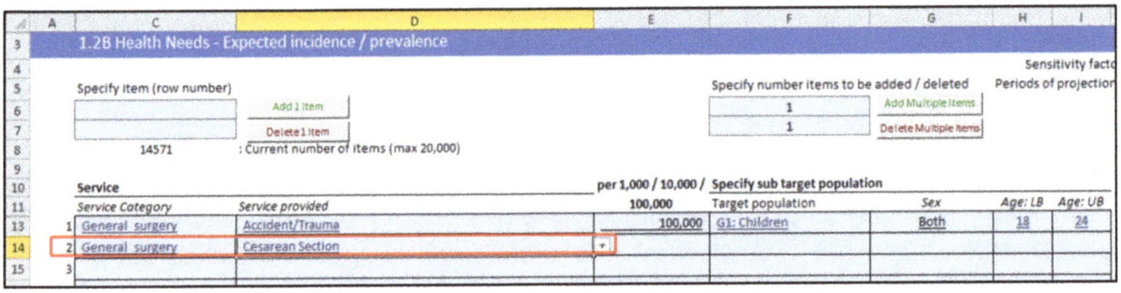

(vi) continue to define entries in **column E** (standardization figure), **column F** (target population), **column G** (Sex), **column H** (lower bound age), and **column I** (upper bound age), accordingly (Figure 134); and

Figure 134: Defining Other Information of New Service in the 1.2B Health Needs Worksheet

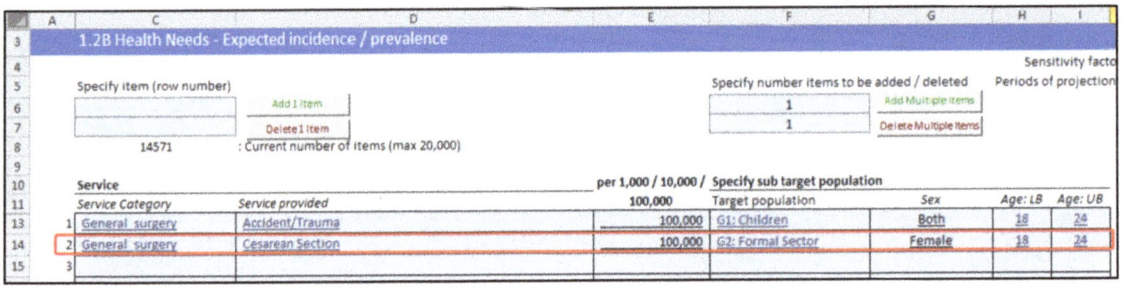

(vii) follow steps 5 and 6 above for the rest of newly added blank rows (Figure 135).

Figure 135: Sample New Service in the 1.2B Health Needs Worksheet

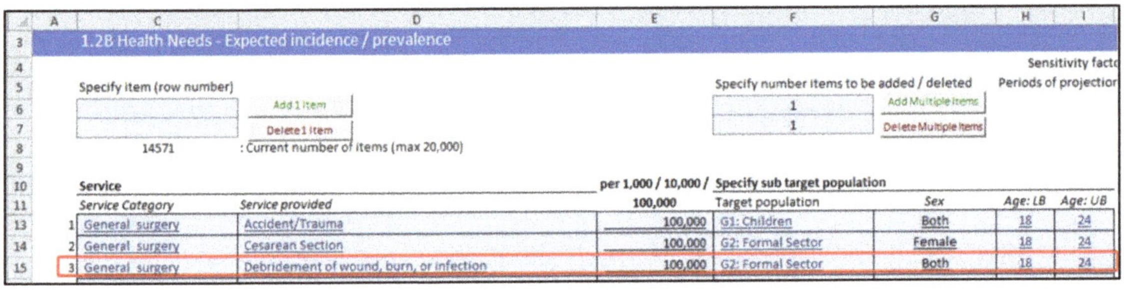

The same steps must be followed if a user wants to delete an existing row (**Steps 1–4** on pages 66–67) or delete multiple rows (**Steps 1–7** on pages 68–69), except that instead of using the <u>Add</u> button, the analyst must use the <u>Delete</u> button.

It is important to note that if the user decides to edit the existing entries in the 1.2A Service Categories worksheet, the entries in the 1.2B Health Needs worksheet must be reviewed and updated as necessary when changes are made in the health services.

For instance, if the user in the 1.2A Service Categories worksheet (Figure 136) renamed the service "Cesarean Section" under "General surgery" category to "CS," the name "Cesarean Section" in the 1.2B Health Needs" worksheet (e.g., item number 2) will be retained and must be updated to "CS" by selecting the new name in the drop-down list. The previous entries in columns E–I are still saved by the program (Figure 137). Thus, if a user assigns a new service in the first row/line number 1, all entries in the said row must be checked for consistency.

Figure 136: Editing Services in the 1.2A Service Category Worksheet

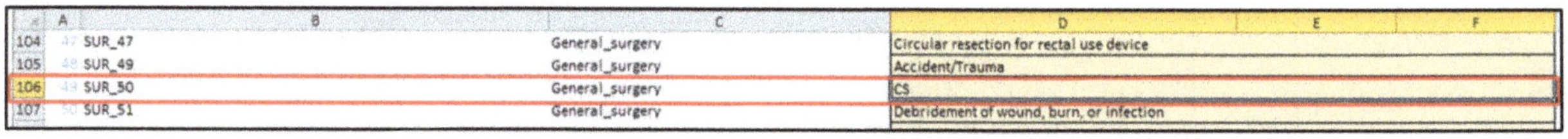

Figure 137: Updating Entries in the 1.2B Health Needs Worksheet

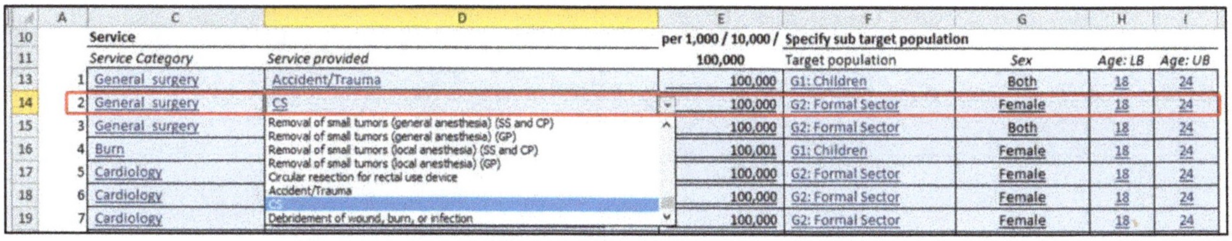

On the other hand, when a service has been deleted in the 1.2A Service Categories worksheet, this will automatically be removed in the 1.2B Health Needs worksheet as well as other related tabs. Figure 138 shows the updated 1.2B Health Needs worksheet when the previously added services (i.e., "Accident/Trauma," "CS," and "Debridement of wound, burn, or infection") were deleted.

Figure 138: Deleted Entries in the 1.2B Health Needs Worksheet

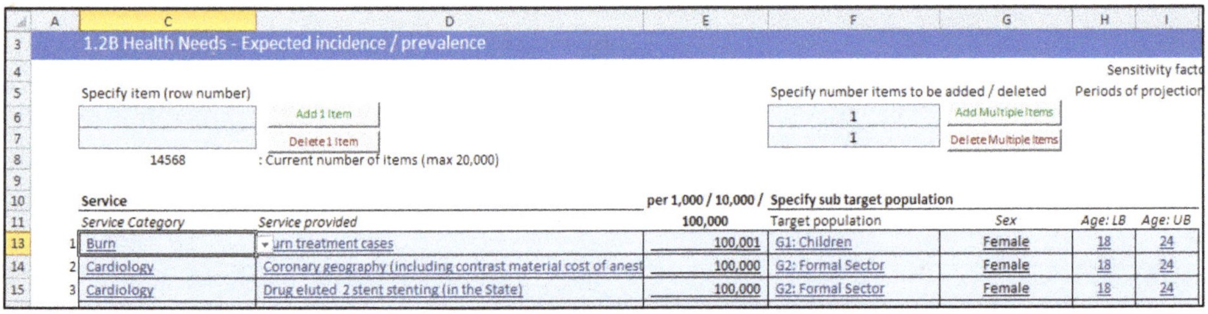

Incidence/Prevalence of the Service

Columns K–Y require the SLAM user to *specify the incidence or prevalence of the service* defined in column D ("Service provided") for the target population characteristics specified in columns F–I ("Target population," "Sex," "Lower bound age," and "Upper bound age"). Up to 15 columns are provided for the *periods of projections.* The number of period is shown in **cell K5**, which is picked up from the 1.0 General Assumptions worksheet. For each period, *the sensitivity factor* by which the incidence is increased (positive percentage) or decreased (negative percentage) can be specified in **row 4** (Figure 139).

Figure 139: Periods of Projections and Incidence/Prevalence of the Service
per Period in the 1.2B Health Needs Worksheet

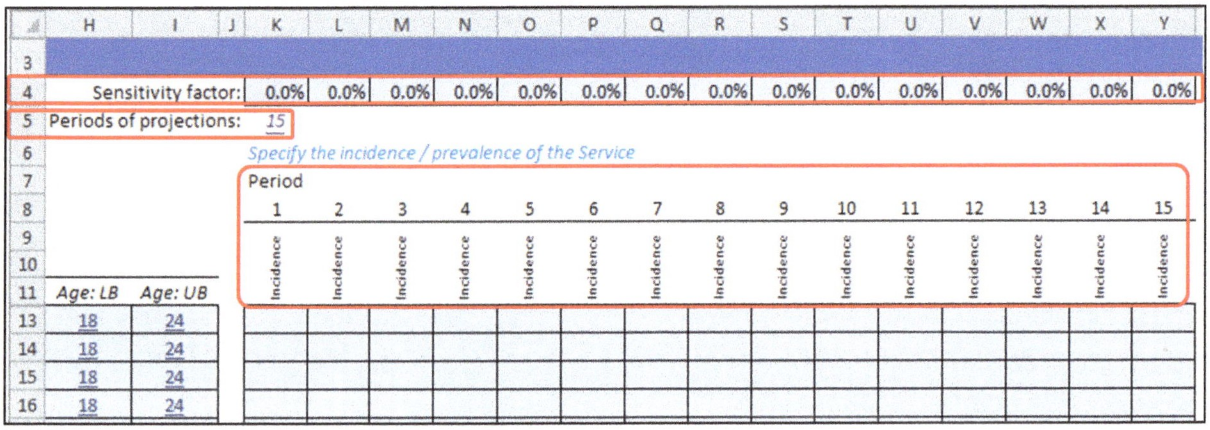

As noted in Assumption 20 (Chapter III-D6) the baseline scenario presumes that incidence and prevalence of all conditions do not change over time.

Inpatient Days of the Service

Columns AA–AO (Figure 140) meanwhile provide space for the SLAM user to specify the estimated number of inpatient days associated with the health services defined in column D ("Service Provided"), if applicable.

Figure 140: Input Cells for Number of Inpatient Days of the Service in the 1.2B Health Needs Worksheet

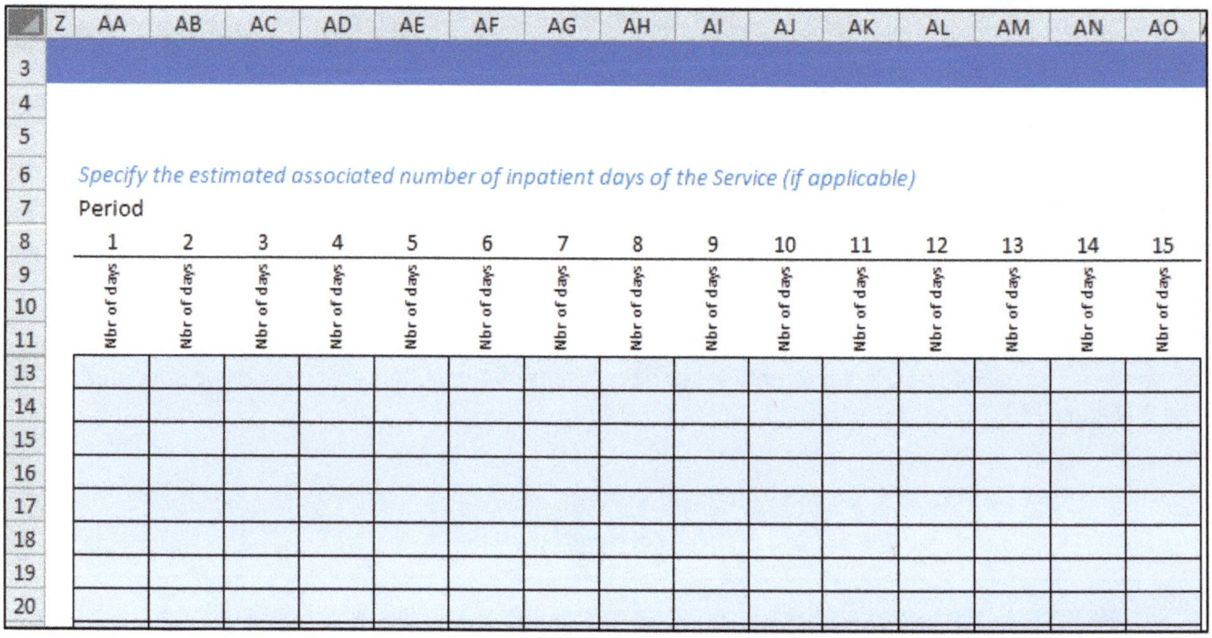

Control, Validation, and Notes

Control or warning cells are provided in **columns AQ–AT** (Figure 141) to inform the users when inconsistencies in various entries are entered.

Figure 141: Control Cells with Warning Texts Columns in the 1.2B Health Needs Worksheet

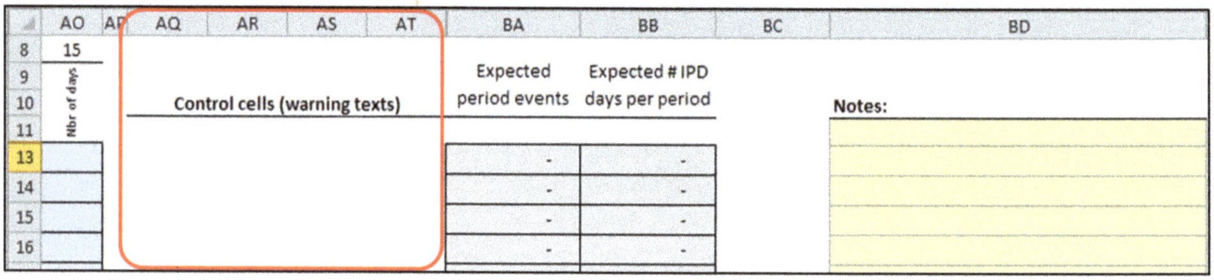

Note: IPD = inpatient days.

Column AQ (Figure 142) requires users to select a group when new rows are added using the <u>Add 1 Item</u> or <u>Add Multiple Items</u> buttons.

Figure 142: Validation Rule for Column AQ in the 1.2B Health Needs Worksheet

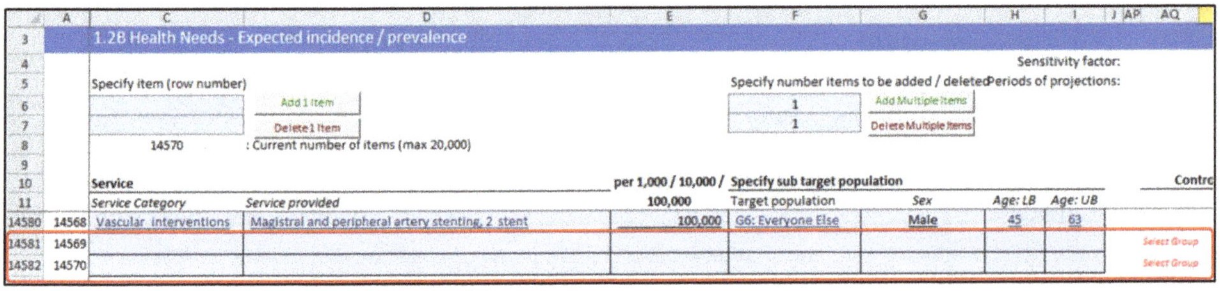

Column AR (Figure 143) informs the user when age lower bound value entered in column H is greater than the upper bound value entered in column I.

Figure 143: Validation Rule for Column AR in the 1.2B Health Needs Worksheet

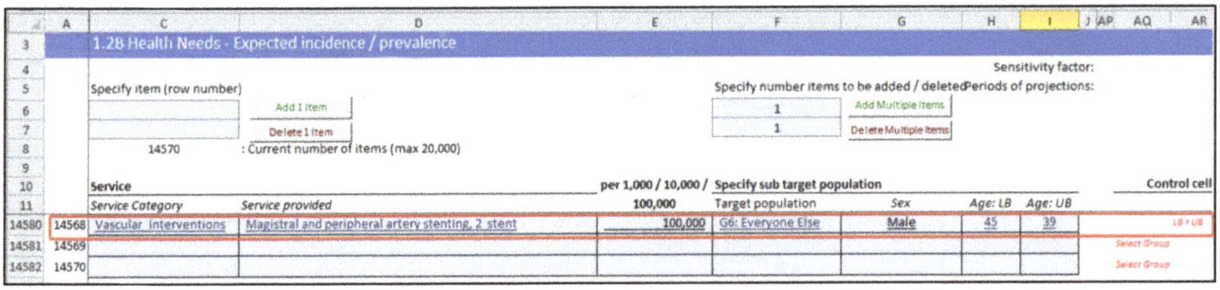

Columns AS–AT ensures that the lower and upper bound values entered in columns H and I, respectively, are consistent with the values in set in the 1.1A Target Populations worksheet. In current SLAM programming, however, the restrictions implemented in columns H and I (selection from drop-down menu identified from the 1.1A Target Population worksheet) already ensures that the rules defined in columns AS and AT are not violated.

Columns BA and BB are provided to compute for the "Expected period events" for Year 1 (Figure 144) and "Expected number of inpatient days (IPD) per period" for Year 1 (Figure 145), respectively. These columns are used for controlling purposes.

Figure 144: Control Cells of the Expected Period Events in the 1.2B Health Events Worksheet

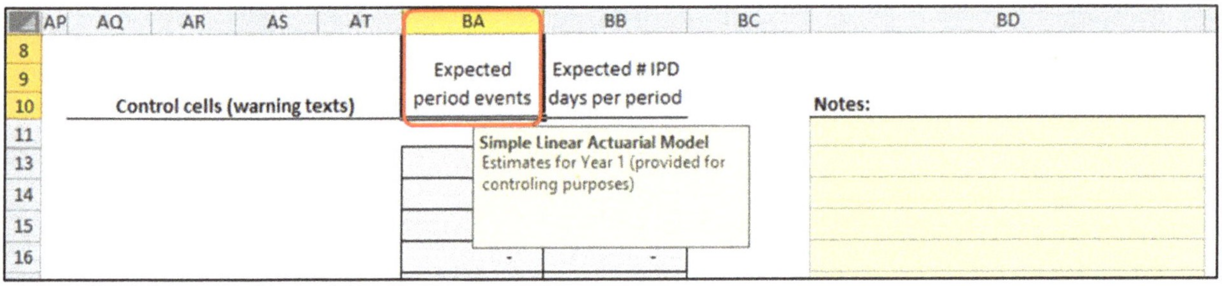

Note: IPD = inpatient days.

Figure 145: Control Cells of Expected Number of Inpatient Days per Period in the 1.2B Health Events Worksheet

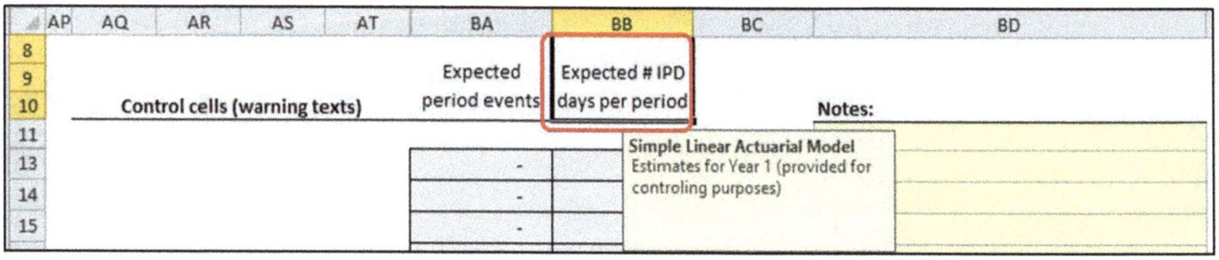

Note: IPD = inpatient days.

Column BD (Figure 146) provides the space for the SLAM user to write notes for other users and analysts.

Figure 146: Input Cells for Notes in the 1.2B Health Events Worksheet

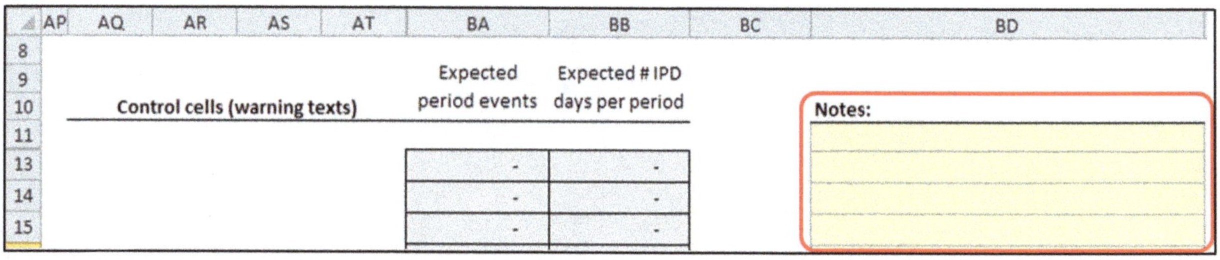

Note: IPD = inpatient days.

E.   The 1.3 Health Supply—Costs Input Sheet

As mentioned previously, for each health service is included in the benefit packages of a health insurance scheme, costs, prices, and tariff of providers will be used by the SLAM program to predict the expected value of future claims from current and future health insurance program members.

This worksheet (Figure 147) allows for the setting up of *costs* per health *service*. Up to five different lists on costs of healthcare services may be defined if the analyst prefers to use different data sources or different reference years. Each list may be activated or deactivated depending on which set of health service costs will be used. If there is more than one provider (e.g., public and private), distribution over various providers will be defined in the 1.4 Benefit Packages worksheet.

Figure 147: Preview of the 1.3 Health Supply—Costs Worksheet

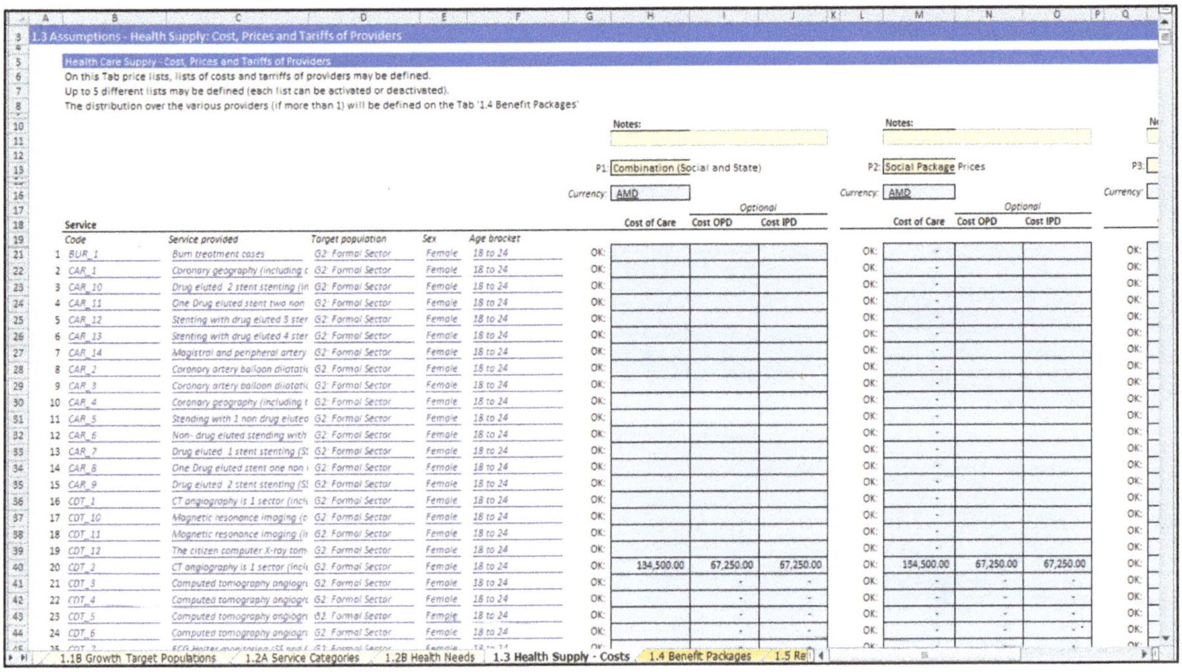

FOR YOUR INFORMATION

Cells found in this worksheet include:

Input Cells

| 100.00 | Input cell, unrestricted |

| 100.00 | Input cell, restricted input (e.g., only positive values/only integers/dates/etc.) |

| 100.00 | Input cell, select option from list |

Free Text Cells

| Note | Input cell to write comments |

Calculation Cells

| 200.00 | Linked and/or Calculation cell (locked); input to cell from another tab |

- Unrestricted input cells that accept alphanumeric keys;
- Restricted input cells for encoding only positive numeric values;
- Restricted input cells for selection from a drop-down list of inputs defined on another worksheet;
- Free text cells for adding corresponding explanations, comments, sources, or other helpful texts pertaining to encoded information; and
- Linked calculation cells (i.e., Code, Service provided, Target population, Sex, Age bracket) that are locked and entries came from another tab.

Service

<u>Columns A to F of this worksheet</u> (Figure 148) refers to the service information linked to, and direct copies of the "1.2B Health Needs" worksheet (Figure 149), specifically column A ("Numbering"), column B ("Code"), column D ("Service Provided"), column F ("Target Population"), column G ("Sex"), and combination of information on column H ("Lower bound age") and column I ("Upper bound age") for the "Age bracket" column F. If the lower bound is undefined from the source worksheet, it is automatically converted into "youngest" in this worksheet. If upper bound is undefined from the source worksheet, it is labeled as the "oldest" in this worksheet.

Figure 148: Columns in 1.3 Health Supply–Costs Worksheet Linked to 1.2B Health Needs Worksheet

	A	B	C	D	E	F	G	H	I	J
17									*Optional*	
18		**Service**						**Cost of Care**	**Cost OPD**	**Cost IPD**
19		*Code*	*Service provided*	*Target population*	*Sex*	*Age bracket*				
21	1	*BUR_1*	*Burn treatment cases*	*G2: Formal Sector*	*Female*	*18 to 24*	OK:			
22	2	*CAR_1*	*Coronary geography (including*	*G2: Formal Sector*	*Female*	*18 to 24*	OK:			
23	3	*CAR_10*	*Drug eluted 2 stent stenting (in*	*G2: Formal Sector*	*Female*	*18 to 24*	OK:			
24	4	*CAR_11*	*One Drug eluted stent two non r*	*G2: Formal Sector*	*Female*	*18 to 24*	OK:			
25	5	*CAR_12*	*Stenting with drug eluted 3 sten*	*G2: Formal Sector*	*Female*	*18 to 24*	OK:			
26	6	*CAR_13*	*Stenting with drug eluted 4 sten*	*G2: Formal Sector*	*Female*	*18 to 24*	OK:			
27	7	*CAR_14*	*Magistral and peripheral artery*	*G2: Formal Sector*	*Female*	*18 to 24*	OK:			
28	8	*CAR_2*	*Coronary artery balloon dilatati*	*G2: Formal Sector*	*Female*	*18 to 24*	OK:			
29	9	*CAR_3*	*Coronary artery balloon dilatati*	*G2: Formal Sector*	*Female*	*18 to 24*	OK:			
30	10	*CAR_4*	*Coronary geography (including*	*G2: Formal Sector*	*Female*	*18 to 24*	OK:			

Figure 149: Source Columns in the 1.2B Health Needs Worksheet

	A	B	C	D	E	F	G	H	I
10		**Service**			**per 1,000 / 10,000 /**	**Specify sub target population**			
11		*Code (*)*	*Service Category*	*Service provided*	**100,000**	Target population	*Sex*	*Age: LB*	*Age: UB*
13	1	BUR_1	Burn	Burn treatment cases	100,000	G2: Formal Sector	Female	18	24
14	2	CAR_1	Cardiology	Coronary geography (including contrast material cost of anest	100,000	G2: Formal Sector	Female	18	24
15	3	CAR_10	Cardiology	Drug eluted 2 stent stenting (in the State)	100,000	G2: Formal Sector	Female	18	24
16	4	CAR_11	Cardiology	One Drug eluted stent two non medical eluted stent	100,000	G2: Formal Sector	Female	18	24
17	5	CAR_12	Cardiology	Stenting with drug eluted 3 stent	100,000	G2: Formal Sector	Female	18	24
18	6	CAR_13	Cardiology	Stenting with drug eluted 4 stent	100,000	G2: Formal Sector	Female	18	24
19	7	CAR_14	Cardiology	Magistral and peripheral artery stenting, the stent	100,000	G2: Formal Sector	Female	18	24
20	8	CAR_2	Cardiology	Coronary artery balloon dilatation using one cylinder	100,000	G2: Formal Sector	Female	18	24

Costs

The next portion of this worksheet is for recording health costs for up to five listings (Figure 150):

- **<u>Columns H, I, J</u>** for "Cost listing 1,"
- **<u>Columns M, N, O</u>** "Cost listing 2,"
- **<u>Columns R, S, T</u>** for "Cost listing 3,"
- **<u>Columns W, X, Y</u>** for "Cost listing 4," and
- **<u>Columns AB, AC, AD</u>** for "Cost listing 5."

Figure 150: Input Cells for Costs per Provider in the 1.3 Health Supply—Costs Worksheet

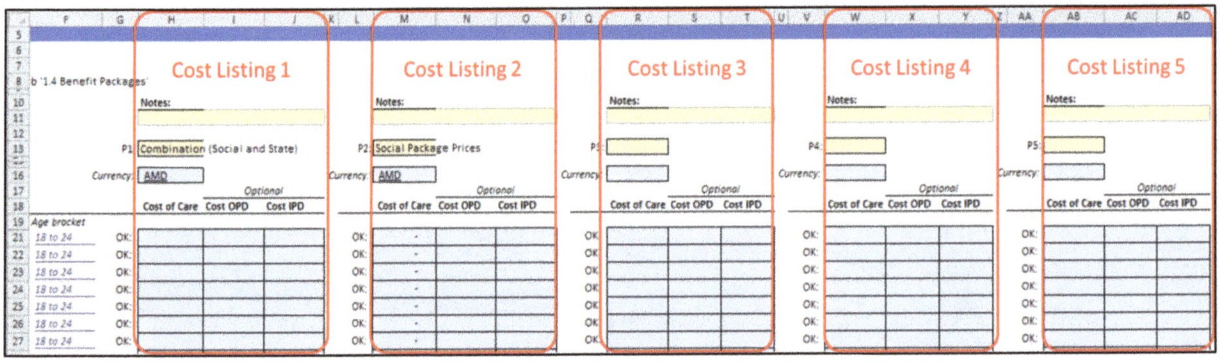

For each cost listing, **row 11** (Figure 151) provides input cells for "Notes" such as the data source and/or reference year of the costs of services to be recorded.

Figure 151: Notes on Costs in the 1.3 Health Supply—Costs Worksheet

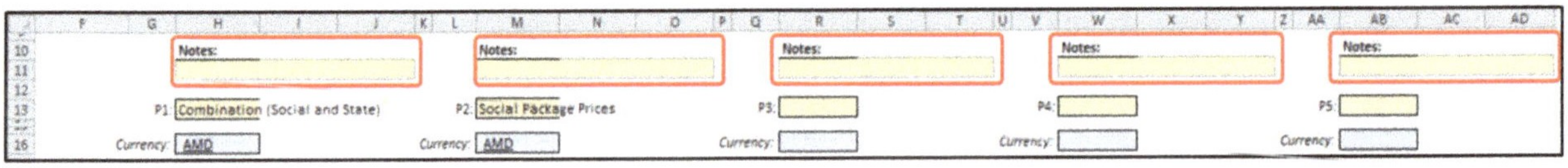

Columns H, M, R, W, and AB in row 13 (Figure 152) provide for the input cells of cost definition or provider (e.g., "Average cost" of providers).

Figure 152: Input Cells of Cost Definition in the 1.3 Health Supply—Costs Worksheet

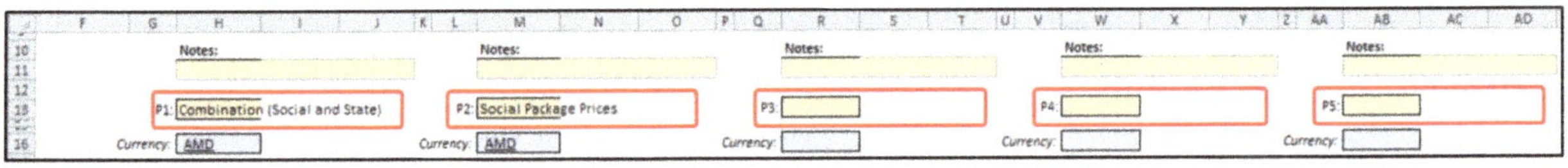

Columns H, M, R, W, and AB in row 16 (Figure 153) provide for the input cells of "Currency" selected from the drop-down menu. The currency options are picked up by the program from the currencies defined in worksheet 1.0 General Assumptions.

Figure 153: Input Cells of Cost Definition in the 1.3 Health Supply—Costs Worksheet

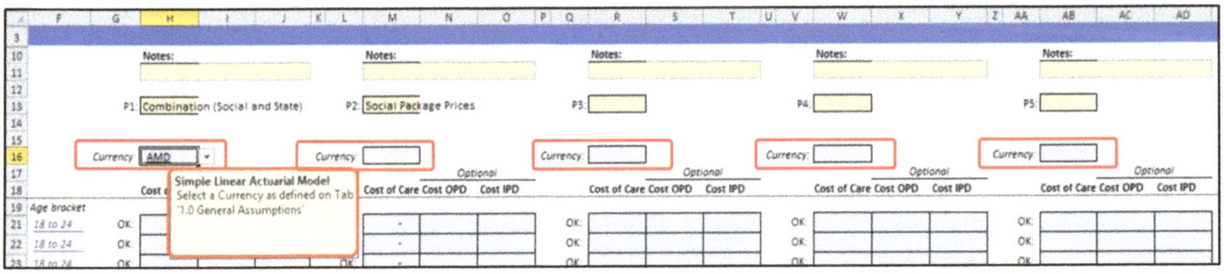

Beginning row 21 provides recording of the costs of services. Specifically, **columns H, M, R, W, and AB** provide input cells for "Cost of Care" (Figure 154).

Figure 154: Input Cells of Cost of Care in the 1.3 Health Supply—Costs Worksheet

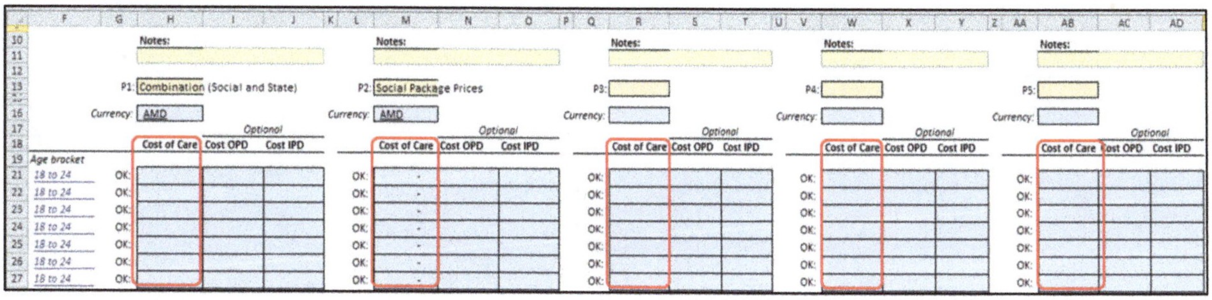

The user may also opt to provide separate outpatient and inpatient costs associated with the health service, if available. Specifically, **columns I, N, S, X, and AC** provide input cells for optional "Cost OPD" or outpatient costs (Figure 155) and **columns I, N, S, X, and AC provide** input cells for optional "Cost IPD" or inpatient costs (Figure 156).

Figure 155: Input Cells of Cost Outpatient Day in the 1.3 Health Supply—Costs Worksheet

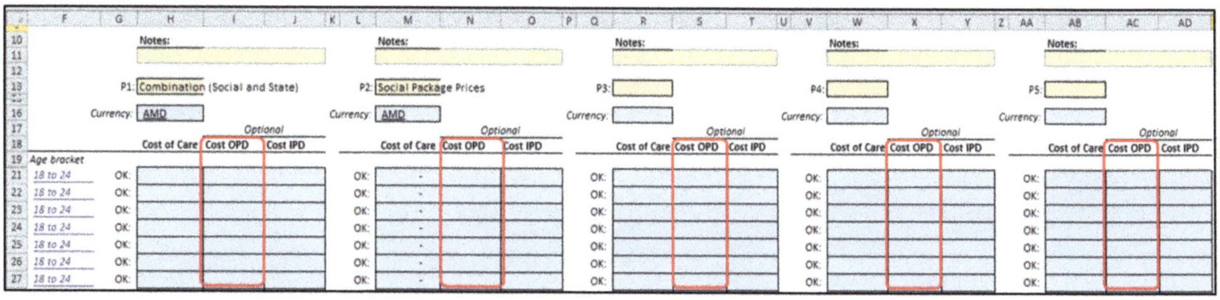

Figure 156: Input Cells of Cost Inpatient Day in the 1.3 Health Supply—Costs Worksheet

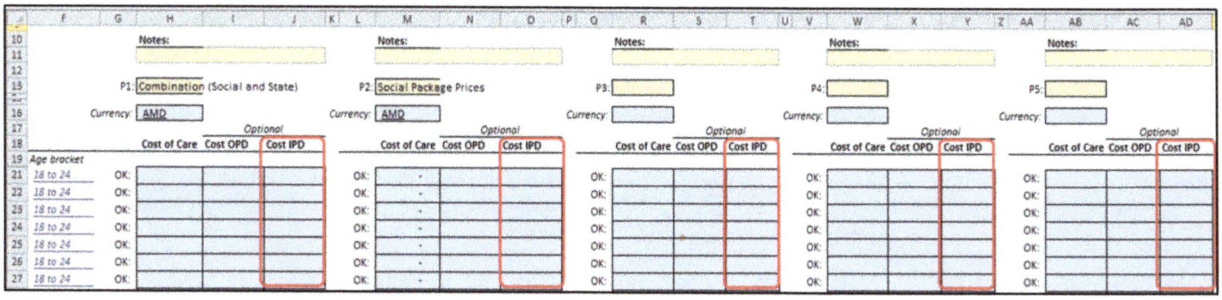

The user must be careful though to ensure that "Cost OPD" is only filled up for outpatient services, while "Cost IPD" for inpatient services.

For verification purposes, verification cells **beginning row 21 under columns G** were included to ensure that if the user inputs data under the "Cost OPD" in column I and/or "Cost IPD" in column J, the total value of the OP and IP costs will not exceed the total "Cost of Care" in column H. If the outpatient and/or inpatient costs breakdown exceeds the total cost, entries under column G will change from "OK" to "Check" remark (Figure 157).

Figure 157: Verification Cells in the 1.3 Health Supply—Costs Worksheet

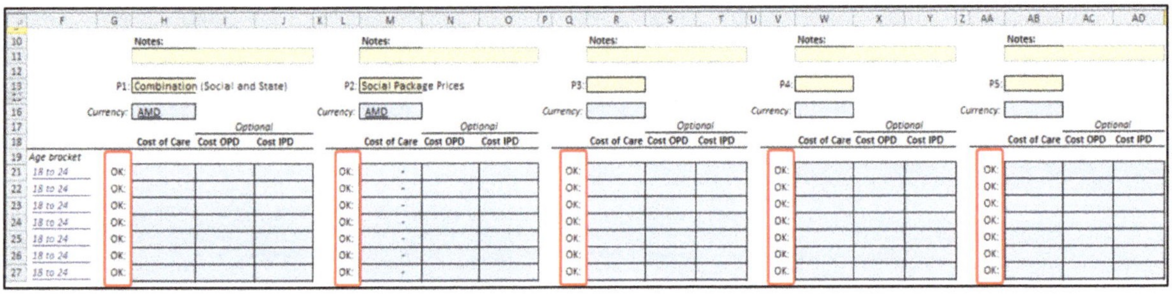

F.   The 1.4 Benefit Packages Input Sheet

This worksheet (Figure 158) provides the list of *Benefit Packages* to be included in the SLAM analysis. It also allows the user to define

- whether the services defined in the 1.2A Service Category worksheet are included in one or more benefit packages,
- where enrollees may utilize healthcare services, and
- whether the enrollee can access inpatient and/or outpatient services.

Figure 158: Preview of the 1.4 Benefit Packages Worksheet

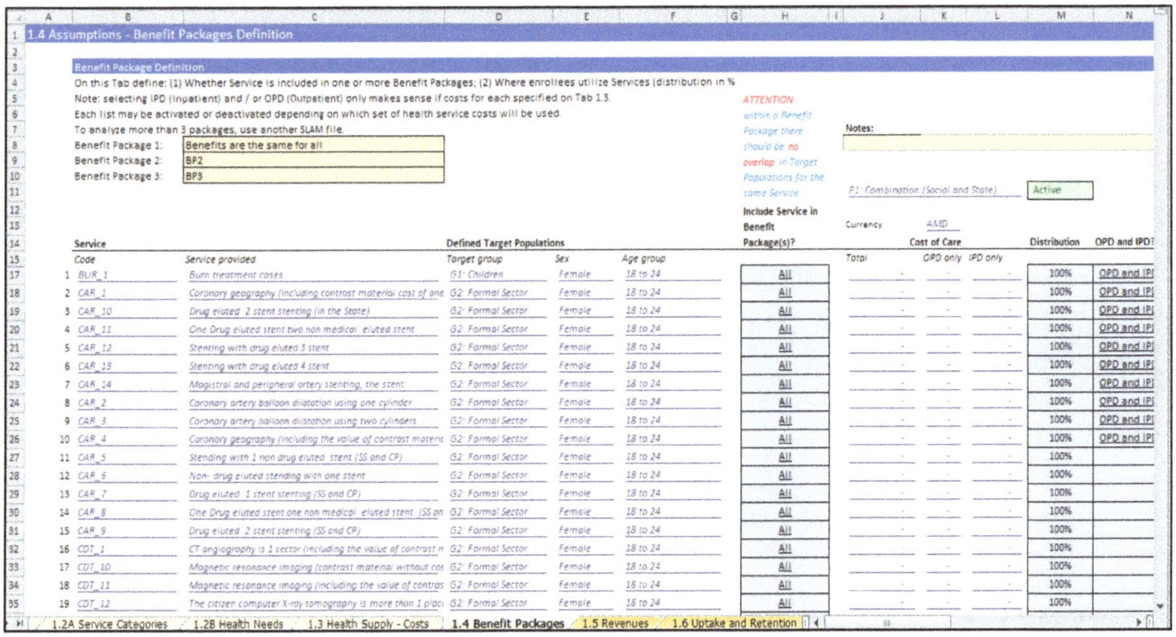

FOR YOUR INFORMATION

Cells found in this worksheet include:

Input Cells

100.00	Input cell, unrestricted
100.00	Input cell, restricted input (e.g., only positive values/only integers/dates/etc.)
100.00	Input cell, select option from list
100.00	Input cell, select option from list, input defined on another sheet
	Input cell *contents ignored* (not included in calculations)
Inactive	*Activation cell* - choose from drop down menu, color changes accordingly

Free Text Cells

Note	Input cell to write comments

Calculation Cells

200.00	Linked and/or Calculation cell (locked); input to cell from another tab

- Unrestricted input cells that accept alphanumeric keys;
- Restricted input cells for encoding only positive numeric values;
- Restricted input cells for selection from a drop-down list;
- Ignored input cells where entries are not considered in calculations and analyses;
- Activation cells which activate or inactive parameters;
- Free text cells for adding corresponding explanations, comments, sources, or other helpful texts pertaining to encoded information; and
- Linked calculation cells (i.e., Code, Service provided, Target population, Sex, Age bracket) that are locked and entries came from another tab.

Benefit Packages

Up to three benefit package(s) can be assessed and recorded in **cells C8, C9 and/or C10** (Figure 159).

Figure 159: Input Cells for Benefit Packages in the 1.4 Benefit Packages Worksheet

Similar with "1.3 Health Supply – Costs" worksheet, **columns A to F of this worksheet** (Figure 160) refers to the service information linked to, and direct copies of the "1.2B Health Needs" worksheet, specifically column A ("Numbering"), column B (Code), column D (Service Provided), column F (Target Population), column G (Sex), and combination of information on column H (Lower bound age) and column I (Upper bound age) for the Age bracket column F.

Figure 160: Linked Service Information in the 1.4 Benefit Packages Worksheet

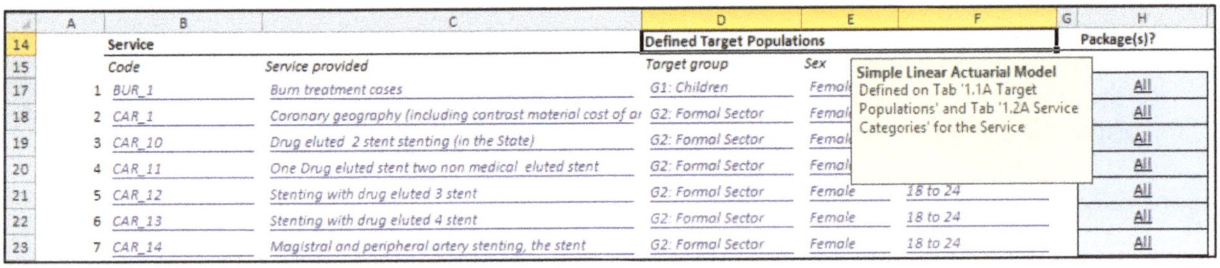

	A	B	C	D	E	F	H
14		Service		Defined Target Populations			Package(s)?
15		Code	Service provided	Target group	Sex		
17	1	BUR_1	Burn treatment cases	G1: Children	Femal		All
18	2	CAR_1	Coronary geography (including contrast material cost of ai	G2: Formal Sector	Femal		All
19	3	CAR_10	Drug eluted 2 stent stenting (in the State)	G2: Formal Sector	Femal		All
20	4	CAR_11	One Drug eluted stent two non medical eluted stent	G2: Formal Sector	Femal		All
21	5	CAR_12	Stenting with drug eluted 3 stent	G2: Formal Sector	Female	18 to 24	All
22	6	CAR_13	Stenting with drug eluted 4 stent	G2: Formal Sector	Female	18 to 24	All
23	7	CAR_14	Magistral and peripheral artery stenting, the stent	G2: Formal Sector	Female	18 to 24	All

Column H (Figure 161) requires the users to determine whether each ***Service provided*** in column C is included in the Benefit Packages defined in cells C8 to C10. A drop-down menu is provided to allow users to select

- "1," "2," or "3" entries indicate that the service is exclusively covered by the first, second, or third Benefit Package, respectively;
- "1 and 2" if the service is covered by the both the first and second Benefit Package;
- "1 and 3" if the service is covered by the both the first and third Benefit Package;
- "2 and 3" if the service is covered by the both the second and third Benefit Package;
- "All" if the service is covered by all Benefit Packages specified; and
- "None" if the service is not covered by any of the three Benefit Packages.

Figure 161: Whether Each Health Service Is Included in Identified Benefit Packages

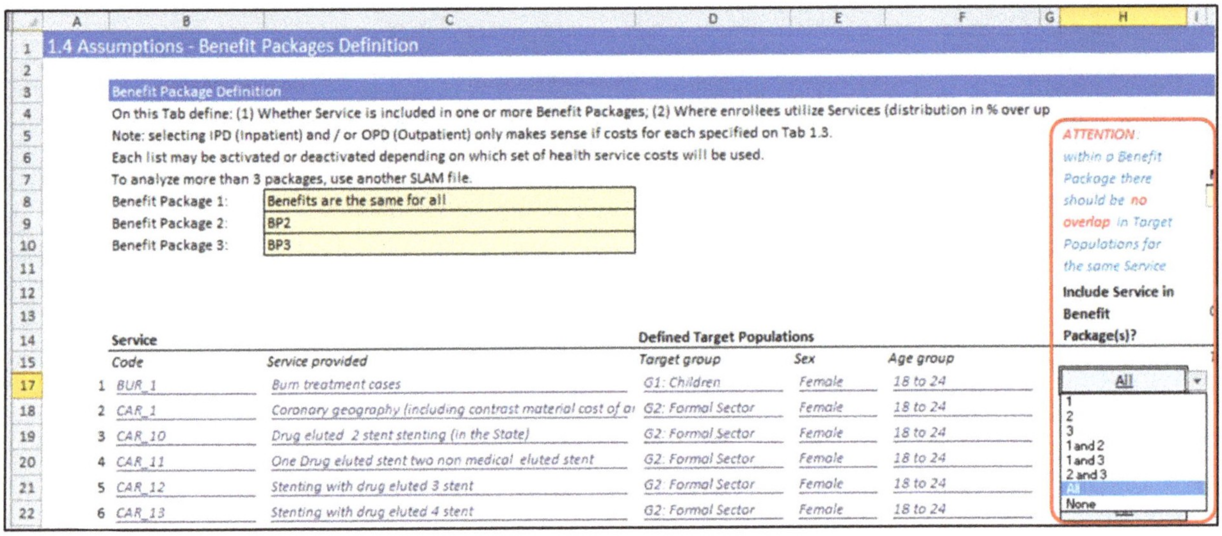

	A	B	C	D	E	F	H
14		Service		Defined Target Populations			
15		Code	Service provided	Target group	Sex	Age group	
17	1	BUR_1	Burn treatment cases	G1: Children	Female	18 to 24	All
18	2	CAR_1	Coronary geography (including contrast material cost of ai	G2: Formal Sector	Female	18 to 24	
19	3	CAR_10	Drug eluted 2 stent stenting (in the State)	G2: Formal Sector	Female	18 to 24	
20	4	CAR_11	One Drug eluted stent two non medical eluted stent	G2: Formal Sector	Female	18 to 24	
21	5	CAR_12	Stenting with drug eluted 3 stent	G2: Formal Sector	Female	18 to 24	
22	6	CAR_13	Stenting with drug eluted 4 stent	G2: Formal Sector	Female	18 to 24	

In tagging the coverage of the services, there is no need to select options in each of the cells in column H. The program allows for copying of cells within the same column of identifying service inclusion in the Benefit Packages.

The SLAM analysis requires that within a Benefit Package, there should be no overlaps in Target Populations for the same service.

Cost of Care and Distribution of Utilization

The next portion of this worksheet displays data fields for up to five providers: (i) the costs of care per service that were defined earlier in 1.3 Health Supply–Costs worksheet; and (ii) input cells for recording of the distribution, where the patients go for the specified services (Figure 162).

Specifically,

- For "Provider 1," **columns J to L** show the linked cost data and **columns M and N** provide the distribution input cells;

- For "Provider 2," **columns P to R** show the linked cost data and **columns S and T** provide the distribution input cells;

- For "Provider 3," **columns V to X** show the linked cost data and **columns Y and Z** provide the distribution input cells;

- For "Provider 4," **columns AB to AD** show the linked cost data and **columns AE and AF** provide the distribution input cells;

- For "Provider 5," **columns AH to AJ** show the linked cost data and **columns AK and AL** provide the distribution input cells.

Figure 162: Data Fields for up to Five Providers in the 1.4 Benefit Packages Worksheet

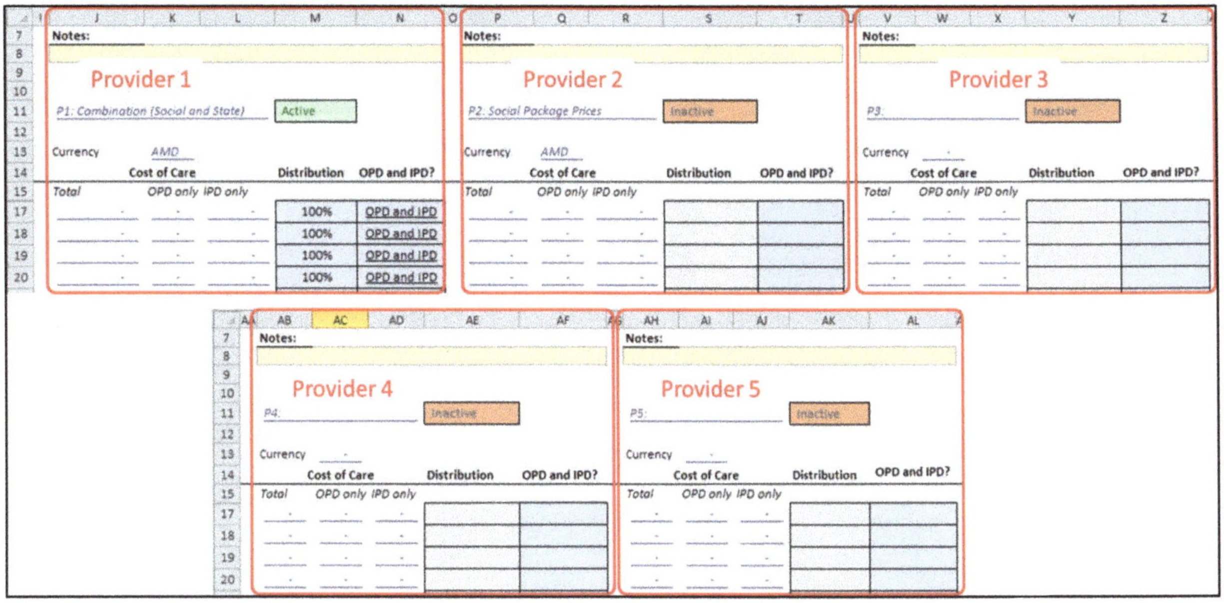

For each provider listing, **row 8** (Figure 163) provides input cells for "Notes" and other remarks to be recorded.

Figure 163: Input Cells on the Notes for Distribution per Provider Listing in the 1.4 Health Supply—Costs Worksheet

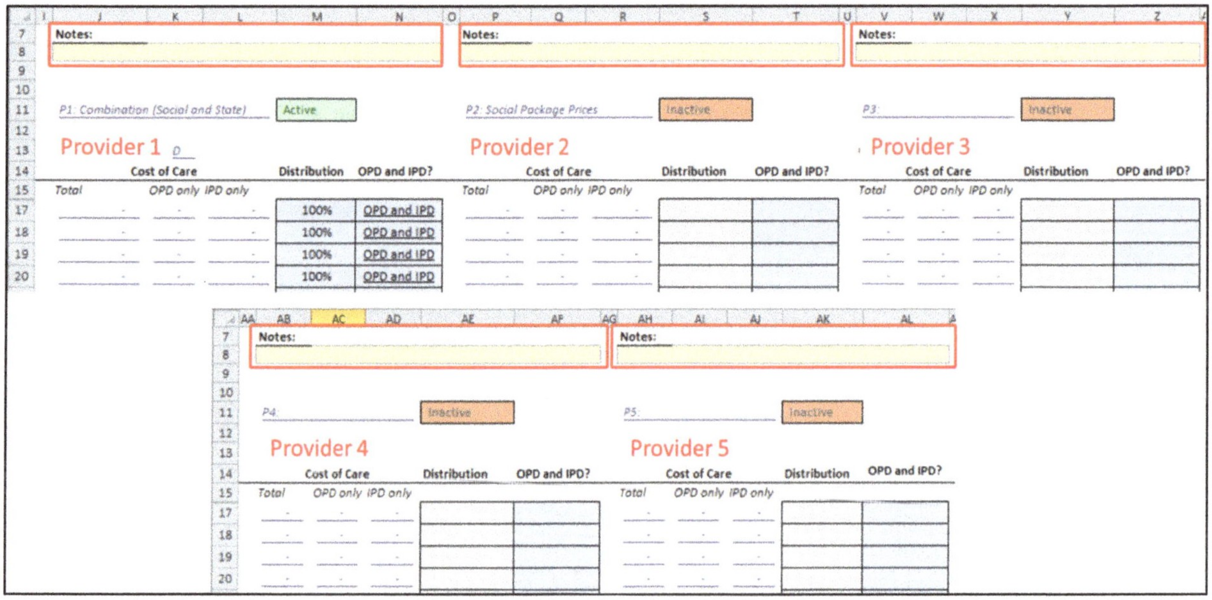

Meanwhile, **row 11** shows the "Provider name" picked up from "1.3 Health Supply Costs" worksheet, specifically **columns J to L** for "P1;" **columns P to R** for "P2," **columns V to X** for "P3;" **columns AB to AD** for "P4;" and **columns AH to AJ** for "P5" (Figure 164).

Figure 164: Linked Cells for Provider Name in the 1.4 Benefit Packages Worksheet

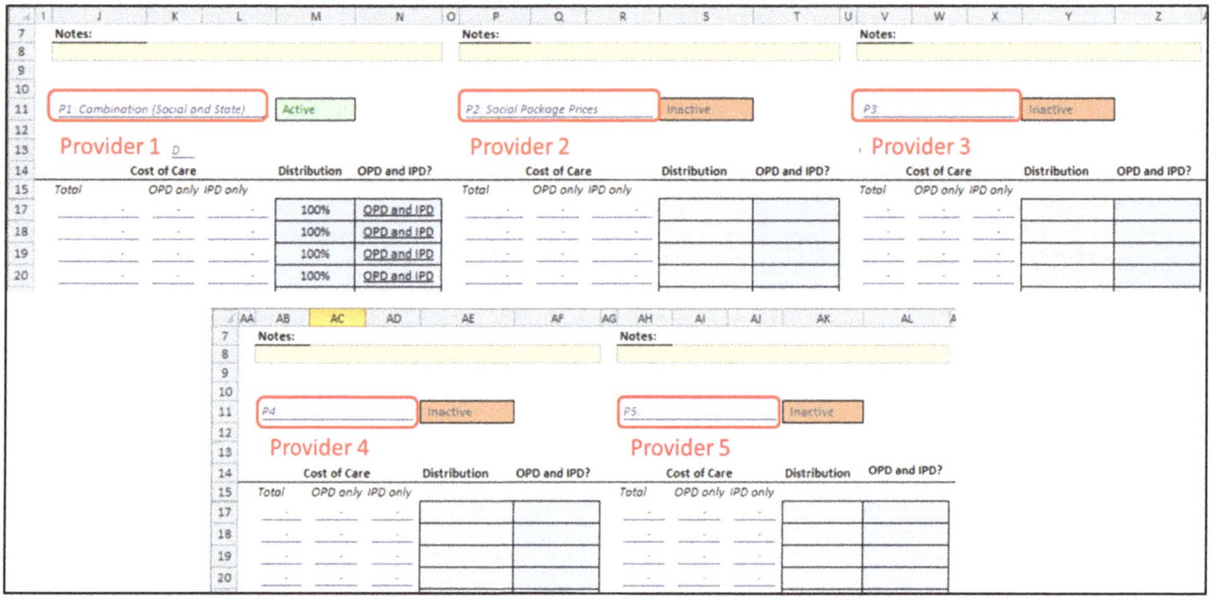

Next to the provider name is an "Activation cell," specifically in **cell M11** for "P1;" **cell S11** for "P2;" **cell Y11** for "P3;" **cell AE11** for "P4;" and **cell AK11** for "P5" (Figure 165).

Figure 165: Activation Cells per Provider Listing in the 1.4 Benefit Packages Worksheet

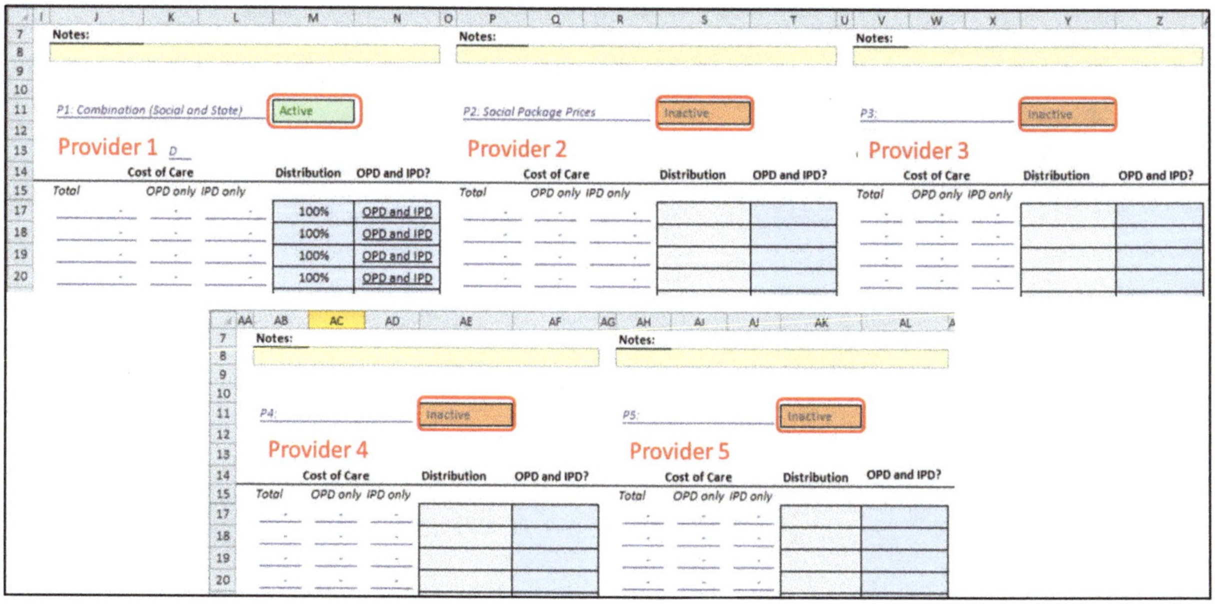

To use the cost data picked up from the 1.3 Health Supply Costs worksheet and specify distribution utilization of the said services for identified providers, the user must set the respective activation cell into active status by using the drop-down list provided (e.g., in "P1"). However, if the cost data is not available for a provider (e.g., in P3–P5), as defined in the 1.3 Health Supply Costs worksheet, their respective activation cell in this 1.4 Benefit Packages worksheet must be set to inactive for the SLAM program to work.

Suppose P2 (i.e., social package prices) that has cost data in the 1.3 Health Supply–Costs worksheet will be used in analysis. Linked data will automatically appear in the 1.4 Benefit Packages worksheet (e.g., columns P–R) if the user selects "Active" in cell S11 and the "Distribution" column (e.g., column S) is filled (Figure 166).

Figure 166: Activating Providers in the 1.4 Benefit Packages Worksheet

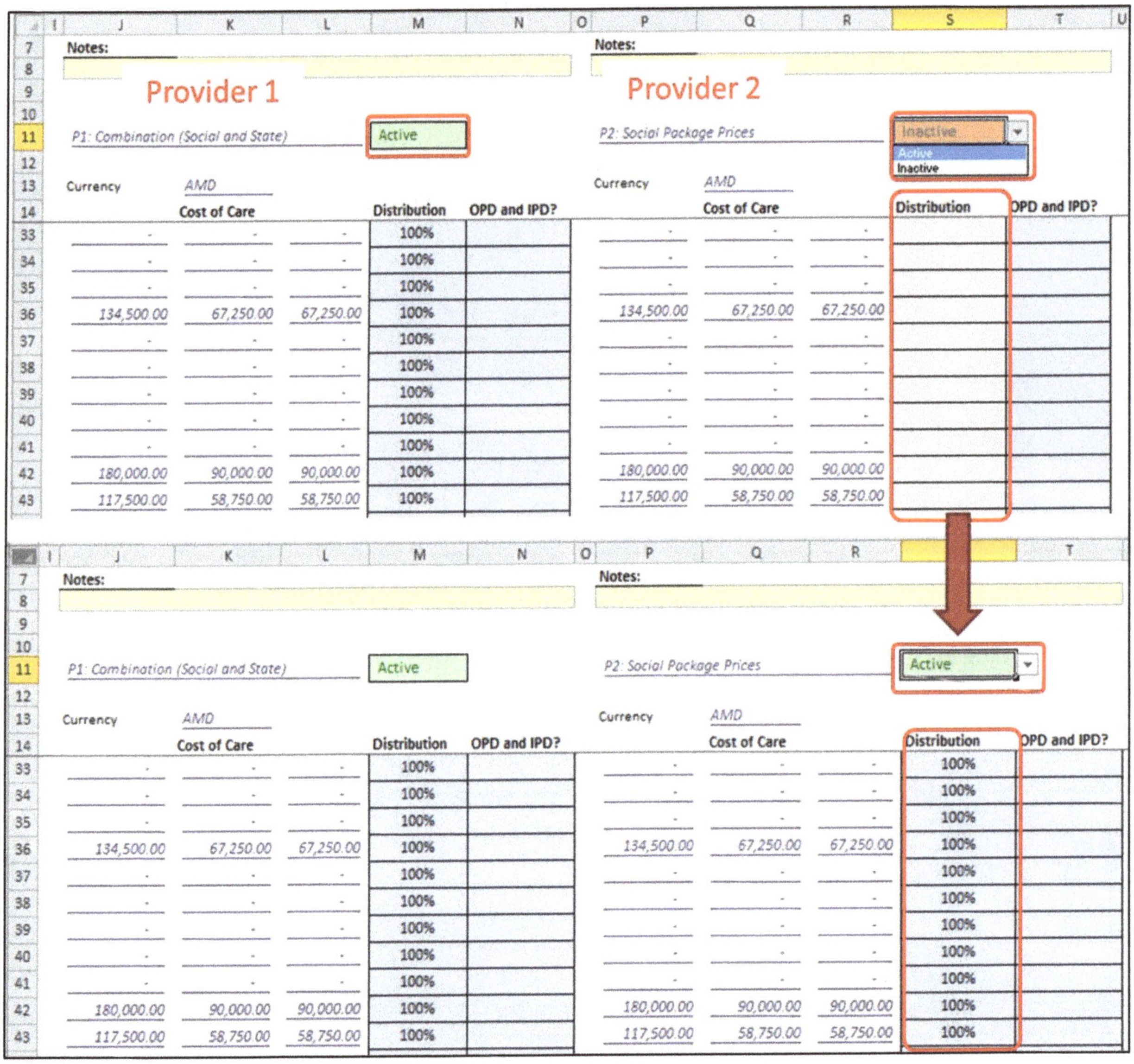

Notes: AMD = Armenian dram, IPD = inpatient days, OPD = outpatient days.

Below the "Provider Name" is the "Currency" picked up by the SLAM program from the 1.0 General Assumptions worksheet. Specifically, it can be seen in **cell K13** for P1, **cell S11** for P2 **cell Y11** for P3, **cell AE11** for P4, and **cell AK11** for P5 (Figure 167).

Figure 167: Linked Cells for Currency in the 1.4 Benefit Packages Worksheet

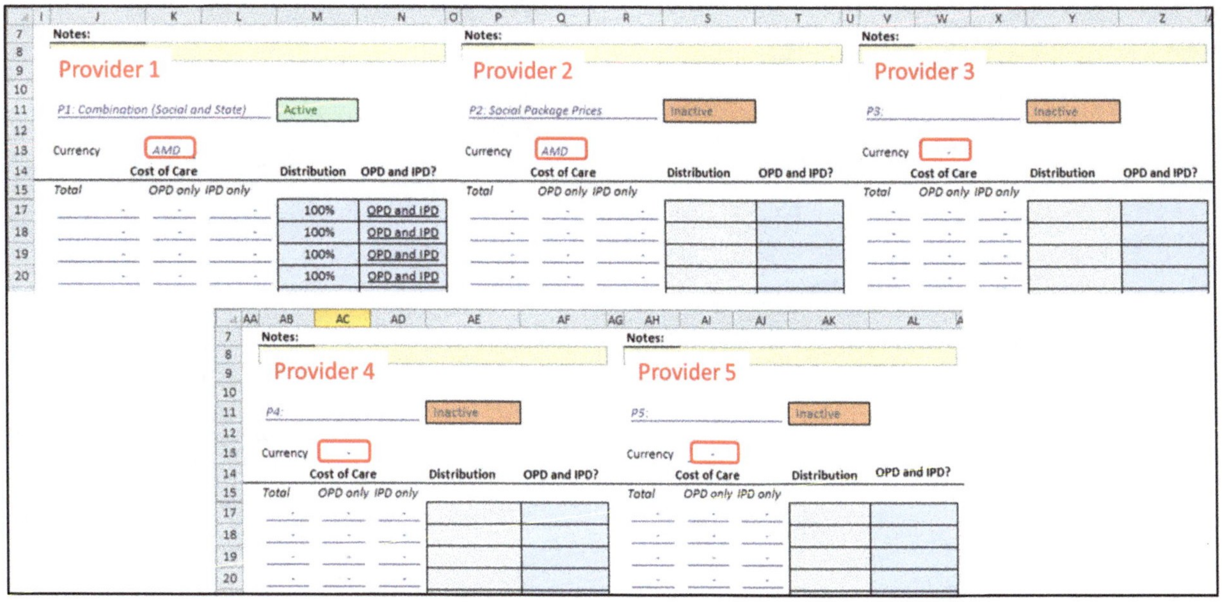

Notes: AMD = Armenian dram, IPD = inpatient days, OPD = outpatient days.

Only beginning in **row 17** can the costs of care and input cells for distribution of utilization be seen. The distribution column (e.g., column M for the first provider) requires the user to define the distribution of where the patients go for the specific services listed in column C (Figure 168).

Figure 168: Input Cells for Distribution of Cost of Care in the 1.4 Benefit Packages Worksheet

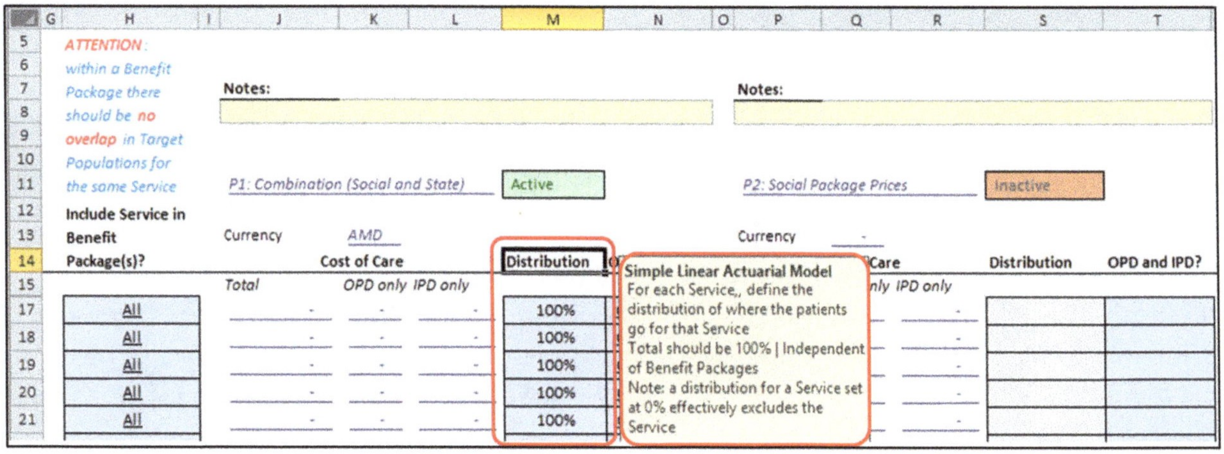

Note: Screenshot contains hidden rows for illustration purposes only.

This means that if costs of care (Figure 169) are available for the first provider (P1, columns J–L), second provider (columns P–R), third provider (columns V–X), fourth provider (columns AB–AD), or fifth provider (columns AH–AJ), percent shares summing to 100% must be distributed to these five costs data.

Figure 169: Linked Cells for Cost of Care in the 1.4 Benefit Packages Worksheet

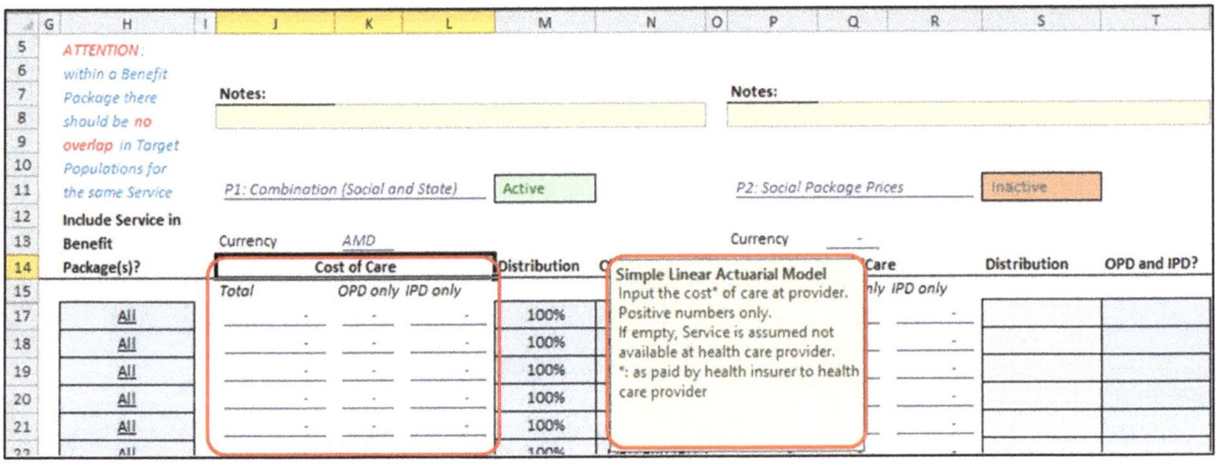

Notes: AMD = Armenian dram, IPD = inpatient days, OPD = outpatient days. Screenshot contains hidden rows for illustration purposes only.

In the example provided in this manual, there is only one provider (e.g., P1: Combination of Social and State). Thus, the entry in Column M for each service defined must be 100% (Figure 169).

Figure 170: Sample Distribution in the 1.4 Benefit Packages Worksheet

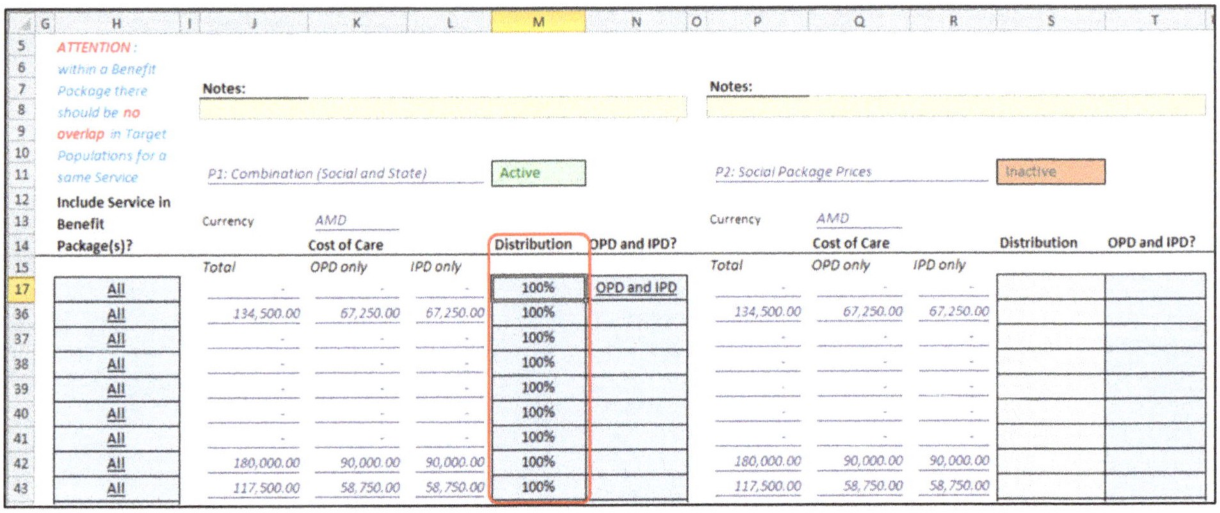

Notes: AMD = Armenian dram, IPD = inpatient days, OPD = outpatient days. Screenshot contains hidden rows for illustration purposes only.

The OPD and IPD column (i.e, column N for the first provider) allows the user to estimate the costs pertaining to the outpatient service (OPD only), inpatient service (IPD only), or both components (OPD and IPD) on each of the defined services. If left empty, the program will assume that OPD and IPD components should be used in the analysis. To ensure that calculations are done for each service component, the costs should be defined in the 1.3 Health Supply–Costs worksheet. This means that if separate costs for OPD and IPD are not available in the health costs tab, then the user must either select OPD and IPD or leave the appropriate cell in column N blank (Figure 171).

Figure 171: Input Cells for Outpatient Days or Inpatient Days Distribution in the 1.4 Benefit Packages Worksheet

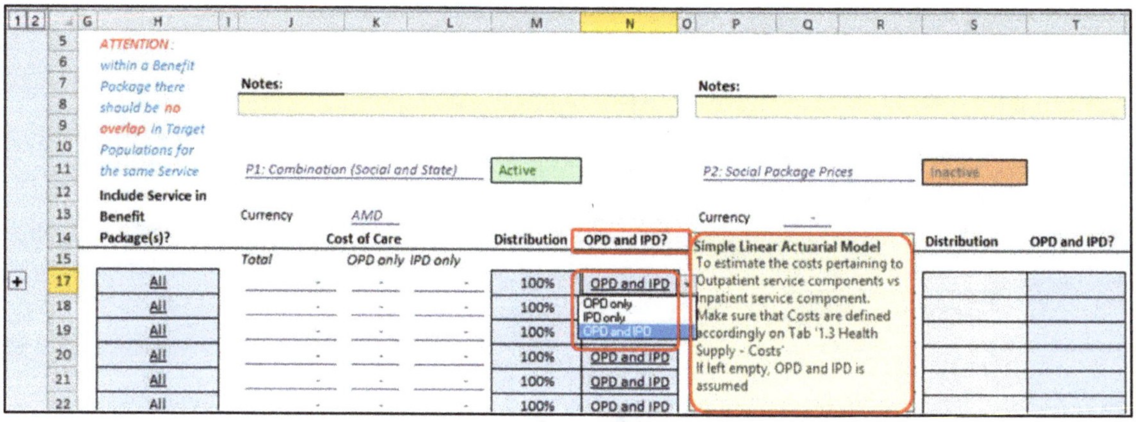

Notes: AMD = Armenian dram, IPD = inpatient days, OPD = outpatient days.

Control and Validation

Column AN (*Indicator Distribution*) is a validation data field that computes the total distribution of percent shares across all five providers. If the set distribution is not 100%, a warning informing the user of the data inconsistency will be displayed in **column AO** ("Warning explanation") (Figure 172).

Figure 172: Warning Explanation Columns in the 1.4 Benefit Packages Worksheet

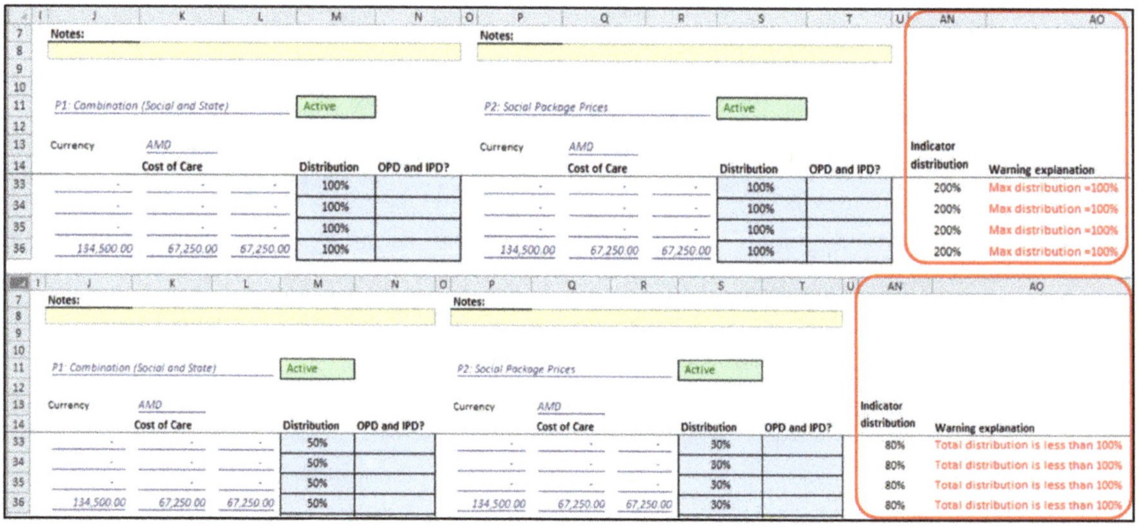

Notes: AMD = Armenian dram, IPD = inpatient days, OPD = outpatient days.

Columns AT–AW (Figure 173) provide the estimation of the indicative results for the first year of the analysis. For each service:

- *Total cost* (column AT) is computed by multiplying the expected annual incidence (column AP) and average total cost per service (column AQ). Column AP is derived from the 1.2B Health Needs worksheet, while AQ is picked up by the program from the total costs from providers 1–5, weighted by the distribution shares assigned to each provider.

- *OPD* cost and *IPD* cost (i.e., columns AU and AV, respectively) are computed the same way *total cost* is calculated when applicable data of these components are available (i.e., cost of care in the 1.3 Health Supply–Costs worksheet).
- *Number of bed days* (column AW) is picked up by the program from the 1.2B Health Needs worksheet.

Figure 173: Indicative Results for the First Year in the 1.4 Benefit Packages Worksheet

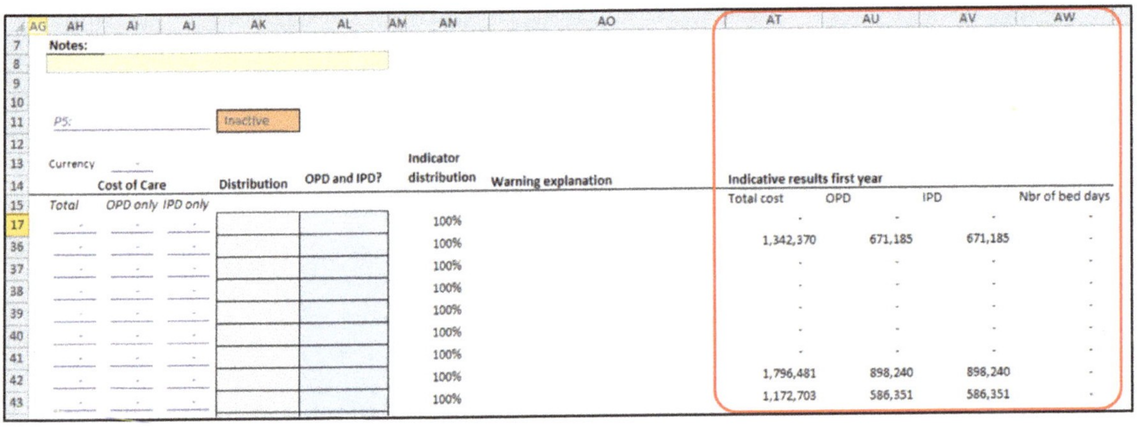

Notes: IPD = inpatient days, OPD = outpatient days.

G.   The 1.5 Revenues Input Sheet

This worksheet (Figure 174) provides the space for inputting the current premiums levied to various member groups. If left empty, the SLAM results in Dashboard and the 3.1 Results worksheets will show the required funds for the healthcare provision to the number of members defined in the 1.1A Target Populations worksheet.

Figure 174: Preview of the 1.5 Revenues Worksheet

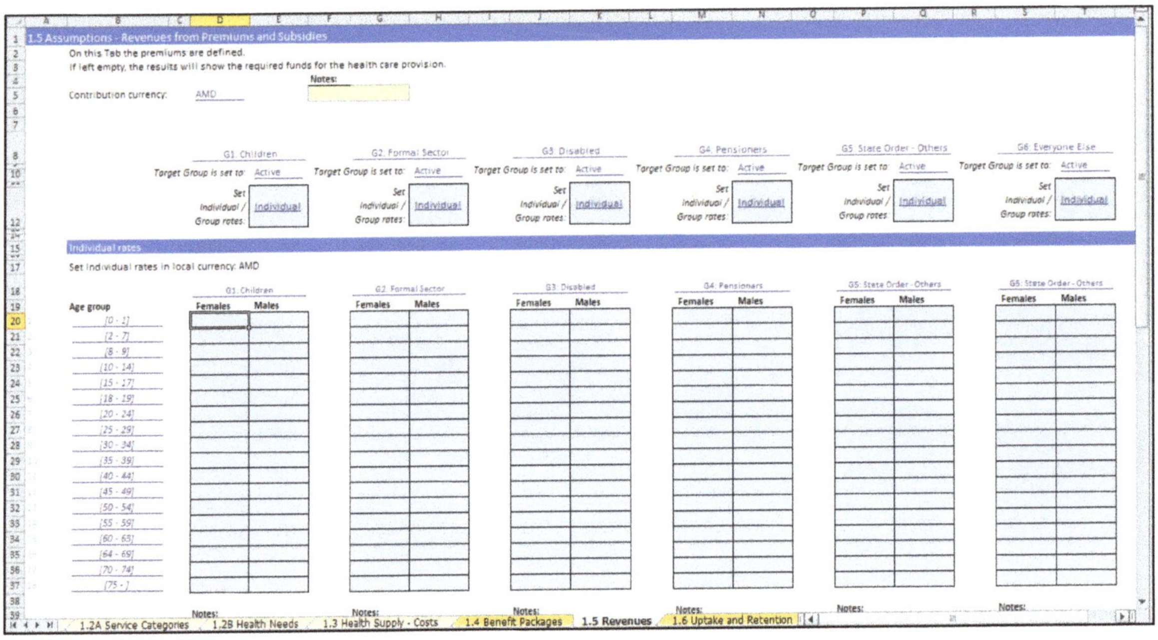

FOR YOUR INFORMATION

Cells found in this worksheet include:

Input Cells

100.00	Input cell, restricted input (e.g., only positive values/only integers/dates/etc.)
100.00	Input cell, select option from list
100.00	Input cell, select option from list, input defined on another sheet
	Input cell *contents ignored* (not included in calculations)

Free Text Cells

Note	Input cell to write comments

Calculation Cells

200.00	Linked and/or Calculation cell (locked); input to cell from another tab
200.00	Output cell (locked)

Buttons

Add Item	Button to perform action such as adding or deleting rows and/or columns, selecting an option or performing an action. Green text on a button means an item is added, red text means an item is deleted

- Restricted input cells for encoding only positive numeric values;
- Restricted input cells for selection from a drop-down list;
- Restricted input cells for selection from a drop-down list of inputs defined on another worksheet;
- Ignored input cells where entries are not considered in calculations and analyses;
- Free text cells for adding corresponding explanations, comments, sources, or other helpful texts pertaining to encoded information;
- Linked calculation cells (i.e., Age bracket) that are locked and entries came from another tab;
- Output cells that are locked for editing and show results of calculations within the worksheet; and
- Buttons with blue text for applying an action.

For discussion purposes, this worksheet is divided into three partitions: (i) prerequisite information, (ii) individual rates, and (iii) group rates.

Prerequisite Information

This portion of the worksheet (Figure 175) shows essential information to be used in defining the revenue rates. Contents of this worksheet include the *contribution currency* in **cell D5**; input cells for *notes* in **cells F5 to G5**; the *target groups* in **row 8**; respective *group status* (i.e., active or inactive) in **row 10**; and restricted input cells for setting *individual or group rates* in **row 12**.

Figure 175: Prerequisite Information of the 1.5 Revenues Worksheet

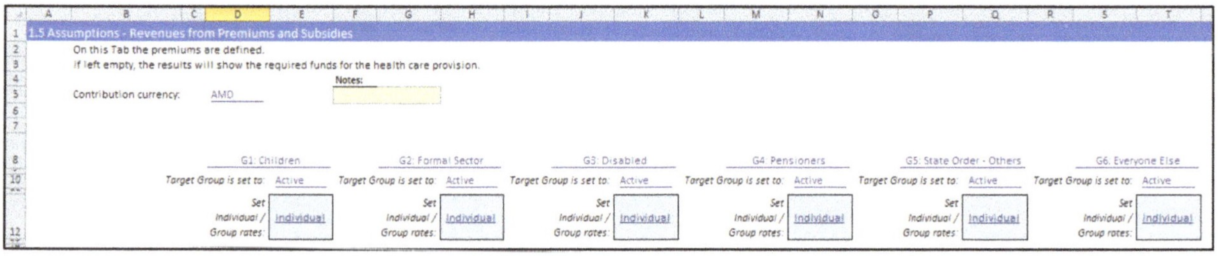

The *contribution currency* in **cell D5** refers to *Currency 1* used for projections defined in the 1.0 General Assumptions worksheet. On the other hand, the user may input notes in unrestricted **cells F5–G5** that accepts alphanumeric characters (Figure 176).

Figure 176: Linked Cell for Contribution Currency and Input Cell for Notes in the 1.5 Revenues Worksheet

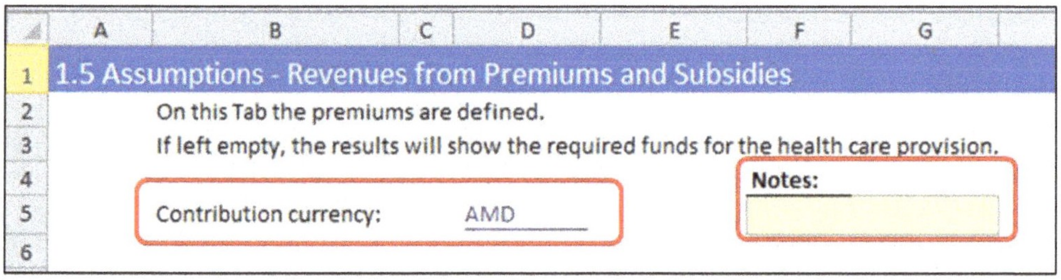

Note: AMD = Armenian dram.

Each *Target Group* of population defined in "1.1A Target Populations" worksheet also has their own partition in this worksheet (Figure 177):

- **Columns D and E** for "Group 1;"
- **Columns G and H** "Group 2;"
- **Columns J and K** for "Group 3;"
- **Columns M and N** for "Group 4;"
- **Columns P and Q** for "Group 5;" and
- **Columns S and T** for "Group 6."

Figure 177: Target Group Portions in the 1.5 Revenues Worksheet

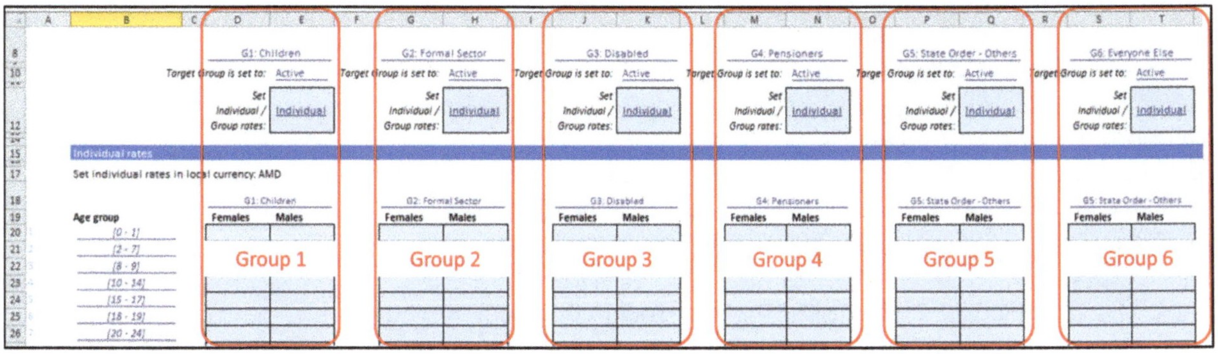

For each target member group, the *target group status* included in the analysis (i.e., active or inactive) is automatically picked up from the 1.1A Target Populations worksheet. It is shown specifically in **cells E10, H10, K10, N10, Q10, and T10** (Figure 178) for the six groups, respectively.

Figure 178: Linked Cells for Target Group Status in the 1.5 Revenues Worksheet

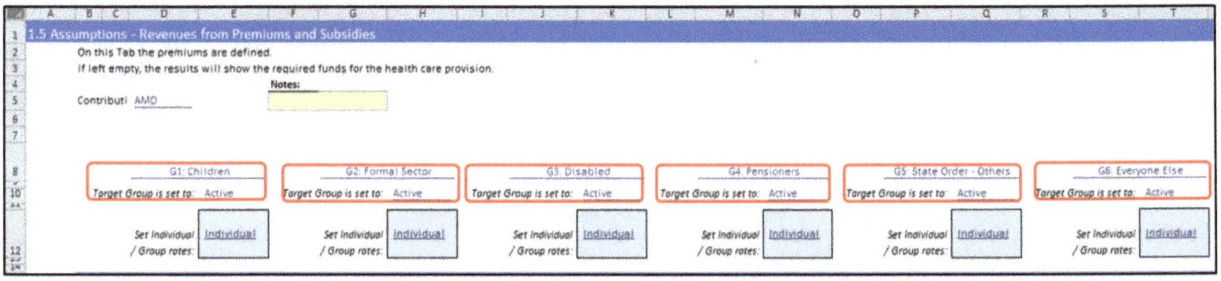

Just below the *target group status,* specifically in **cells E12, H12, K12, N12, Q12, and T12** (Figure 179), the user will be asked to determine for each subpopulation, through a drop-down menu, whether the premium rate is for individual members ("Individual") or a group of members ("Group").

Figure 179: Input Cells for Setting Individual or Group Rates in the 1.5 Revenues Worksheet

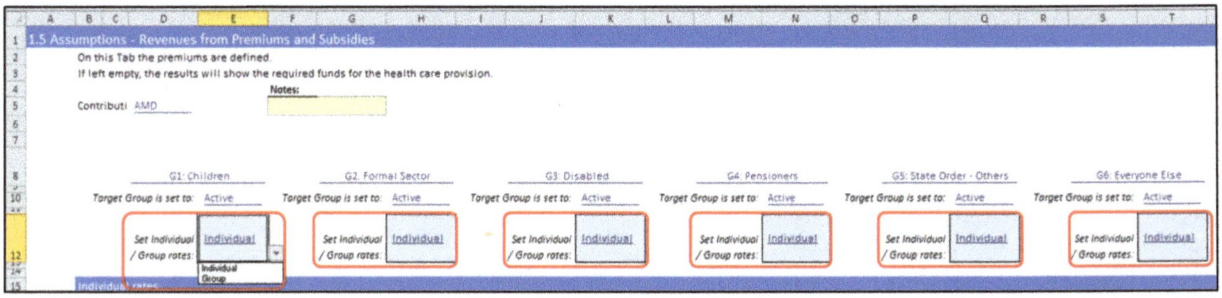

Individual Rates

The *individual rates* per *target group* by *age bracket* and *sex* must be recorded in **rows 20–37** (Figure 180). *Age bracket* data under **column B** (Figure 181) is also picked up from the "1.1A Target Populations" worksheet.

Figure 180: Input Cells for Individual Rates per Target Group by Age Bracket and Sex in 1.5 Revenues Worksheet

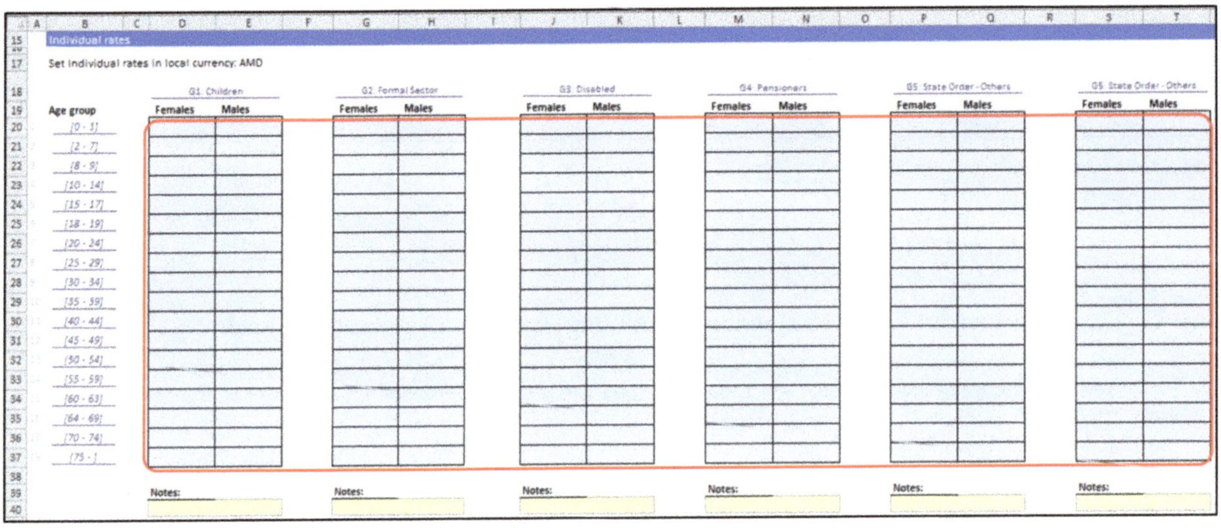

Figure 181: Age Bracket Linked Cells in 1.5 Revenues Worksheet

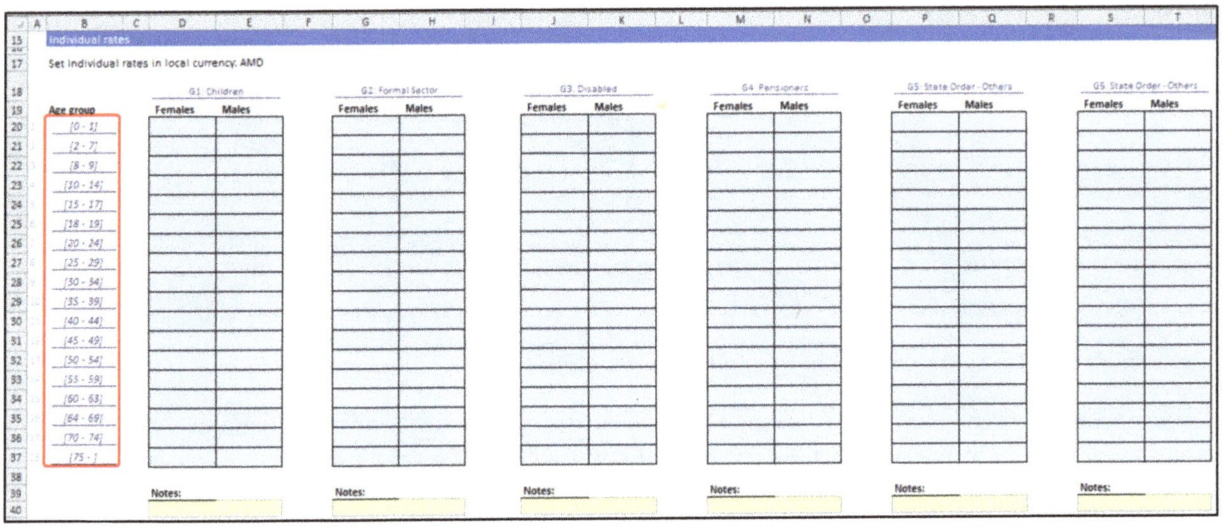

For each age group, the user must define the current premium rates collected by the health insurance program. The cells are restricted to accept only positive values for premium rates (Figure 182).

Figure 182: Restricted Cells to Accept Only Positive Values for Premium Rates

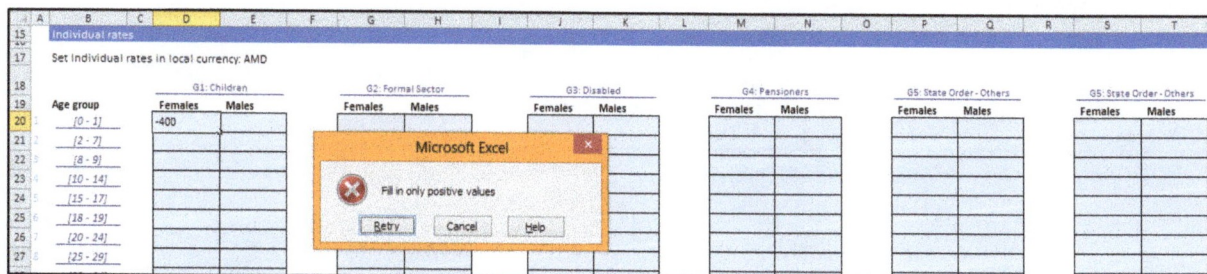

Note: AMD = Armenian dram.

Meanwhile, **row 40** provides space for recording specific notes per group (Figure 183).

Figure 183: Input Cells for Notes on Individual Rates in the 1.5 Revenues Worksheet

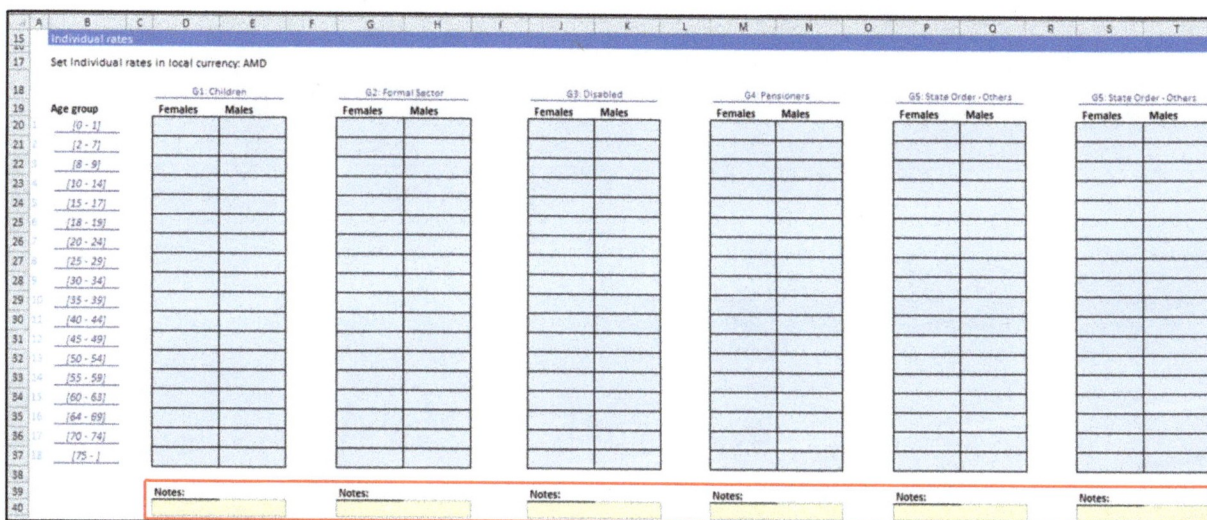

Note: AMD = Armenian dram.

Group Rates

An example of health insurance premiums applied for as a *group rate* is a family wherein the coverage of the family head ("principal") extends to his/her spouse and young children ("dependents").

If the group option is selected as the set rate in **row 12** drop-down list (Figure 184), then the user must record information for group rates beginning row 42 (Figure 185).

Figure 184: Input Cells for Setting Up Rates in the 1.5 Revenues Worksheet

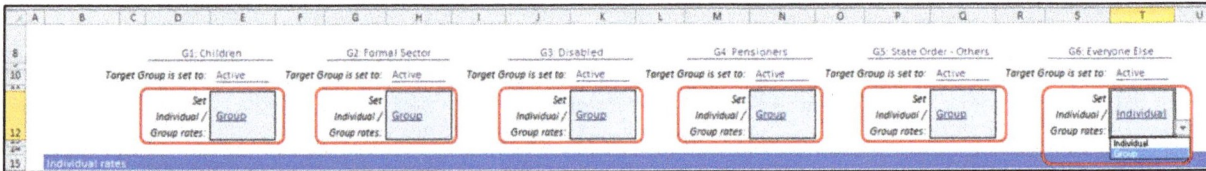

Figure 185: Set Group Rates Portion in the 1.5 Revenues Worksheet

For instance, the "Group" option is selected in **cell E12** for "G1: Ever enrolled population" (Figure 186).

Figure 186: Setting Up Group Rates in 1.5 Revenues Worksheet

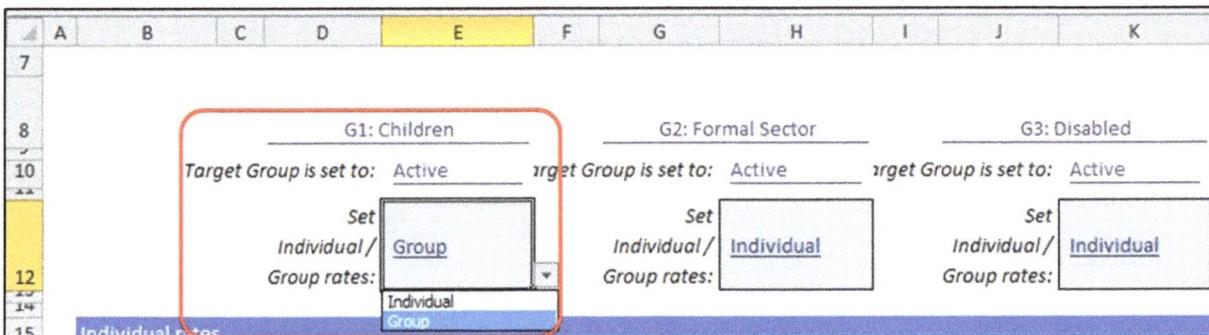

Rows 48 and below under columns D and E are then activated (Figure 187).

Figure 187: Input Cells for Group Rates in the 1.5 Revenues Worksheet

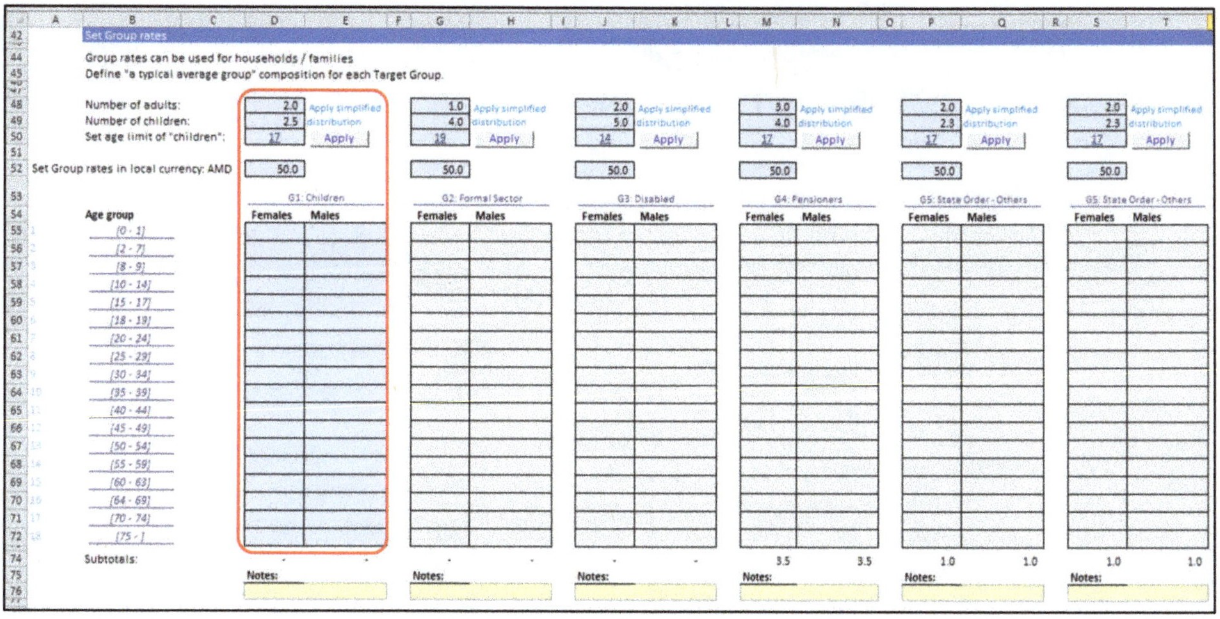

Before inputting the premium rates, beginning **row 55**, the user is required to define a *typical average group* composition for each *target group*. This includes information on the number of adults (**row 48**), number of children (**row 49**), and the maximum age for children (**row 50**).

For example, a "typical group" could be composed of two adults (i.e., head and spouse) and two children with a maximum age of 17 selected from the age drop-down list (Figure 188).

Figure 188: Input Cells for Typical Average Group in the 1.5 Revenues Worksheet

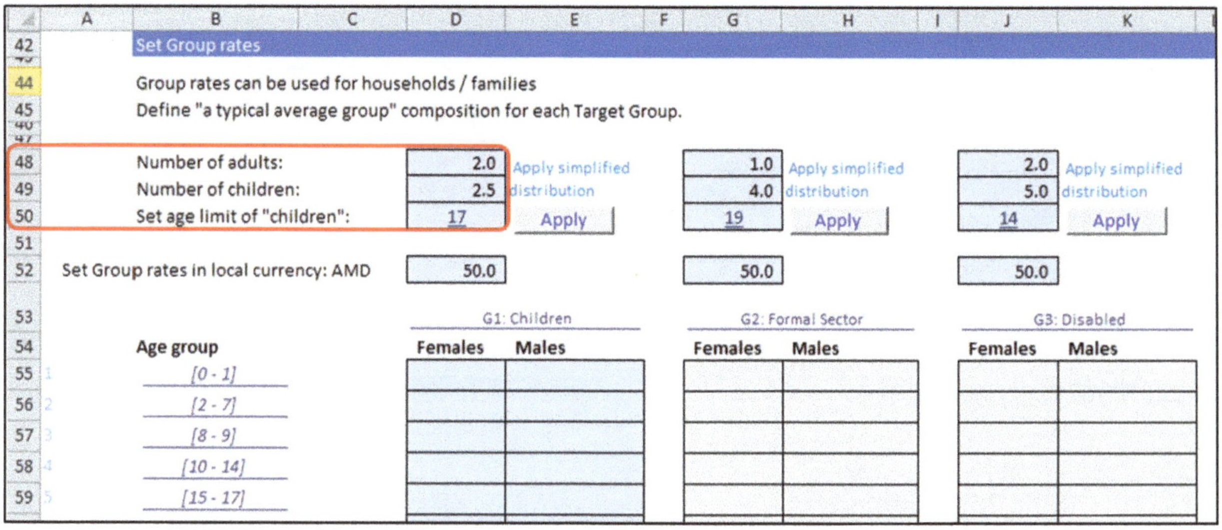

Note: AMD = Armenian dram.

After completing the required information, the user must click the **Apply** button (Figure 189).

Figure 189: The Apply Buttons in Visual Basic for Applications

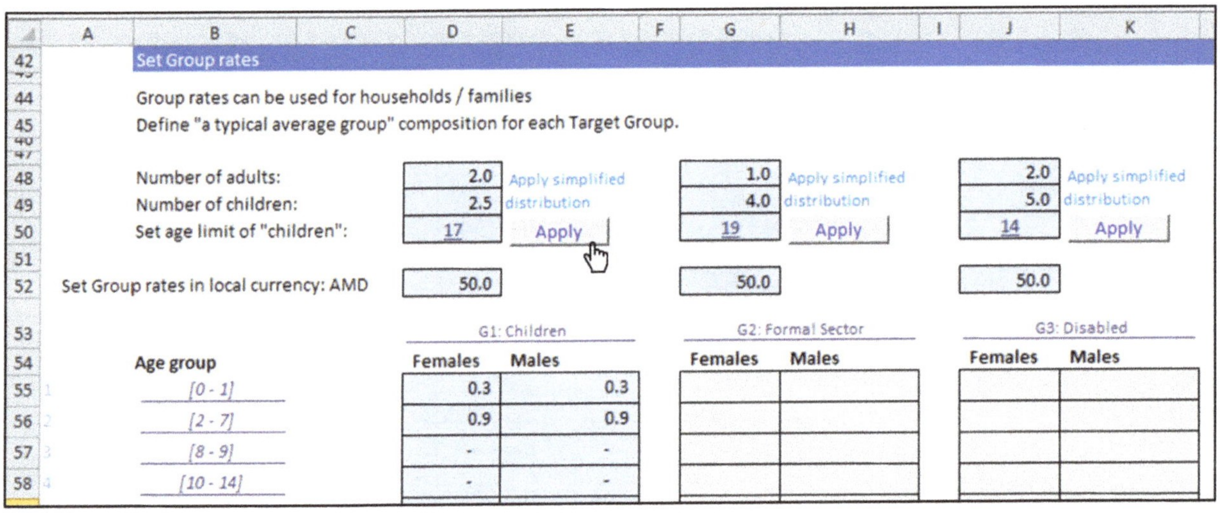

Note: AMD = Armenian dram.

This Visual Basic for Applications (VBA) button applies a simple distribution of the number of the members defined for the "typical average group" over the age groups (Figure 190). The model does not consider the distribution between females and males. It also does not take into consideration which age groups are not covered. For instance, since Group 1 is defined as "children," even if the set age limit of "children" is 17, only those applicable age brackets of the "children" group will be covered by the distribution.

Figure 190: Applying Simplified Distributions in 1.5 Revenues Worksheet

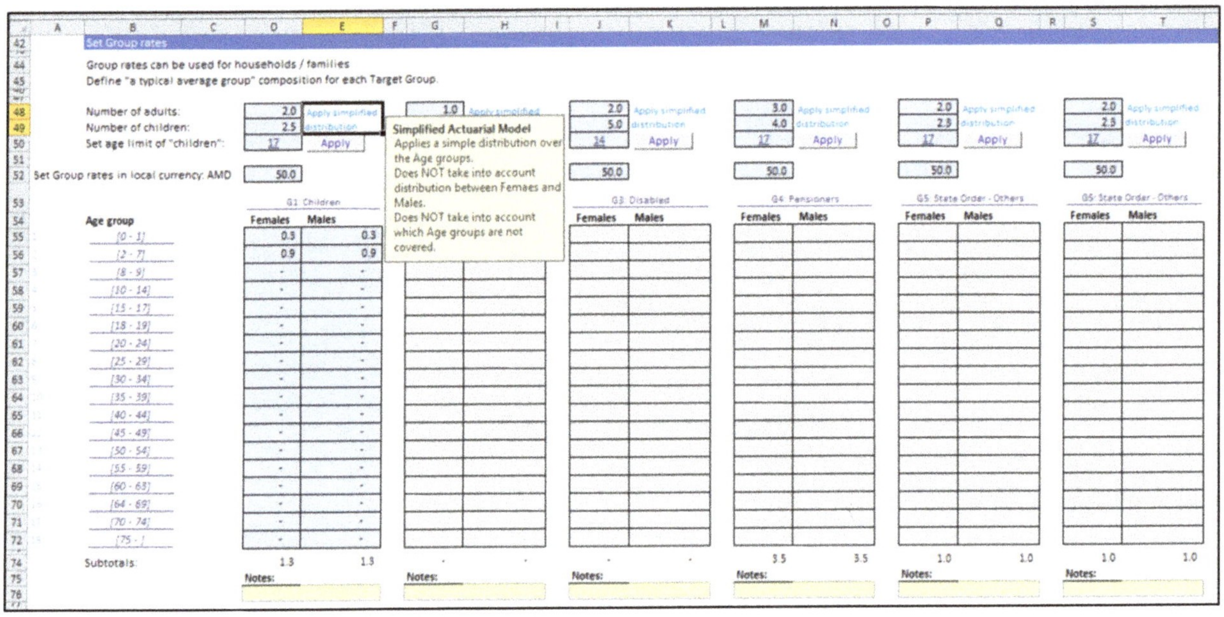

Note: AMD = Armenian dram.

The user must then input the ***group rate in local currency*** in **row 52** (Figure 191).

Figure 191: Input Cell for Group Rates in Local Currency in the 1.5 Revenues Worksheet

Row	A–C	D	E	G	H	J	K
42	Set Group rates						
44	Group rates can be used for households / families						
45	Define "a typical average group" composition for each Target Group.						
48	Number of adults:	2.0	Apply simplified	1.0	Apply simplified	2.0	Apply simplified
49	Number of children:	2.5	distribution	4.0	distribution	5.0	distribution
50	Set age limit of "children":	17	Apply	19	Apply	14	Apply
51							
52	Set Group rates in local currency: AMD	50.0		50.0		50.0	
53		G1: Children		G2: Formal Sector		G3: Disabled	
54	Age group	Females	Males	Females	Males	Females	Males
55	1 [0 - 1]	0.3	0.3				
56	2 [2 - 7]	0.9	0.9				
57	3 [8 - 9]	-	-				
58	4 [10 - 14]	-	-				

Note: AMD = Armenian dram.

To check for the appropriate distribution of members, **row 74** is provided for the calculation of ***subtotals*** (Figure 192).

Figure 192: Subtotals Output Cells in the 1.5 Revenues Worksheet

Row	A–C	D	E	G	H	J	K
42	Set Group rates						
44	Group rates can be used for households / families						
45	Define "a typical average group" composition for each Target Group.						
48	Number of adults:	2.0	Apply simplified	1.0	Apply simplified	2.0	Apply simplified
49	Number of children:	2.5	distribution	4.0	distribution	5.0	distribution
50	Set age limit of "children":	17	Apply	19	Apply	14	Apply
51							
52	Set Group rates in local currency: AMD	50.0		50.0		50.0	
53		G1: Children		G2: Formal Sector		G3: Disabled	
54	Age group	Females	Males	Females	Males	Females	Males
55	1 [0 - 1]	0.3	0.3				
56	2 [2 - 7]	0.9	0.9				
57	3 [8 - 9]	-	-				
58	4 [10 - 14]	-	-				
59	5 [15 - 17]	-	-				
74	Subtotals:	1.3	1.3	-	-	-	-
75		Notes:		Notes:		Notes:	
76							

Note: AMD = Armenian dram.

Meanwhile, **row 76** allows for the recording of any ***notes*** or remarks regarding the assumption on the number of adults, children, age limit set for the children, and group rates (Figure 193).

Figure 193: Prerequisite Information in the 1.6 Uptake and Retention Worksheet

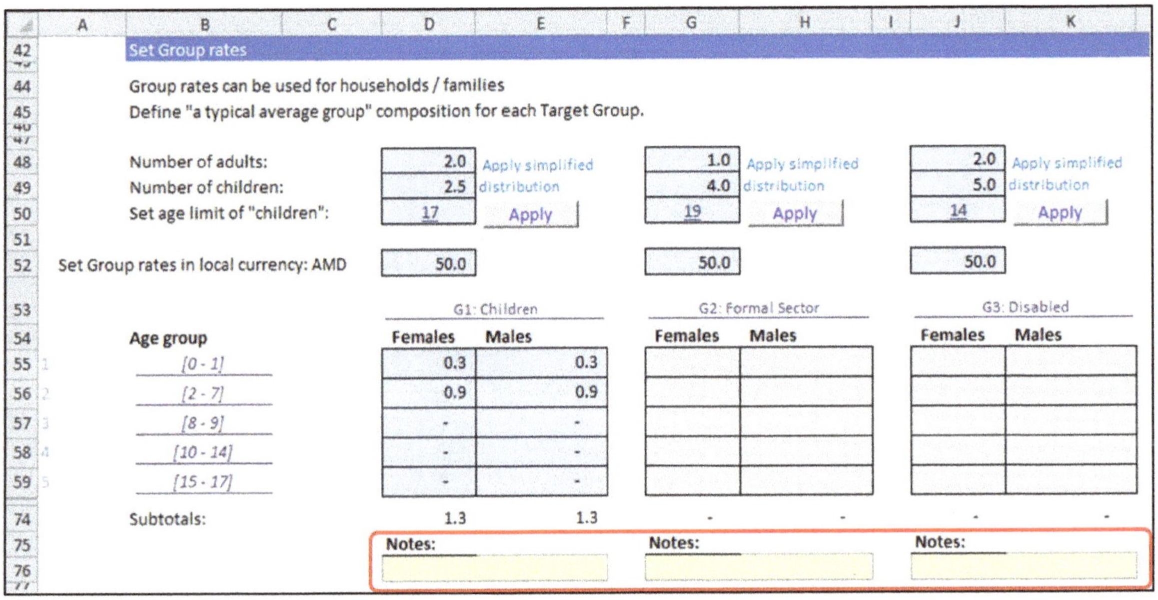

H.   The 1.6 Uptake and Retention Input Sheet

This worksheet (Figure 194) allows for setting up the number or percentage of members of the target population that are new enrollees and then re-enroll at the end the specified period of enrollment.

Figure 194: Preview of the 1.6 Uptake and Retention Worksheet

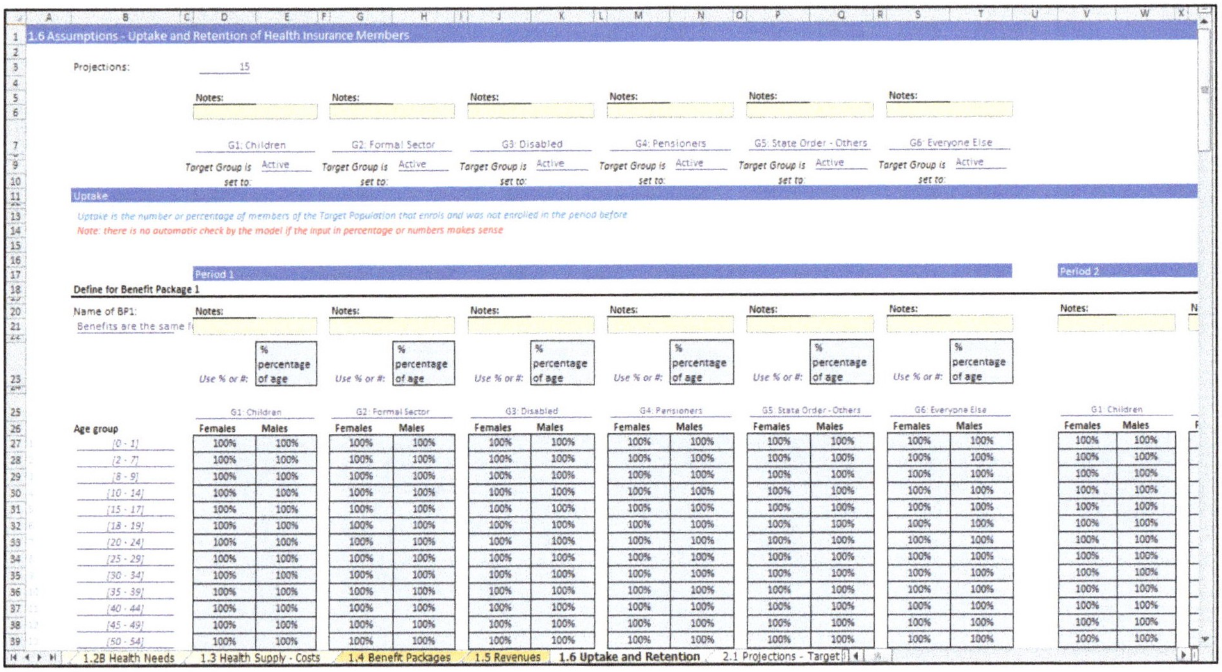

FOR YOUR INFORMATION

Cells found in this worksheet include:

Input Cells

| 100.00 | Input cell, restricted input (e.g., only positive values/only integers/dates/etc.) |

| 100.00 | Input cell, select option from list |

Free Text Cells

| Note | Input cell to write comments |

Calculation Cells

| 200.00 | Linked and/or Calculation cell (locked), input to cell from another tab |

- Restricted input cells for encoding only positive numeric values;
- Restricted input cells for selection from a drop-down list;
- Free text cells for adding corresponding explanations, comments, sources, or other helpful texts pertaining to encoded information; and
- Linked calculation cells (i.e., Period of Projections, Target Group Names and Status, Benefit Package Names, and Age bracket) that are locked and entries came from another tab.

This worksheet can be divided into three partitions: (i) prerequisite information, (ii) uptake assumptions, and (iii) retention assumptions.

Prerequisite Information

This portion of the worksheet (Figure 195) shows essential information to be used in defining uptake and retention rates. Contents of this worksheet include the *Period of Projections* in **cell D3**; input cells for *Notes* in **row 6**; the *Target Groups* in **row 7**; and respective *Group Status* (i.e., active or inactive) in **row 9**. The projection period is linked from the 1.0 General Assumptions worksheet, while the target groups and their status are defined from the 1.1A Target Populations worksheet.

Figure 195: Prerequisite Information in the 1.6 Uptake and Retention Worksheet

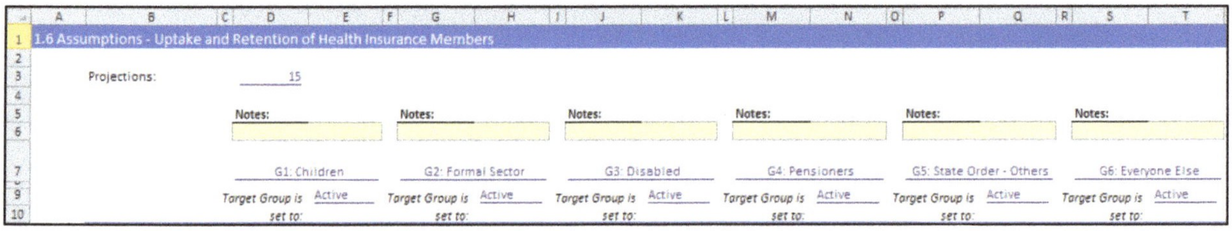

Uptake

The *uptake* portion of the worksheet is from row 11 up to row 105 (Figure 196).

Figure 196: Uptake for each Target Group and Period in the 1.6 Uptake and Retention Worksheet

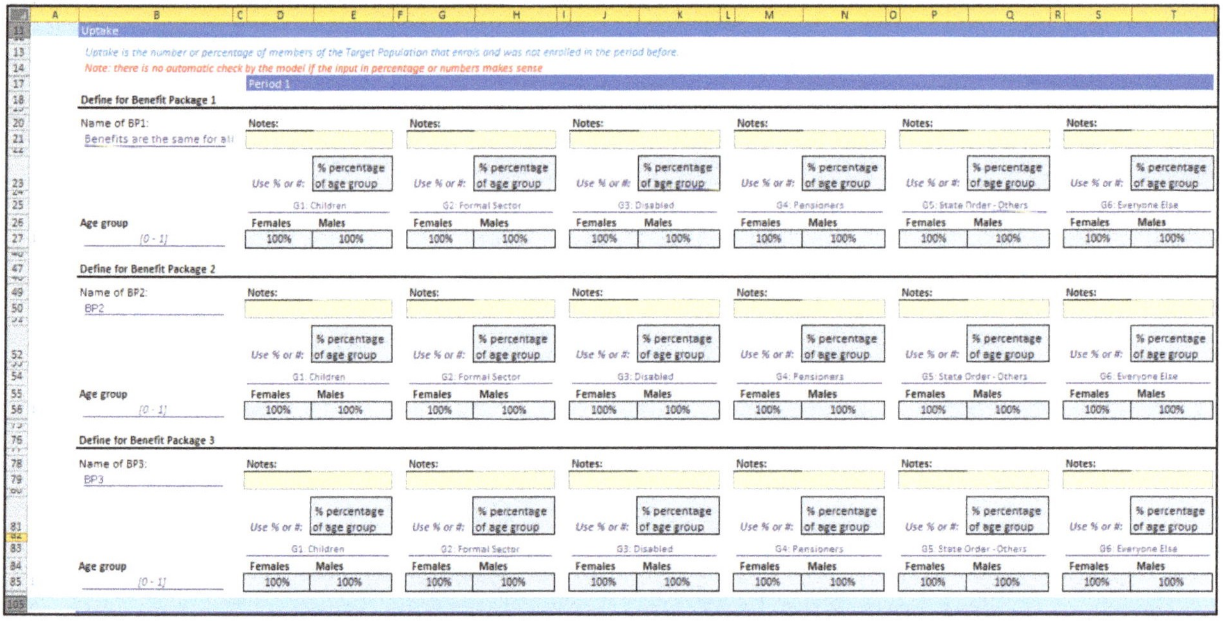

Note: Screenshot contains hidden rows for illustration purposes only.

Up to three panels (i.e., one for each benefit package listed in the 1.4 Benefit Packages worksheet) are provided for recording uptake data. Specifically,

- **Rows 18–46** pertain to the panel for Benefit Package 1 (Figure 197),
- **Rows 47–75** pertain to the panel for Benefit Package 2 (Figure 198), and
- **Rows 76–105** pertain to the panel for Benefit Package 3 (Figure 199).

Figure 197: Uptake Panel for Benefit Package 1 in the 1.6 Uptake and Retention Worksheet

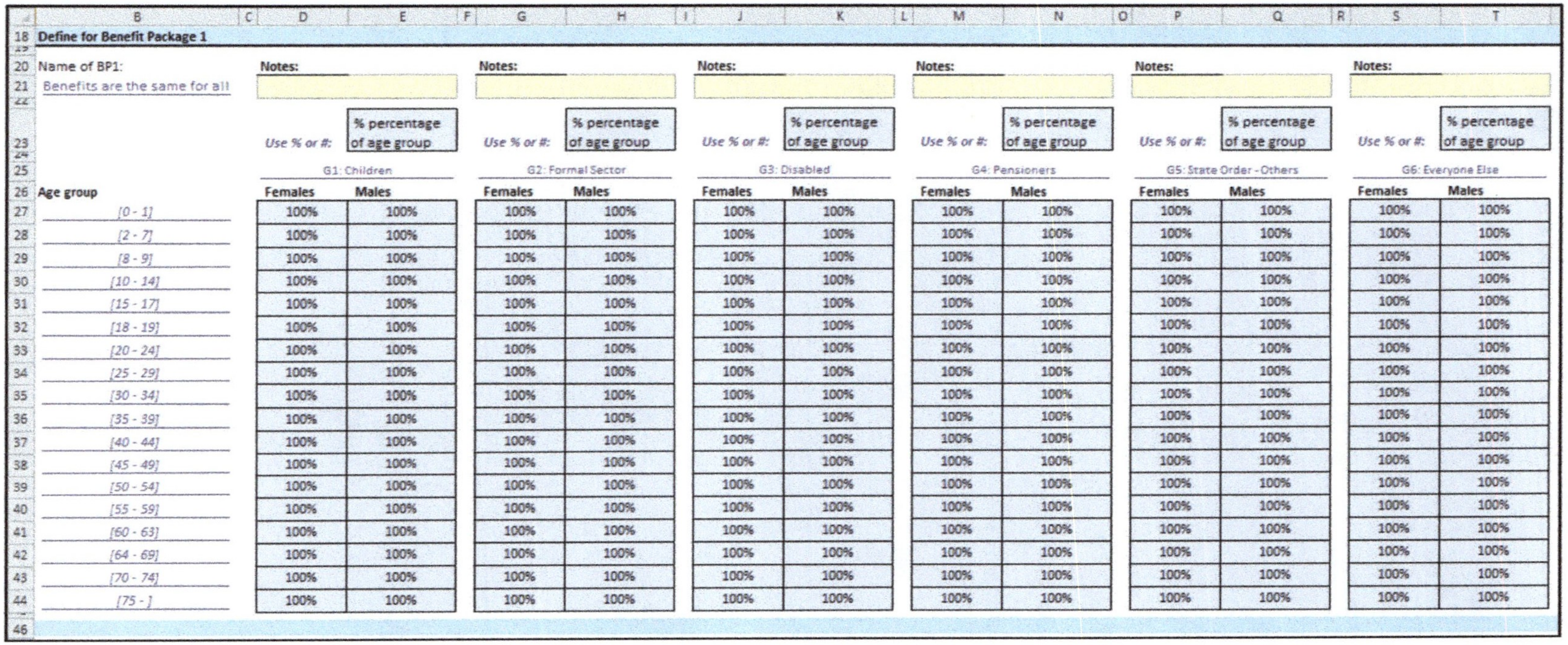

Figure 198: Uptake Panel for Benefit Package 2 in the 1.6 Uptake and Retention Worksheet

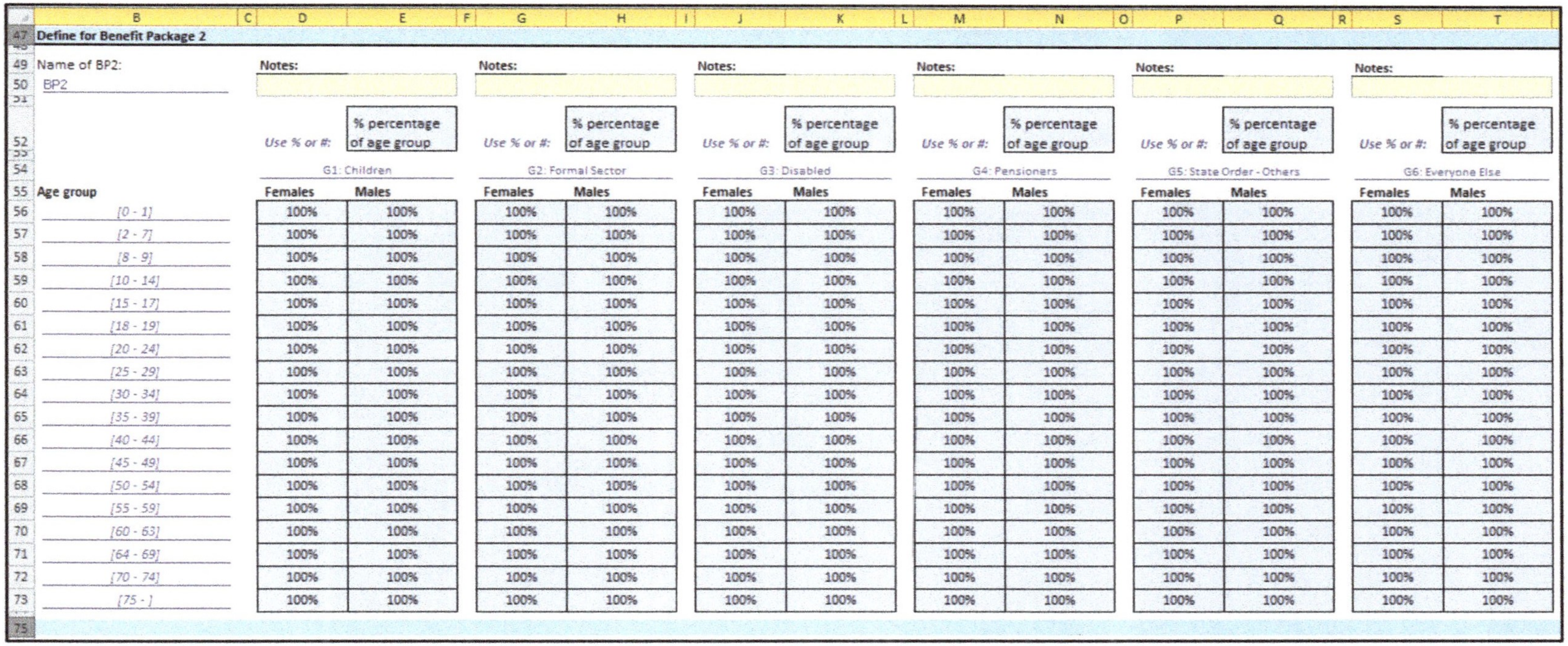

Figure 199: Uptake Panel for Benefit Package 3 in the 1.6 Uptake and Retention Worksheet

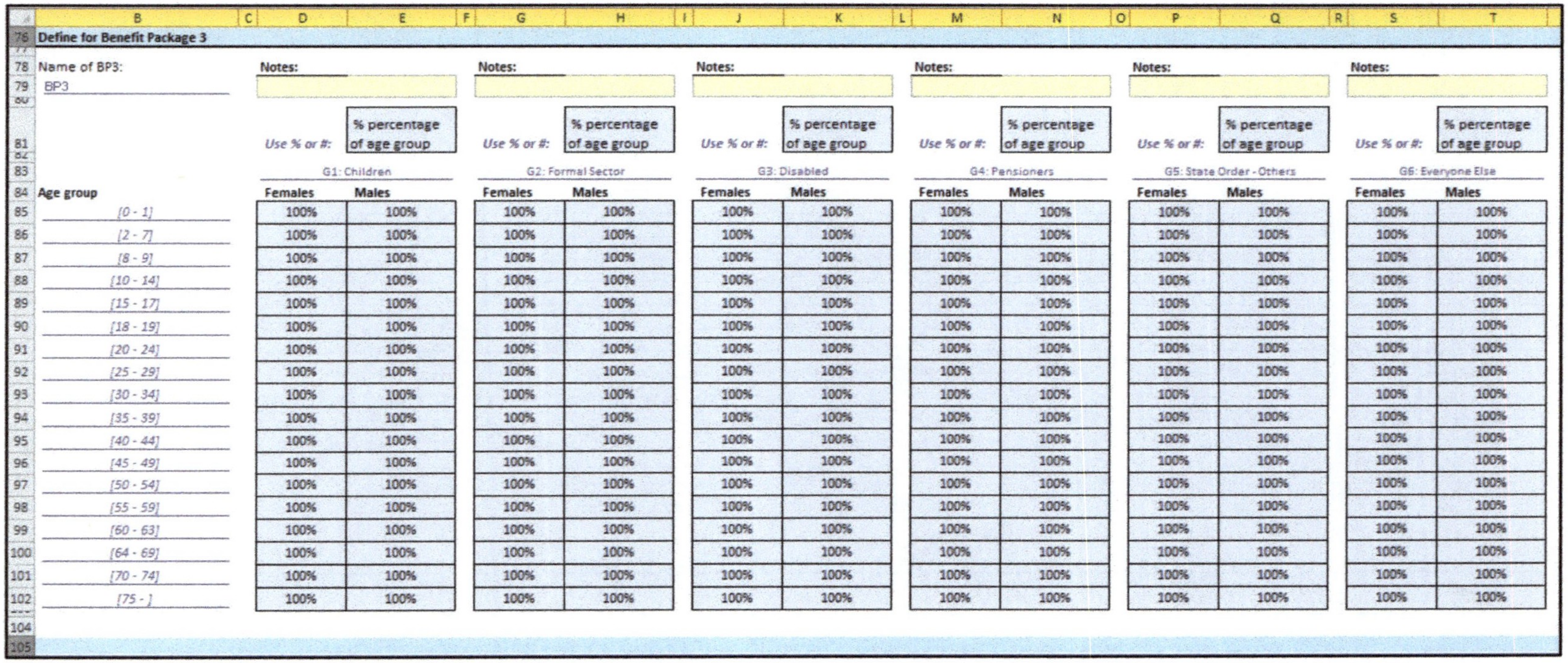

The name of the Benefit Packages is automatically displayed in the upper left corner of each panel (i.e., **cell B21** for Benefit Package 1; **cell B50** for Benefit Package 2; and **cell B79** for Benefit Package 3 [Figure 200]). These names are picked up from the 1.4 Benefit Packages worksheet.

Figure 200: Benefit Package Names for Uptake in 1.6 Uptake and Retention Worksheet

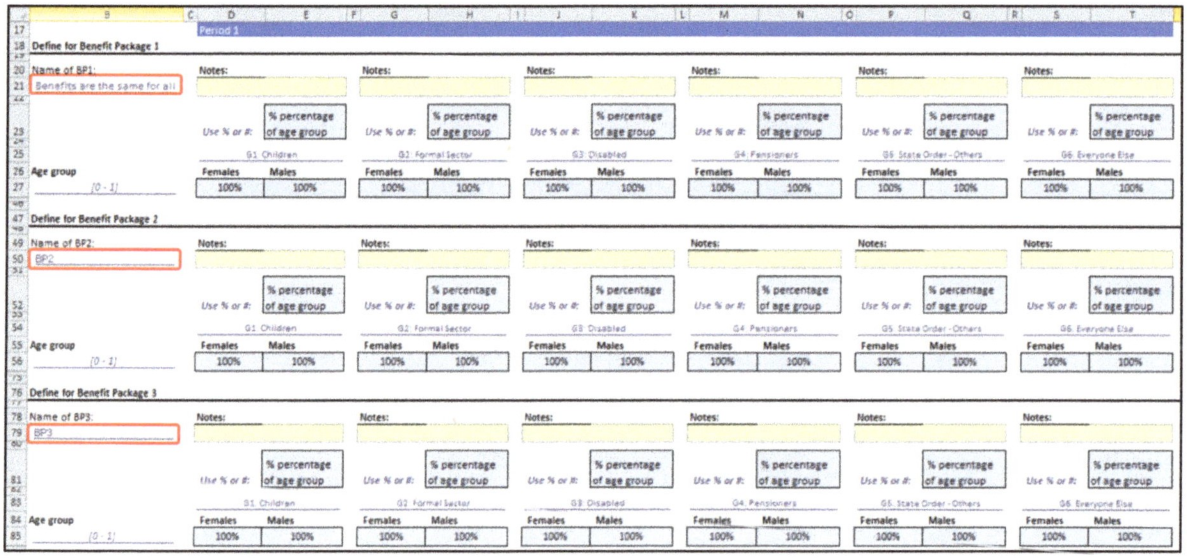

Note: Screenshot contains hidden rows for illustration purposes only.

Within the row next to the name of the benefit packages are free text cells for inputs to *notes* on uptake assumptions per target group in each period. Specifically, these are **row 21** for Benefit Package 1; **row 50** for Benefit Package 2; and **row 79** for Benefit Package 3 (Figure 201).

Figure 201: Uptake Notes in the 1.6 Uptake and Retention Worksheet

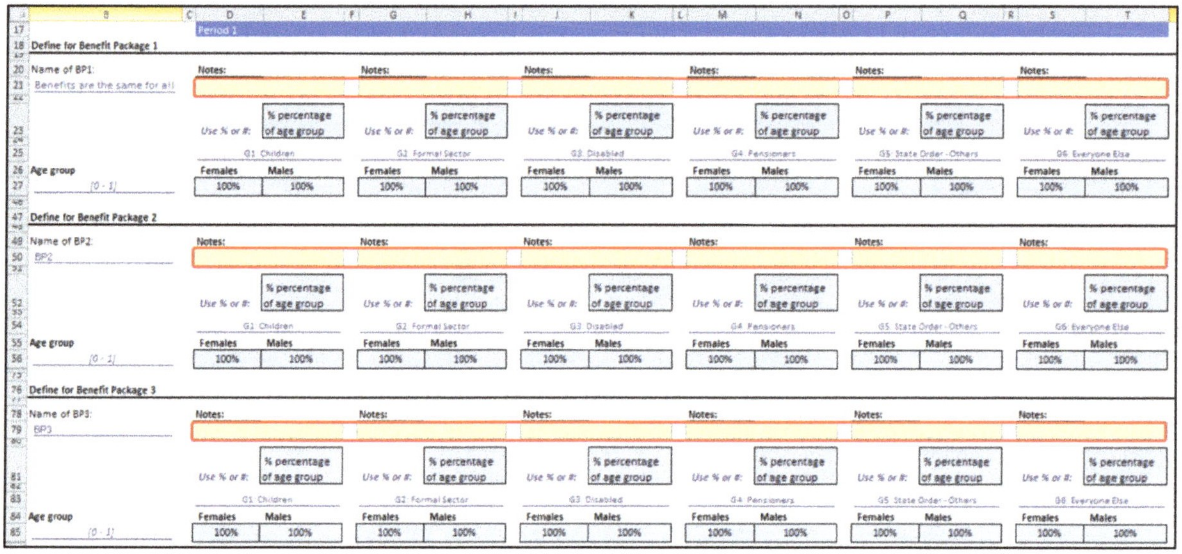

Note: Screenshot contains hidden rows for illustration purposes only.

The uptake can then be defined as either the percentage of the members of the Target Member Group by age bracket, or the number of persons per age group. This is set in the drop-down menu located in **row 23** for "Benefit Package 1;" **row 52** for "Benefit Package 2;" and **row 81** for "Benefit Package 3" (Figure 202).

Figure 202: Setting Up the Uptake Definition in the 1.6 Uptake and Retention Worksheet

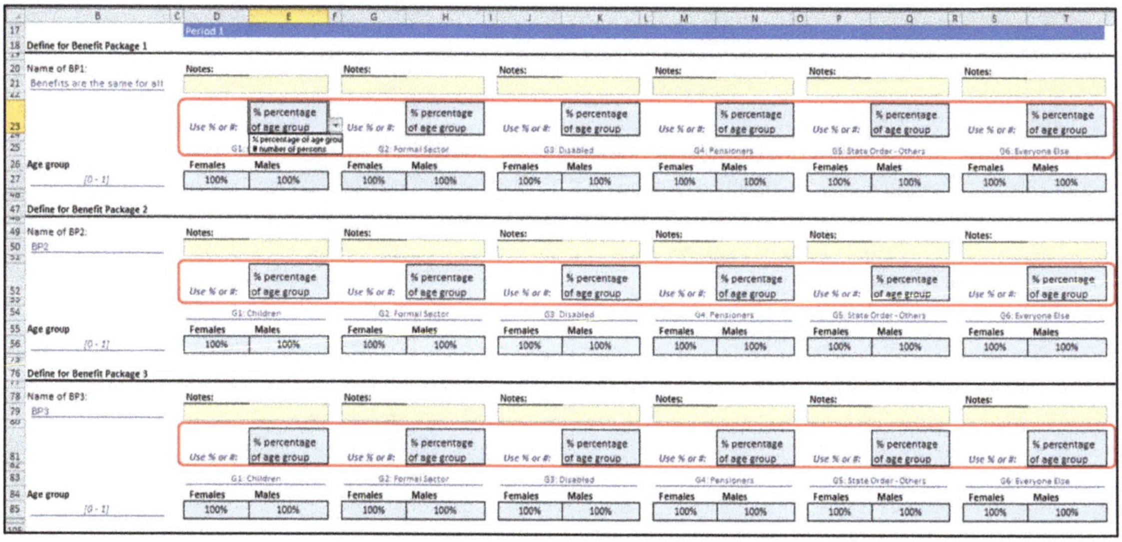

Note: Screenshot above contains hidden rows for illustration purposes only.

Just below the uptake definition setting and for each *target group* and each *period*, the user is required to record the uptake information by *age bracket* and *sex*. Specifically, these input cells for uptake data begin **row 27** for Benefit Package 1; **row 56** for Benefit Package 2; and **row 85** for Benefit Package 3. The user must be careful in inputting data here since there are no built-in automatic checks for these uptake cells (Figure 203).

Figure 203: Input Cells for Uptake Numbers or Percentages in the 1.6 Uptake and Retention Worksheet

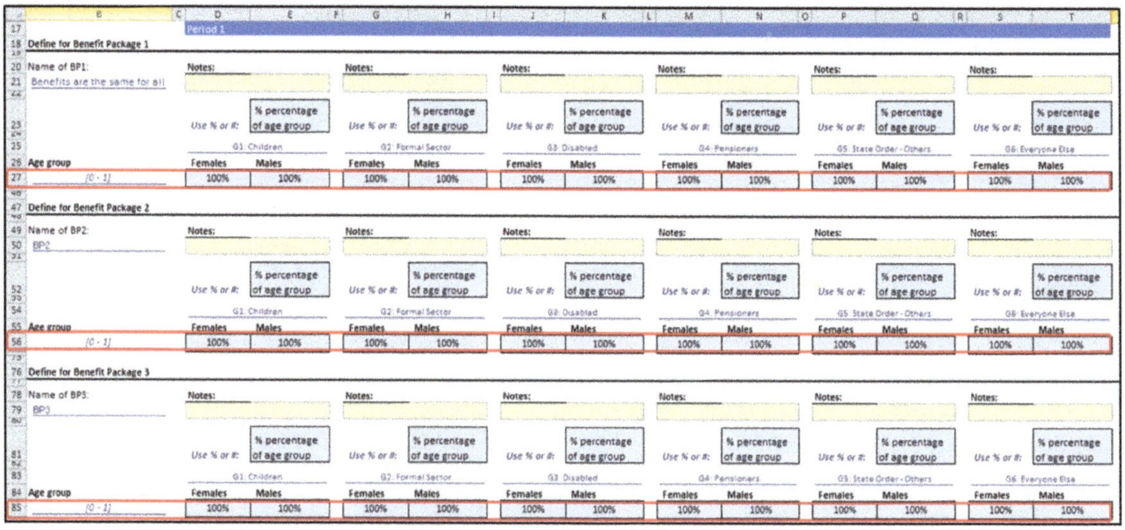

Note: Screenshot contains hidden rows for illustration purposes only.

Retention

The *retention* portion of the worksheet includes rows 106–195 (Figure 204).

Figure 204: Retention Portion for Each Target Group and Period in the 1.6 Uptake and Retention Worksheet

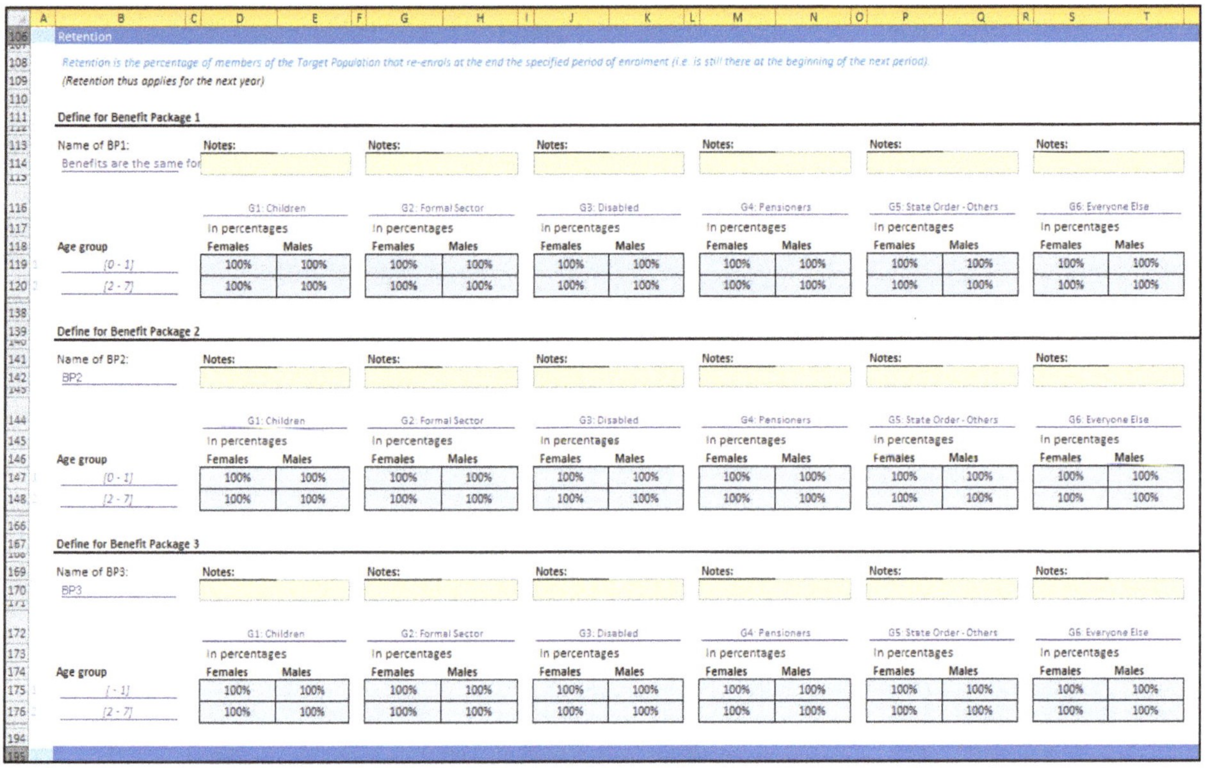

Note: Screenshot contains hidden rows for illustration purposes only.

Similar to the uptake portion, up to three panels—one for each benefit package listed in the 1.4 Benefit Packages worksheet—are provided for the recording of the "Retention" data. Specifically,

- **Rows 111–138** pertain to the panel for Benefit Package 1 (Figure 205),
- **Rows 139–166** pertain to the panel for Benefit Package 1 (Figure 206), and
- **Rows 167–195** pertain to the panel for Benefit Package 3 (Figure 207).

Figure 205: Retention Panel for Benefit Package 1 in the 1.6 Uptake and Retention Worksheet

Define for Benefit Package 1

Name of BP1:

Benefits are the same for all

Notes:

Age group	G1 Children		G2 Formal Sector		G3 Disabled		G4 Pensioners		G5 State Order - Others		G6 Everyone Else	
	In percentages		In percentages		In percentages		In percentages		In percentages		In percentages	
	Females	Males	Females	Males	Females	Males	Females	Males	Females	Males	Females	Males
[0 - 1]	100%	100%	100%	100%	100%	100%	100%	100%	100%	100%	100%	100%
[2 - 7]	100%	100%	100%	100%	100%	100%	100%	100%	100%	100%	100%	100%
[8 - 9]	100%	100%	100%	100%	100%	100%	100%	100%	100%	100%	100%	100%
[10 - 14]	100%	100%	100%	100%	100%	100%	100%	100%	100%	100%	100%	100%
[15 - 17]	100%	100%	100%	100%	100%	100%	100%	100%	100%	100%	100%	100%
[18 - 19]	100%	100%	100%	100%	100%	100%	100%	100%	100%	100%	100%	100%
[20 - 24]	100%	100%	100%	100%	100%	100%	100%	100%	100%	100%	100%	100%
[25 - 29]	100%	100%	100%	100%	100%	100%	100%	100%	100%	100%	100%	100%
[30 - 34]	100%	100%	100%	100%	100%	100%	100%	100%	100%	100%	100%	100%
[35 - 39]	100%	100%	100%	100%	100%	100%	100%	100%	100%	100%	100%	100%
[40 - 44]	100%	100%	100%	100%	100%	100%	100%	100%	100%	100%	100%	100%
[45 - 49]	100%	100%	100%	100%	100%	100%	100%	100%	100%	100%	100%	100%
[50 - 54]	100%	100%	100%	100%	100%	100%	100%	100%	100%	100%	100%	100%
[55 - 59]	100%	100%	100%	100%	100%	100%	100%	100%	100%	100%	100%	100%
[60 - 63]	100%	100%	100%	100%	100%	100%	100%	100%	100%	100%	100%	100%
[64 - 69]	100%	100%	100%	100%	100%	100%	100%	100%	100%	100%	100%	100%
[70 - 74]	100%	100%	100%	100%	100%	100%	100%	100%	100%	100%	100%	100%
[75 -]	100%	100%	100%	100%	100%	100%	100%	100%	100%	100%	100%	100%

Notes: (for G2, G3, G4, G5, G6)

Figure 206: Retention Panel for Benefit Package 2 in the 1.6 Uptake and Retention Worksheet

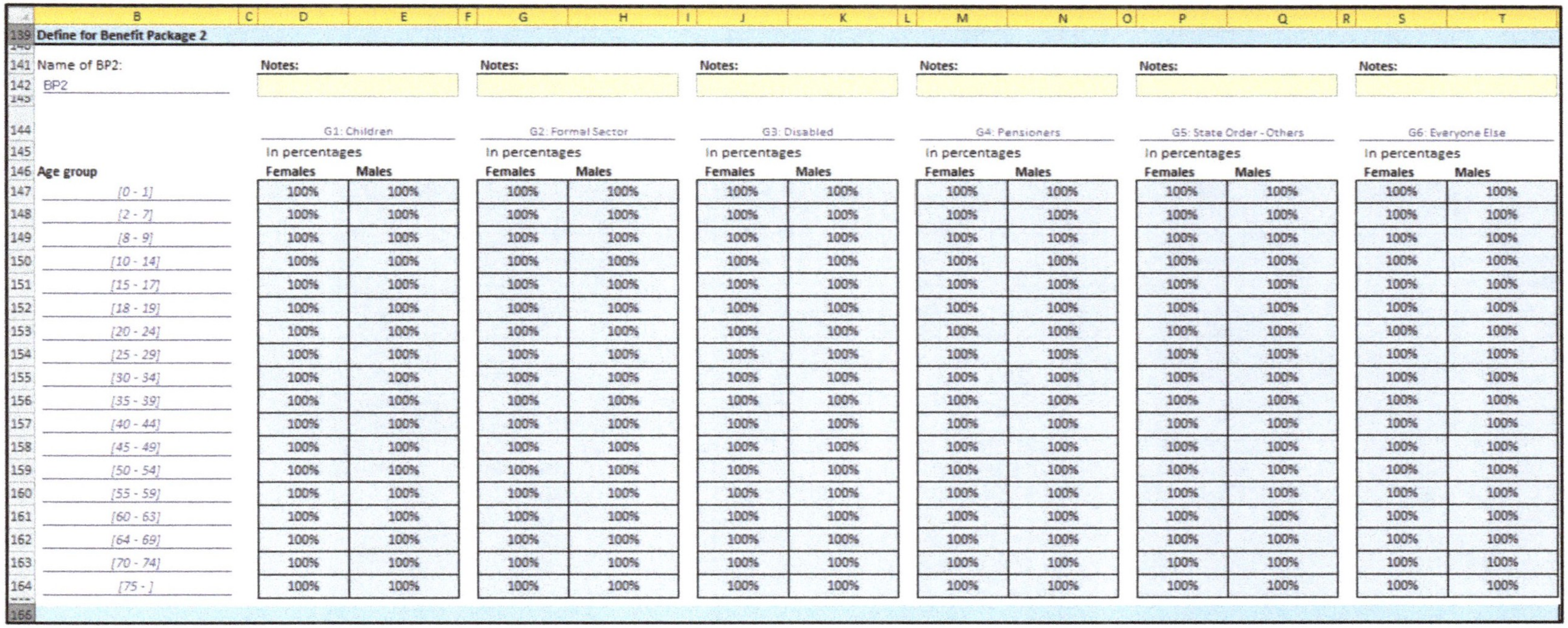

Figure 207: Retention Panel for Benefit Package 3 in the 1.6 Uptake and Retention Worksheet

The name of the benefit packages is automatically displayed in the upper left corner of each panel (i.e., **cell B114** for Benefit Package 1; **cell B142** for Benefit Package 2; and **cell B170** for Benefit Package 3 [Figure 208]). These names are picked up from the 1.4 Benefit Packages worksheet.

Figure 208: Benefit Package Names for Retention in the 1.6 Uptake and Retention Worksheet

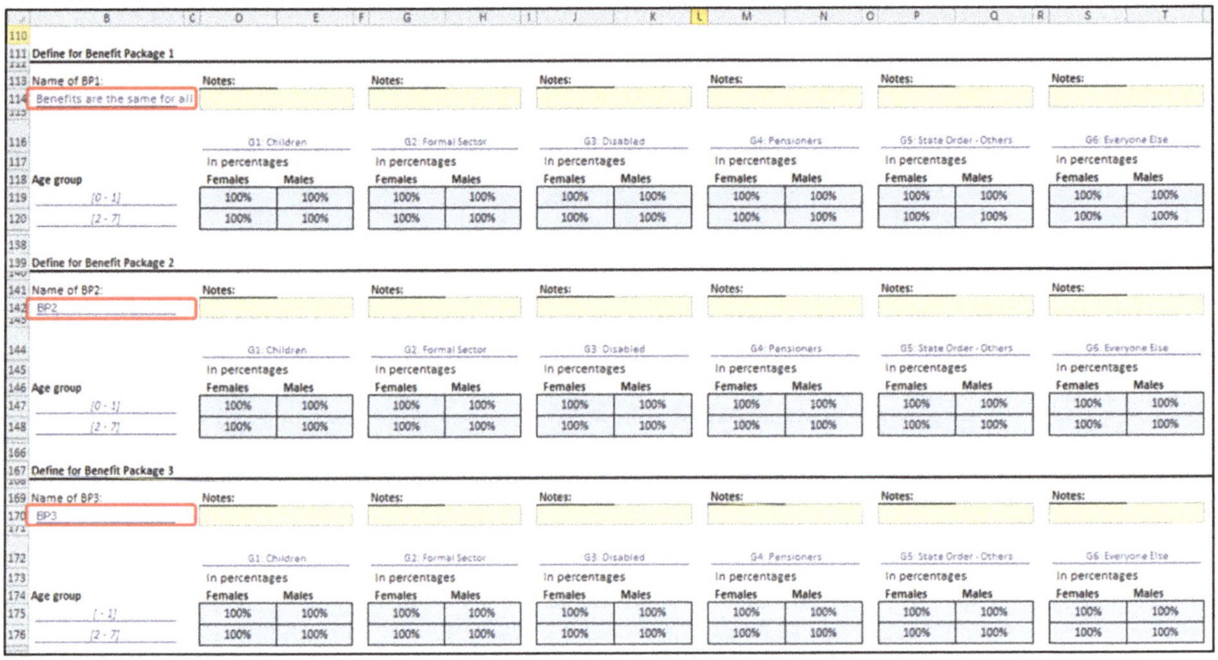

Note: Screenshot contains hidden rows for illustration purposes only.

Within the row next to the name of the benefit packages are free text cells for inputs to *notes* on uptake assumptions per target group for each period. Specifically, these are **row 114** for Benefit Package 1; **row 142** for Benefit Package 2; and **row 170** for Benefit Package 3 (Figure 209).

Figure 209: Retention Notes in 1.6 Uptake and Retention Worksheet

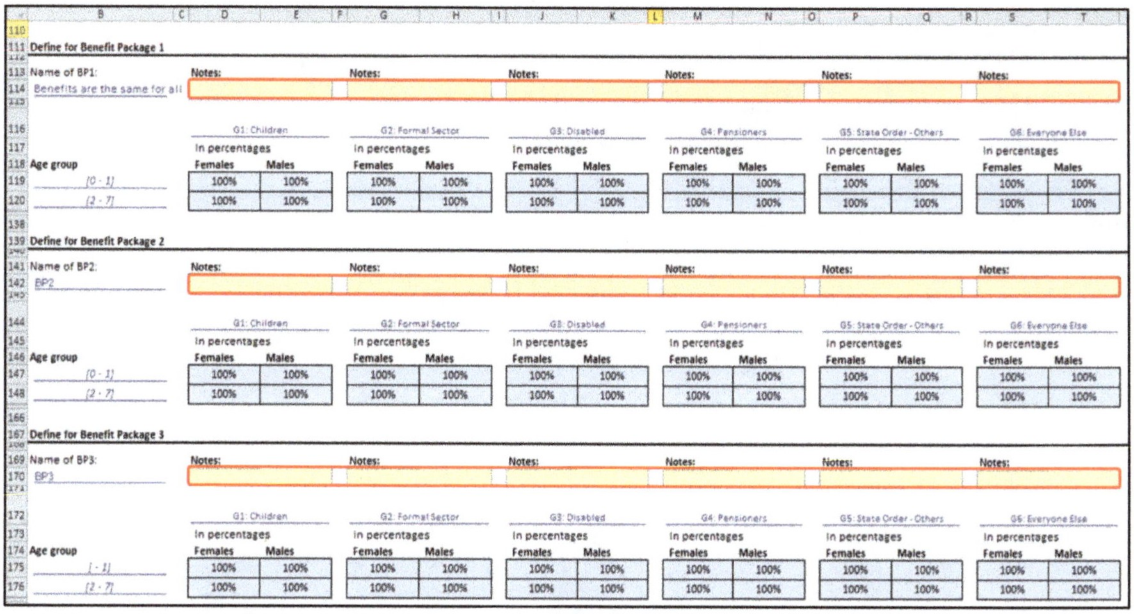

Note: Screenshot contains hidden rows for illustration purposes only.

Just below the benefit package names and notes for each *target group* and each *period*, the user is required to record the retention rates by *age bracket* and *sex*. Specifically, these input cells for retention data begin with **row 119** for Benefit Package 1, **row 147** for Benefit Package 2, and **row 175** for Benefit Package 3. Retention data should be recorded as the percentage of members of the target population that re-enrolls at the end of the specific period of enrollment. Thus, retention rates are applied to the next year (Figure 210).

Figure 210: Input Cells for Retention Percentages in 1.6 Uptake and Retention Worksheet

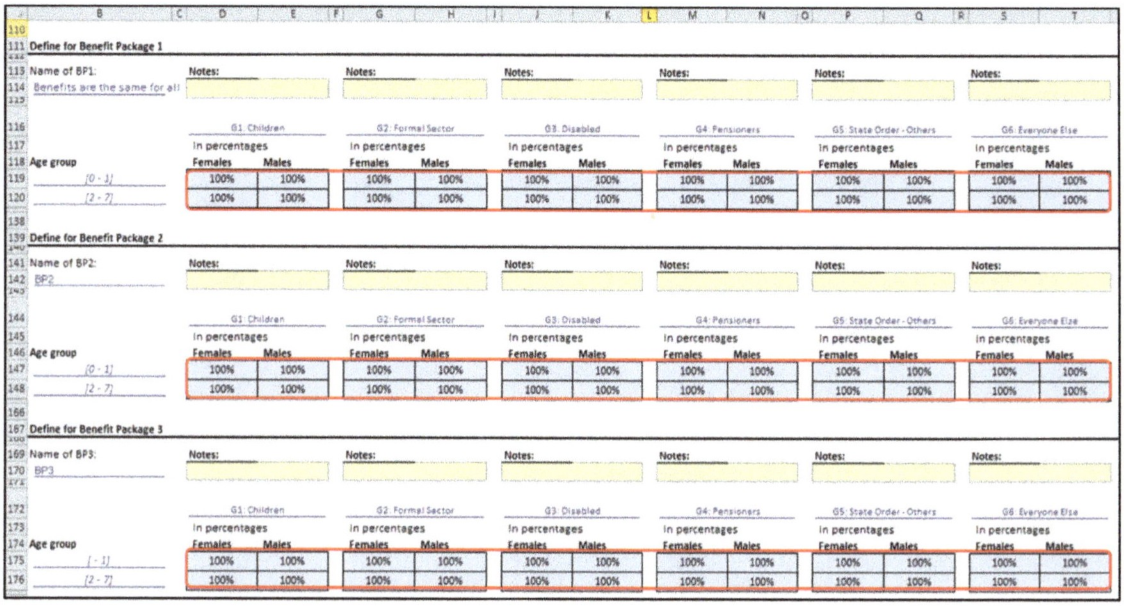

Note: The screenshot above contains hidden rows for illustration purposes only.

CHAPTER V

Results of the SLAM File

This chapter describes the 2.0 Generate Results, 3.1 Results," and Dashboard worksheets that show the results, summary tables, and charts of baseline scenario estimates in the SLAM file.

In this chapter, variables and parameters are denoted in *blue italics*, buttons are described in red underlined, while emphasized information are in **black underlined**.

A.   The 2.0 Generate Results Worksheet

This locked worksheet (Figure 211) provides a Generate Results button that updates the 3.1 Results. worksheet.

Figure 211: Preview of the 2.0 Generate Results Worksheet

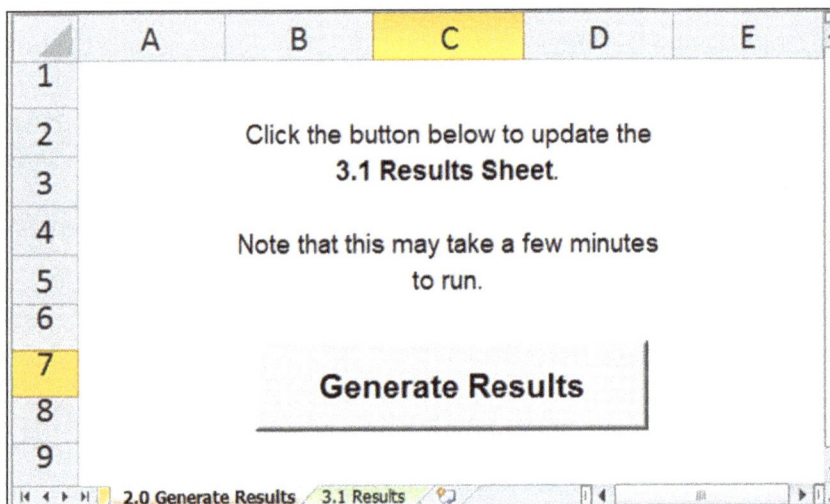

Clicking the general results button runs for a few minutes before showing the 3.1 Results worksheet with a Generating Results message box (Figure 212). A successful updating will return to the 2.0 Generate Results worksheet and only then can the user move on to the updated 3.1 Results tab reflecting the settings defined in the input worksheets.

Figure 212: Generating Results Message Box from the 2.0 Generate Results Worksheet

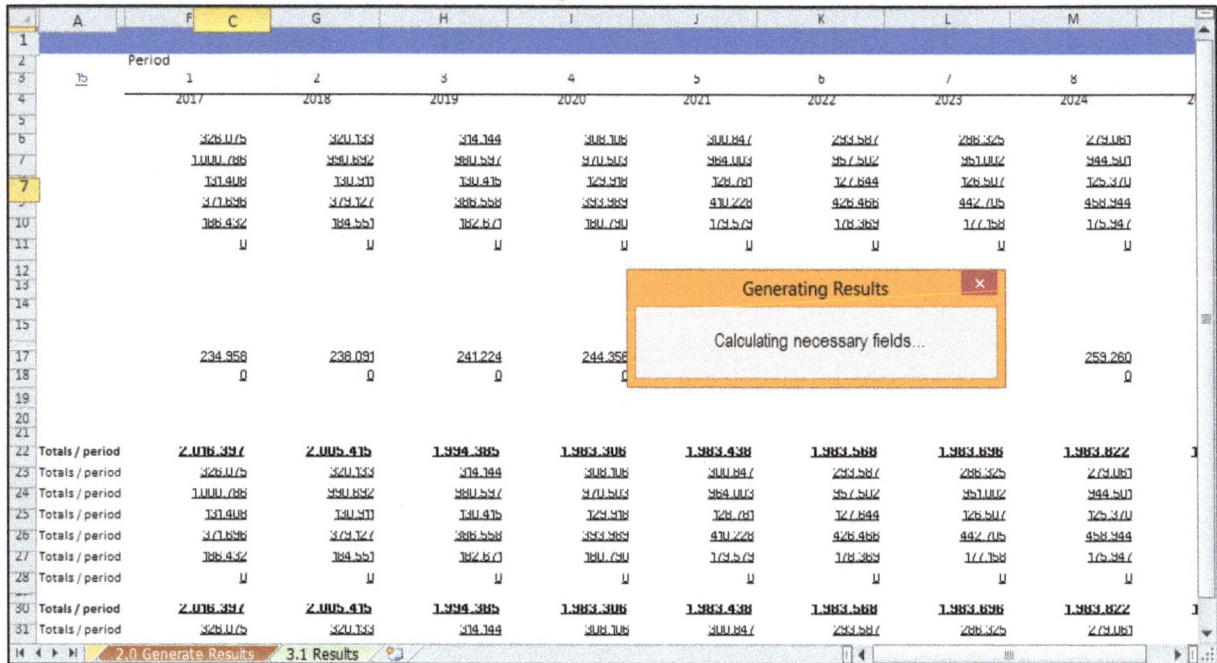

B.   The 3.1 Results Worksheet

This locked worksheet summarizes the projections on the target population and active members, health expenditures, revenues from premiums, cash flow, financial indicators, and analysis cash flow per member type (Figure 213). Specifically, portions of this worksheet include the following:

- **Rows 1–11** for population projections (Figure 214);
- **Rows 13–18** for health needs (Figure 215);
- **Rows 21–44** for enrollment projections (Figure 216);
- **Rows 46–71** for expenditures projections (Figure 217);
- **Rows 73–110** for revenue projections exclusive of risk loading and/or profit margin (Figure 218);
- **Rows 112–139** for revenue projections inclusive of risk loading and/or profit margin and/or premium increase (Figure 219);

- **Rows 141–164** for cash flow projections (Figure 220);
- **Rows 167–170** for discounted cash flow (Figure 221);
- **Rows 172–195** for expenditures per enrollee (Figure 222);
- **Rows 197–220** for revenues per enrollee (Figure 223);
- **Rows 222–245** for cash flow per enrollee (Figure 224);
- **Rows 247–270** for cash flow as % of revenues (Figure 225); and
- **Rows 272–295** for revenue as % of expenditures (Figure 226).

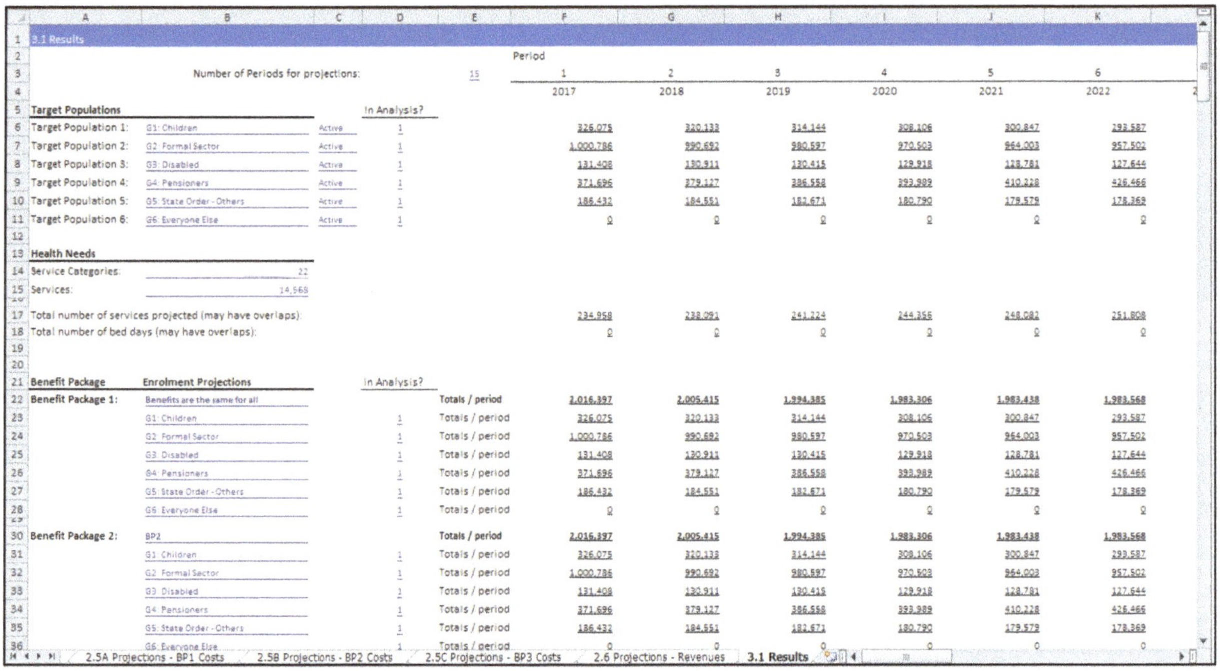

Figure 213: Preview of the 3.1 Results Worksheet

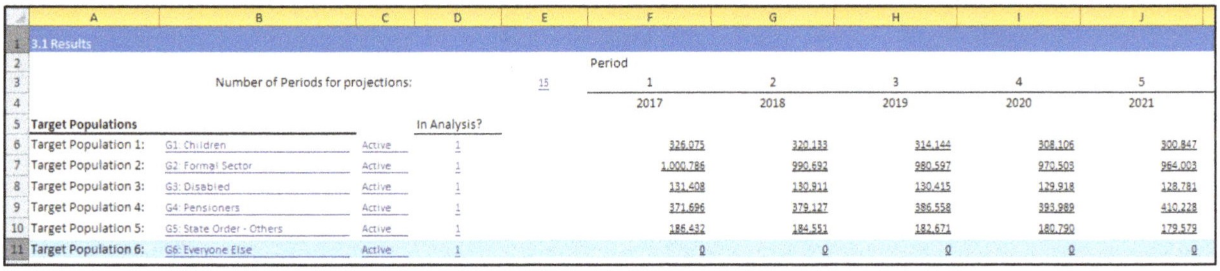

Figure 214: The Population Projection in the 3.1 Results Worksheet

Figure 215: Health Needs in the 3.1 Results Worksheet

	A	B	C	D	E	F	G	H	I	J
1	3.1 Results									
2						Period				
3		Number of Periods for projections:			15	1	2	3	4	5
4						2017	2018	2019	2020	2021
13	Health Needs									
14	Service Categories:			22						
15	Services:			14,568						
17	Total number of services projected (may have overlaps):					234,958	238,091	241,224	244,356	248,082
18	Total number of bed days (may have overlaps):					0	0	0	0	0

Figure 216: Enrollment Projections in the 3.1 Results Worksheet

	A	B	C	D	E	F	G	H	I	J
21	Benefit Package	Enrolment Projections		In Analysis?						
22	Benefit Package 1:	Benefits are the same for all			Totals / period	2,016,397	2,005,415	1,994,385	1,983,306	1,983,438
23		G1: Children		1	Totals / period	326,075	320,133	314,144	308,106	300,847
24		G2: Formal Sector		1	Totals / period	1,000,786	990,692	980,597	970,503	964,003
25		G3: Disabled		1	Totals / period	131,408	130,911	130,415	129,918	128,781
26		G4: Pensioners		1	Totals / period	371,696	379,127	386,558	393,989	410,228
27		G5: State Order - Others		1	Totals / period	186,432	184,551	182,671	180,790	179,579
28		G6: Everyone Else		1	Totals / period	0	0	0	0	0
30	Benefit Package 2:	BP2			Totals / period	2,016,397	2,005,415	1,994,385	1,983,306	1,983,438
31		G1: Children		1	Totals / period	326,075	320,133	314,144	308,106	300,847
32		G2: Formal Sector		1	Totals / period	1,000,786	990,692	980,597	970,503	964,003
33		G3: Disabled		1	Totals / period	131,408	130,911	130,415	129,918	128,781
34		G4: Pensioners		1	Totals / period	371,696	379,127	386,558	393,989	410,228
35		G5: State Order - Others		1	Totals / period	186,432	184,551	182,671	180,790	179,579
36		G6: Everyone Else		1	Totals / period	0	0	0	0	0
38	Benefit Package 3:	BP3			Totals / period	2,016,397	2,005,415	1,994,385	1,983,306	1,983,438
39		G1: Children		1	Totals / period	326,075	320,133	314,144	308,106	300,847
40		G2: Formal Sector		1	Totals / period	1,000,786	990,692	980,597	970,503	964,003
41		G3: Disabled		1	Totals / period	131,408	130,911	130,415	129,918	128,781
42		G4: Pensioners		1	Totals / period	371,696	379,127	386,558	393,989	410,228
43		G5: State Order - Others		1	Totals / period	186,432	184,551	182,671	180,790	179,579
44		G6: Everyone Else		1	Totals / period	0	0	0	0	0

Figure 217: Expenditures Projections in the 3.1 Results Worksheet

	A	B	C	D	E	F	G	H	I	J
21	Benefit Package	Enrolment Projections		In Analysis?						
22	Benefit Package 1:	Benefits are the same for all			Totals / period	2,016,397	2,005,415	1,994,385	1,983,306	1,983,438
23		G1: Children		1	Totals / period	326,075	320,133	314,144	308,106	300,847
24		G2: Formal Sector		1	Totals / period	1,000,786	990,692	980,597	970,503	964,003
25		G3: Disabled		1	Totals / period	131,408	130,911	130,415	129,918	128,781
26		G4: Pensioners		1	Totals / period	371,696	379,127	386,558	393,989	410,228
27		G5: State Order - Others		1	Totals / period	186,432	184,551	182,671	180,790	179,579
28		G6: Everyone Else		1	Totals / period	0	0	0	0	0
30	Benefit Package 2:	BP2			Totals / period	2,016,397	2,005,415	1,994,385	1,983,306	1,983,438
31		G1: Children		1	Totals / period	326,075	320,133	314,144	308,106	300,847
32		G2: Formal Sector		1	Totals / period	1,000,786	990,692	980,597	970,503	964,003
33		G3: Disabled		1	Totals / period	131,408	130,911	130,415	129,918	128,781
34		G4: Pensioners		1	Totals / period	371,696	379,127	386,558	393,989	410,228
35		G5: State Order - Others		1	Totals / period	186,432	184,551	182,671	180,790	179,579
36		G6: Everyone Else		1	Totals / period	0	0	0	0	0
38	Benefit Package 3:	BP3			Totals / period	2,016,397	2,005,415	1,994,385	1,983,306	1,983,438
39		G1: Children		1	Totals / period	326,075	320,133	314,144	308,106	300,847
40		G2: Formal Sector		1	Totals / period	1,000,786	990,692	980,597	970,503	964,003
41		G3: Disabled		1	Totals / period	131,408	130,911	130,415	129,918	128,781
42		G4: Pensioners		1	Totals / period	371,696	379,127	386,558	393,989	410,228
43		G5: State Order - Others		1	Totals / period	186,432	184,551	182,671	180,790	179,579
44		G6: Everyone Else		1	Totals / period	0	0	0	0	0

Figure 218: Revenue Projections Exclusive of Risk Loading and/or Profit Margin in the 3.1 Results Worksheet

	A	B	C	D	E	F	G	H	I	J	K	L	M	N
73	Benefit Package	Revenue Projections		In Analysis?		EXCLUSIVE OF RISK LOADING AND / OR PROFIT MARGIN								
74	Benefit Package 1:	Benefits are the same for all			AMD	8.173.157	8.140.379	8.069.223	8.059.926	8.103.983	8.153.980	8.203.990	8.250.878	8.29
75		G1: Children		1	AMD	8.173.157	8.140.379	8.069.223	8.059.926	8.103.983	8.153.980	8.203.990	8.250.878	8.
76		G2: Formal Sector		1	AMD	0	0	0	0	0	0	0	0	
77		G3: Disabled		1	AMD	0	0	0	0	0	0	0	0	
78		G4: Pensioners		1	AMD	0	0	0	0	0	0	0	0	
79		G5: State Order - Others		1	AMD	0	0	0	0	0	0	0	0	
80		G6: Everyone Else		1	AMD	0	0	0	0	0	0	0	0	
82	Benefit Package 2:	BP2			AMD	8.173.157	8.140.379	8.069.223	8.059.926	8.103.983	8.153.980	8.203.990	8.250.878	8.29
83		G1: Children		1	AMD	8.173.157	8.140.379	8.069.223	8.059.926	8.103.983	8.153.980	8.203.990	8.250.878	8.
84		G2: Formal Sector		1	AMD	0	0	0	0	0	0	0	0	
85		G3: Disabled		1	AMD	0	0	0	0	0	0	0	0	
86		G4: Pensioners		1	AMD	0	0	0	0	0	0	0	0	
87		G5: State Order - Others		1	AMD	0	0	0	0	0	0	0	0	
88		G6: Everyone Else		1	AMD	0	0	0	0	0	0	0	0	
90	Benefit Package 3:	BP3			AMD	8.173.157	8.140.379	8.069.223	8.059.926	8.103.983	8.153.980	8.203.990	8.250.878	8.29
91		G1: Children		1	AMD	8.173.157	8.140.379	8.069.223	8.059.926	8.103.983	8.153.980	8.203.990	8.250.878	8.
92		G2: Formal Sector		1	AMD	0	0	0	0	0	0	0	0	
93		G3: Disabled		1	AMD	0	0	0	0	0	0	0	0	
94		G4: Pensioners		1	AMD	0	0	0	0	0	0	0	0	
95		G5: State Order - Others		1	AMD	0	0	0	0	0	0	0	0	
96		G6: Everyone Else		1	AMD	0	0	0	0	0	0	0	0	
98	Cash flow				BP1	(48,190,679,232)	(49,695,626,321)	(51,046,256,528)	(52,881,446,332)	(55,035,463,696)	(57,352,363,277)	(59,803,523,839)	(62,376,698,533)	(65,056,01
99					BP2	(48,190,679,232)	(49,695,626,321)	(51,046,256,528)	(52,881,446,332)	(55,035,463,696)	(57,352,363,277)	(59,803,523,839)	(62,376,698,533)	(65,056,01
100					BP3	(48,190,679,232)	(49,695,626,321)	(51,046,256,528)	(52,881,446,332)	(55,035,463,696)	(57,352,363,277)	(59,803,523,839)	(62,376,698,533)	(65,056,01
101														
102	Risk loading		0.00%	Premiums		100.0%	100.0%	100.0%	100.0%	100.0%	100.0%	100.0%	100.0%	1
103	Admin		0.00%	Premiums		100.0%	100.0%	100.0%	100.0%	100.0%	100.0%	100.0%	100.0%	1
104	Profit Margin, not applied to Positive Cashflow		0.00%	Positive Cashflow		100.0%	100.0%	100.0%	100.0%	100.0%	100.0%	100.0%	100.0%	1
105	Premium increase		0.00%	First period only	100.00%	100.0%	100.0%	100.0%	100.0%	100.0%	100.0%	100.0%	100.0%	1
106	Total Premium, excluding Profit on Positive Cashflow					100.0%	100.0%	100.0%	100.0%	100.0%	100.0%	100.0%	100.0%	1
107														
108	Profit Margin, applied to Positive Cashflow				BP1	0	0	0	0	0	0	0	0	
109					BP2	0	0	0	0	0	0	0	0	
110					BP3	0	0	0	0	0	0	0	0	

Figure 219: Revenue Projections Inclusive of Risk Loading and/or Profit Margin and/or Premium Increase in the 3.1 Results Worksheet

	A	B	C	D	E	F	G	H	I	J
112	Benefit Package	Revenue Projections		In Analysis?		INCLUSIVE OF RISK LOADING AND / OR PROFIT MARGIN AND / OR PREMIUM INCREASE				
113	Benefit Package 1:	Benefits are the same for all			AMD	8.173.157	8.140.379	8.069.223	8.059.926	8.103.983
114		G1: Children		1	AMD	8,173,157	8,140,379	8,069,223	8,059,926	8,103,983
115		G2: Formal Sector		1	AMD	0	0	0	0	0
116		G3: Disabled		1	AMD	0	0	0	0	0
117		G4: Pensioners		1	AMD	0	0	0	0	0
118		G5: State Order - Others		1	AMD	0	0	0	0	0
119		G6: Everyone Else		1	AMD	0	0	0	0	0
120										
121	Benefit Package 2:	BP2			AMD	8.173.157	8.140.379	8.069.223	8.059.926	8.103.983
122		G1: Children		1	AMD	8,173,157	8,140,379	8,069,223	8,059,926	8,103,983
123		G2: Formal Sector		1	AMD	0	0	0	0	0
124		G3: Disabled		1	AMD	0	0	0	0	0
125		G4: Pensioners		1	AMD	0	0	0	0	0
126		G5: State Order - Others		1	AMD	0	0	0	0	0
127		G6: Everyone Else		1	AMD	0	0	0	0	0
128										
129	Benefit Package 3:	BP3			AMD	8.173.157	8.140.379	8.069.223	8.059.926	8.103.983
130		G1: Children		1	AMD	8,173,157	8,140,379	8,069,223	8,059,926	8,103,983
131		G2: Formal Sector		1	AMD	0	0	0	0	0
132		G3: Disabled		1	AMD	0	0	0	0	0
133		G4: Pensioners		1	AMD	0	0	0	0	0
134		G5: State Order - Others		1	AMD	0	0	0	0	0
135		G6: Everyone Else		1	AMD	0	0	0	0	0
136										
137	*Risk+Profit+Premium_I*	*Benefit Package 1:*				0	0	0	0	0
138		*Benefit Package 2:*				0	0	0	0	0
139		*Benefit Package 3:*				0	0	0	0	0

Figure 220: Cash Flow Projections in the 3.1 Results Worksheet

	A	B	C	D	E	F	G	H	I	J
141	Benefit Package	Cash Flow Projections		in Analysis?						
142	Benefit Package 1:	Benefits are the same for all			AMD	(48,190,679,232)	(49,695,626,321)	(51,046,256,528)	(52,881,446,332)	(55,035,463,696)
143		G1: Children		1	AMD	(7,836,655,191)	(7,815,360,322)	(7,757,563,268)	(7,759,641,864)	(7,804,877,436)
144		G2: Formal Sector		1	AMD	(23,512,569,074)	(23,926,645,568)	(24,251,899,485)	(24,791,025,746)	(25,364,994,888)
145		G3: Disabled		1	AMD	(2,815,819,682)	(2,873,613,935)	(2,921,119,363)	(2,994,817,430)	(3,056,163,464)
146		G4: Pensioners		1	AMD	(11,995,643,792)	(13,020,360,782)	(14,034,301,921)	(15,214,827,706)	(16,637,120,130)
147		G5: State Order - Others		1	AMD	(2,029,991,492)	(2,059,645,716)	(2,081,372,492)	(2,121,133,586)	(2,172,307,778)
148		G6: Everyone Else		1	AMD	0	0	0	0	0
149										
150	Benefit Package 2:	BP2			AMD	(48,190,679,232)	(49,695,626,321)	(51,046,256,528)	(52,881,446,332)	(55,035,463,696)
151		G1: Children		1	AMD	(7,836,655,191)	(7,815,360,322)	(7,757,563,268)	(7,759,641,864)	(7,804,877,436)
152		G2: Formal Sector		1	AMD	(23,512,569,074)	(23,926,645,568)	(24,251,899,485)	(24,791,025,746)	(25,364,994,888)
153		G3: Disabled		1	AMD	(2,815,819,682)	(2,873,613,935)	(2,921,119,363)	(2,994,817,430)	(3,056,163,464)
154		G4: Pensioners		1	AMD	(11,995,643,792)	(13,020,360,782)	(14,034,301,921)	(15,214,827,706)	(16,637,120,130)
155		G5: State Order - Others		1	AMD	(2,029,991,492)	(2,059,645,716)	(2,081,372,492)	(2,121,133,586)	(2,172,307,778)
156		G6: Everyone Else		1	AMD	0	0	0	0	0
157										
158	Benefit Package 3:	BP3			AMD	(48,190,679,232)	(49,695,626,321)	(51,046,256,528)	(52,881,446,332)	(55,035,463,696)
159		G1: Children		1	AMD	(7,836,655,191)	(7,815,360,322)	(7,757,563,268)	(7,759,641,864)	(7,804,877,436)
160		G2: Formal Sector		1	AMD	(23,512,569,074)	(23,926,645,568)	(24,251,899,485)	(24,791,025,746)	(25,364,994,888)
161		G3: Disabled		1	AMD	(2,815,819,682)	(2,873,613,935)	(2,921,119,363)	(2,994,817,430)	(3,056,163,464)
162		G4: Pensioners		1	AMD	(11,995,643,792)	(13,020,360,782)	(14,034,301,921)	(15,214,827,706)	(16,637,120,130)
163		G5: State Order - Others		1	AMD	(2,029,991,492)	(2,059,645,716)	(2,081,372,492)	(2,121,133,586)	(2,172,307,778)
164		G6: Everyone Else		1	AMD	0	0	0	0	0

Figure 221: The Discounted Cash Flow in the 3.1 Results Worksheet

	A	B	C	D	E	F	G	H	I	J
167	Benefit Package	Discounted Cash Flow	2%	15.00						
168	Benefit Package 1:	Benefits are the same for all		(797,269,402,416)	AMD	(47,245,763,953)	(47,765,884,584)	(48,102,027,622)	(48,854,282,315)	(49,847,315,103)
169	Benefit Package 2:	BP2		(797,269,402,416)	AMD	(47,245,763,953)	(47,765,884,584)	(48,102,027,622)	(48,854,282,315)	(49,847,315,103)
170	Benefit Package 3:	BP3		(797,269,402,416)	AMD	(47,245,763,953)	(47,765,884,584)	(48,102,027,622)	(48,854,282,315)	(49,847,315,103)

Figure 222: Expenditures per Enrollee in the 3.1 Results Worksheet

	A	B	C	D	E	F	G	H	I	J
172	Benefit Package	Expenditures per Enrollee		In Analysis?						
173	Benefit Package 1:	Benefits are the same for all			AMD	23,903	24,785	25,599	26,667	27,752
174		G1: Children		1	AMD	24,058	24,438	24,720	25,211	25,970
175		G2: Formal Sector		1	AMD	23,494	24,151	24,732	25,545	26,312
176		G3: Disabled		1	AMD	21,428	21,951	22,399	23,052	23,731
177		G4: Pensioners		1	AMD	32,273	34,343	36,306	38,617	40,556
178		G5: State Order - Others		1	AMD	10,889	11,160	11,394	11,733	12,097
179		G6: Everyone Else		1	AMD	0	0	0	0	0
180										
181	Benefit Package 2:	BP2			AMD	23,903	24,785	25,599	26,667	27,752
182		G1: Children		1	AMD	24,058	24,438	24,720	25,211	25,970
183		G2: Formal Sector		1	AMD	23,494	24,151	24,732	25,545	26,312
184		G3: Disabled		1	AMD	21,428	21,951	22,399	23,052	23,731
185		G4: Pensioners		1	AMD	32,273	34,343	36,306	38,617	40,556
186		G5: State Order - Others		1	AMD	10,889	11,160	11,394	11,733	12,097
187		G6: Everyone Else		1	AMD	0	0	0	0	0
188										
189	Benefit Package 3:	BP3			AMD	23,903	24,785	25,599	26,667	27,752
190		G1: Children		1	AMD	24,058	24,438	24,720	25,211	25,970
191		G2: Formal Sector		1	AMD	23,494	24,151	24,732	25,545	26,312
192		G3: Disabled		1	AMD	21,428	21,951	22,399	23,052	23,731
193		G4: Pensioners		1	AMD	32,273	34,343	36,306	38,617	40,556
194		G5: State Order - Others		1	AMD	10,889	11,160	11,394	11,733	12,097
195		G6: Everyone Else		1	AMD	0	0	0	0	0

Figure 223: Revenues per Enrollee in the 3.1 Results Worksheet

	A	B	C	D	E	F	G	H	I	J
197	Benefit Package	Revenues per Enrollee		In Analysis?						
198	Benefit Package 1:	Benefits are the same for all			AMD	4	4	4	4	4
199		G1: Children		1	AMD	25	25	26	26	27
200		G2: Formal Sector		1	AMD	0	0	0	0	0
201		G3: Disabled		1	AMD	0	0	0	0	0
202		G4: Pensioners		1	AMD	0	0	0	0	0
203		G5: State Order - Others		1	AMD	0	0	0	0	0
204		G6: Everyone Else		1	AMD	0	0	0	0	0
205										
206	Benefit Package 2:	BP2			AMD	4	4	4	4	4
207		G1: Children		1	AMD	25	25	26	26	27
208		G2: Formal Sector		1	AMD	0	0	0	0	0
209		G3: Disabled		1	AMD	0	0	0	0	0
210		G4: Pensioners		1	AMD	0	0	0	0	0
211		G5: State Order - Others		1	AMD	0	0	0	0	0
212		G6: Everyone Else		1	AMD	0	0	0	0	0
213										
214	Benefit Package 3:	BP3			AMD	4	4	4	4	4
215		G1: Children		1	AMD	25	25	26	26	27
216		G2: Formal Sector		1	AMD	0	0	0	0	0
217		G3: Disabled		1	AMD	0	0	0	0	0
218		G4: Pensioners		1	AMD	0	0	0	0	0
219		G5: State Order - Others		1	AMD	0	0	0	0	0
220		G6: Everyone Else		1	AMD	0	0	0	0	0

Figure 224: Cash Flow per Enrollee in the 3.1 Results Worksheet

	A	B	C	D	E	F	G	H	I	J
222	Benefit Package	Cash Flow per Enrollee		In Analysis?						
223	Benefit Package 1:	Benefits are the same for all			AMD	(23,899)	(24,781)	(25,595)	(26,663)	(27,748)
224		G1: Children		1	AMD	(24,033)	(24,413)	(24,694)	(25,185)	(25,943)
225		G2: Formal Sector		1	AMD	(23,494)	(24,151)	(24,732)	(25,545)	(26,312)
226		G3: Disabled		1	AMD	(21,428)	(21,951)	(22,399)	(23,052)	(23,731)
227		G4: Pensioners		1	AMD	(32,273)	(34,343)	(36,306)	(38,617)	(40,556)
228		G5: State Order - Others		1	AMD	(10,889)	(11,160)	(11,394)	(11,733)	(12,097)
229		G6: Everyone Else		1	AMD	0	0	0	0	0
230										
231	Benefit Package 2:	BP2			AMD	(23,899)	(24,781)	(25,595)	(26,663)	(27,748)
232		G1: Children		1	AMD	(24,033)	(24,413)	(24,694)	(25,185)	(25,943)
233		G2: Formal Sector		1	AMD	(23,494)	(24,151)	(24,732)	(25,545)	(26,312)
234		G3: Disabled		1	AMD	(21,428)	(21,951)	(22,399)	(23,052)	(23,731)
235		G4: Pensioners		1	AMD	(32,273)	(34,343)	(36,306)	(38,617)	(40,556)
236		G5: State Order - Others		1	AMD	(10,889)	(11,160)	(11,394)	(11,733)	(12,097)
237		G6: Everyone Else		1	AMD	0	0	0	0	0
238										
239	Benefit Package 3:	BP3			AMD	(23,899)	(24,781)	(25,595)	(26,663)	(27,748)
240		G1: Children		1	AMD	(24,033)	(24,413)	(24,694)	(25,185)	(25,943)
241		G2: Formal Sector		1	AMD	(23,494)	(24,151)	(24,732)	(25,545)	(26,312)
242		G3: Disabled		1	AMD	(21,428)	(21,951)	(22,399)	(23,052)	(23,731)
243		G4: Pensioners		1	AMD	(32,273)	(34,343)	(36,306)	(38,617)	(40,556)
244		G5: State Order - Others		1	AMD	(10,889)	(11,160)	(11,394)	(11,733)	(12,097)
245		G6: Everyone Else		1	AMD	0	0	0	0	0

Figure 225: Cash Flow as % of Revenues in the 3.1 Results Worksheet

	A	B	C	D	E	F	G	H	I	J
247	Benefit Package	Cash Flow as % of Revenues		In Analysis?						
248	Benefit Package 1:	Benefits are the same for all			ratio	(5,896.21)	(6,104.83)	(6,326.04)	(6,561.03)	(6,791.16)
249		G1: Children		1	ratio	(958.83)	(960.07)	(961.38)	(962.74)	(963.09)
250		G2: Formal Sector		1	ratio	0.00	0.00	0.00	0.00	0.00
251		G3: Disabled		1	ratio	0.00	0.00	0.00	0.00	0.00
252		G4: Pensioners		1	ratio	0.00	0.00	0.00	0.00	0.00
253		G5: State Order - Others		1	ratio	0.00	0.00	0.00	0.00	0.00
254		G6: Everyone Else		1	ratio	0.00	0.00	0.00	0.00	0.00
255										
256	Benefit Package 2:	BP2			ratio	(5,896.21)	(6,104.83)	(6,326.04)	(6,561.03)	(6,791.16)
257		G1: Children		1	ratio	(958.83)	(960.07)	(961.38)	(962.74)	(963.09)
258		G2: Formal Sector		1	ratio	0.00	0.00	0.00	0.00	0.00
259		G3: Disabled		1	ratio	0.00	0.00	0.00	0.00	0.00
260		G4: Pensioners		1	ratio	0.00	0.00	0.00	0.00	0.00
261		G5: State Order - Others		1	ratio	0.00	0.00	0.00	0.00	0.00
262		G6: Everyone Else		1	ratio	0.00	0.00	0.00	0.00	0.00
263										
264	Benefit Package 3:	BP3			ratio	(5,896.21)	(6,104.83)	(6,326.04)	(6,561.03)	(6,791.16)
265		G1: Children		1	ratio	(958.83)	(960.07)	(961.38)	(962.74)	(963.09)
266		G2: Formal Sector		1	ratio	0.00	0.00	0.00	0.00	0.00
267		G3: Disabled		1	ratio	0.00	0.00	0.00	0.00	0.00
268		G4: Pensioners		1	ratio	0.00	0.00	0.00	0.00	0.00
269		G5: State Order - Others		1	ratio	0.00	0.00	0.00	0.00	0.00
270		G6: Everyone Else		1	ratio	0.00	0.00	0.00	0.00	0.00

Figure 226: Revenues as % of Expenditures in the 3.1 Results Worksheet

	A	B	C	D	E	F	G	H	I	J
272	Benefit Package	Revenue as % of Expenditures		In Analysis?						
273	Benefit Package 1:	Benefits are the same for all			ratio	0.00	0.00	0.00	0.00	0.00
274		G1: Children		1	ratio	0.00	0.00	0.00	0.00	0.00
275		G2: Formal Sector		1	ratio	0.00	0.00	0.00	0.00	0.00
276		G3: Disabled		1	ratio	0.00	0.00	0.00	0.00	0.00
277		G4: Pensioners		1	ratio	0.00	0.00	0.00	0.00	0.00
278		G5: State Order - Others		1	ratio	0.00	0.00	0.00	0.00	0.00
279		G6: Everyone Else		1	ratio	0.00	0.00	0.00	0.00	0.00
280										
281	Benefit Package 2:	BP2			ratio	0.00	0.00	0.00	0.00	0.00
282		G1: Children		1	ratio	0.00	0.00	0.00	0.00	0.00
283		G2: Formal Sector		1	ratio	0.00	0.00	0.00	0.00	0.00
284		G3: Disabled		1	ratio	0.00	0.00	0.00	0.00	0.00
285		G4: Pensioners		1	ratio	0.00	0.00	0.00	0.00	0.00
286		G5: State Order - Others		1	ratio	0.00	0.00	0.00	0.00	0.00
287		G6: Everyone Else		1	ratio	0.00	0.00	0.00	0.00	0.00
288										
289	Benefit Package 3:	BP3			ratio	0.00	0.00	0.00	0.00	0.00
290		G1: Children		1	ratio	0.00	0.00	0.00	0.00	0.00
291		G2: Formal Sector		1	ratio	0.00	0.00	0.00	0.00	0.00
292		G3: Disabled		1	ratio	0.00	0.00	0.00	0.00	0.00
293		G4: Pensioners		1	ratio	0.00	0.00	0.00	0.00	0.00
294		G5: State Order - Others		1	ratio	0.00	0.00	0.00	0.00	0.00
295		G6: Everyone Else		1	ratio	0.00	0.00	0.00	0.00	0.00

However, the user is advised to use the Dashboard worksheet to view the formatted table results with accompanying graphs for analysis. See next section for description of the Dashboard worksheet, followed by a discussion of viewing results using the Dashboard.

C.   The Dashboard Worksheet

This worksheet shows the formatted results of the SLAM analysis (Figure 227). By design, it is used as quick overview for managers to see the output of the actuarial modeling. Users may also modify the target groups to be included in the analysis by using the "Include in analysis?" option in the drop-down menus.

Figure 227: Preview of the Dashboard Worksheet

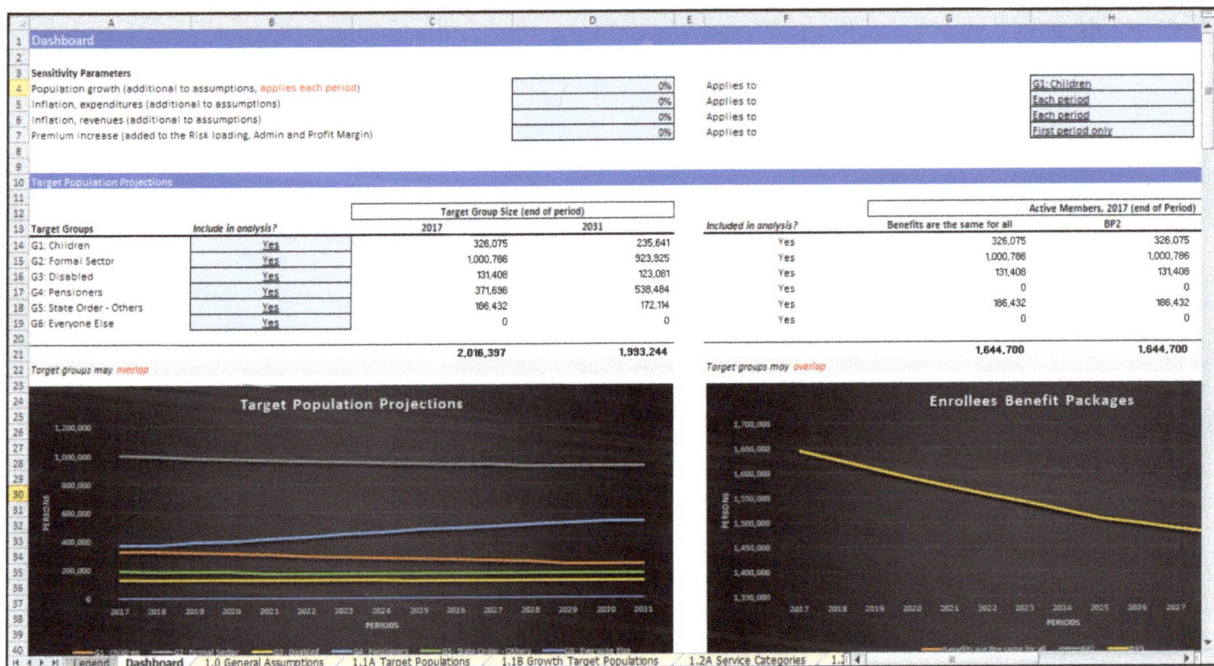

FOR YOUR INFORMATION

Input cells found in this worksheet include:

Input Cells	
100.00	Input cell, restricted input (e.g., only positive values/only integers/dates/etc.)
100.00	Input cell, select option from list

Restrictions in input cells in this worksheet include encoding only positive numeric values or selection from a drop-down list.

The SLAM Dashboard has four partitions: (i) sensitivity parameters, (ii) target population projections, (iii) expenditures and revenue projections, and (iv) ratios, as detailed below.

Sensitivity Parameters

In this partition, users can input specifications to be reflected in the dashboard (Figure 228). This information is in addition to the set assumptions discussed in Chapter II-D. The parameters include *population growth* of each period (**cell D4**) for an identified subpopulation (**cell H4**); *inflation for expenditures* (**cell D5**) and *inflation for revenues* (**cell D6**) for the first period only or for each period (**cells H5 and H6**); and the *premium increase* (**cell D7**) added to the risk loading, admin and profit margin, for the first period only or for each period (**cell H7**).

Figure 228: The Sensitivity Parameters Partition in the Dashboard Worksheet

Sensitivity analysis will be discussed in detail in Chapter VI.

Target Population Projections

In this partition, users set whether a target group of population will be included in the analysis shown in the dashboard (**cells B14–B19**) (Figure 229). It also shows data table and consequent chart on *target group size* by end of the first period and end of the last period per *target group* (Figure 230), as well as *active members under each benefit package* by end of the first period and end of the last period per *target group* (Figure 231).

Figure 229: Preview of the Target Population Projections Partition in the Dashboard Worksheet

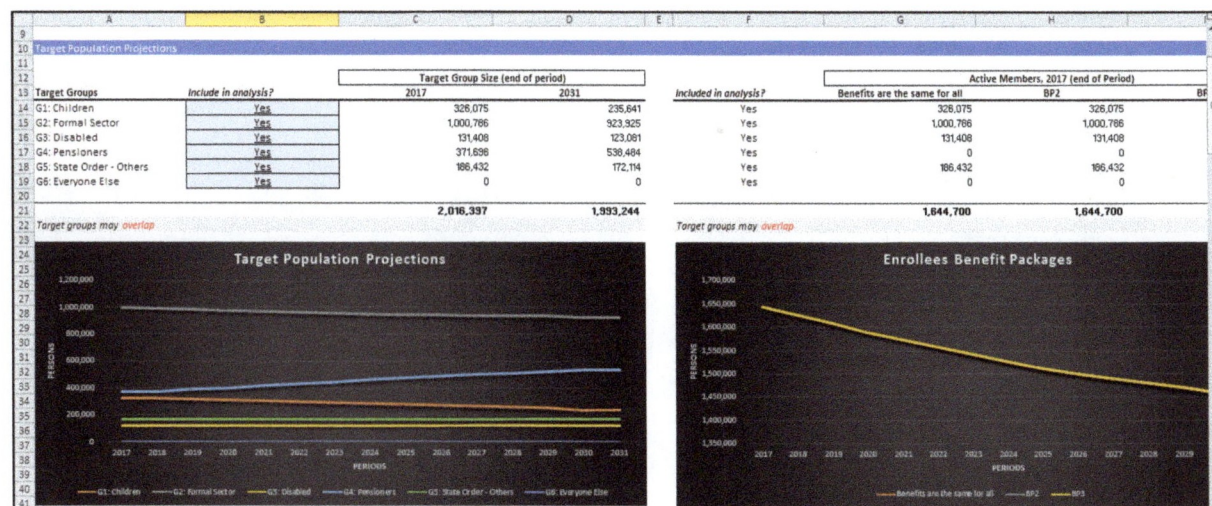

Figure 230: Target Group Size Table and Chart in the Target Population Projections Partition

	A	B	C	D
10	**Target Population Projections**			
11				
12			**Target Group Size (end of period)**	
13	**Target Groups**	*Include in analysis?*	**2017**	**2031**
14	G1: Children	Yes	326,075	235,641
15	G2: Formal Sector	Yes	1,000,786	923,925
16	G3: Disabled	Yes	131,408	123,081
17	G4: Pensioners	Yes	371,696	538,484
18	G5: State Order - Others	Yes	186,432	172,114
19	G6: Everyone Else	Yes	0	0
21			2,016,397	1,993,244
22	*Target groups may* overlap			

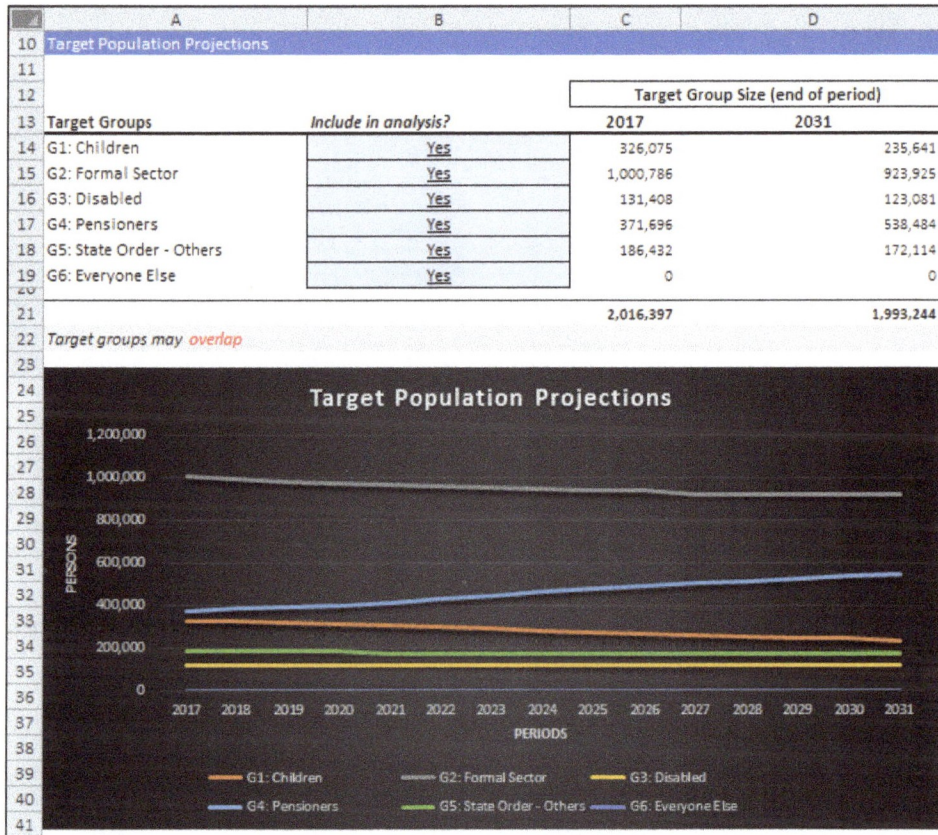

Figure 231: Active Members Table and Chart in the Target Population Projections Partition

	Included in analysis?	Active Members, 2017 (end of Period)			Active Members, 2031 (end of Period)		
		Benefits are the same for all	BP2	BP3	Benefits are the same for all	BP2	BP3
14	Yes	326,075	326,075	326,075	235,641	235,641	235,641
15	Yes	1,000,786	1,000,786	1,000,786	923,925	923,925	923,925
16	Yes	131,408	131,408	131,408	123,081	123,081	123,081
17	Yes	0	0	0	0	0	0
18	Yes	186,432	186,432	186,432	172,114	172,114	172,114
19	Yes	0	0	0	0	0	0
21		1,644,700	1,644,700	1,644,700	1,454,760	1,454,760	1,454,760
22	*Target groups may* overlap						

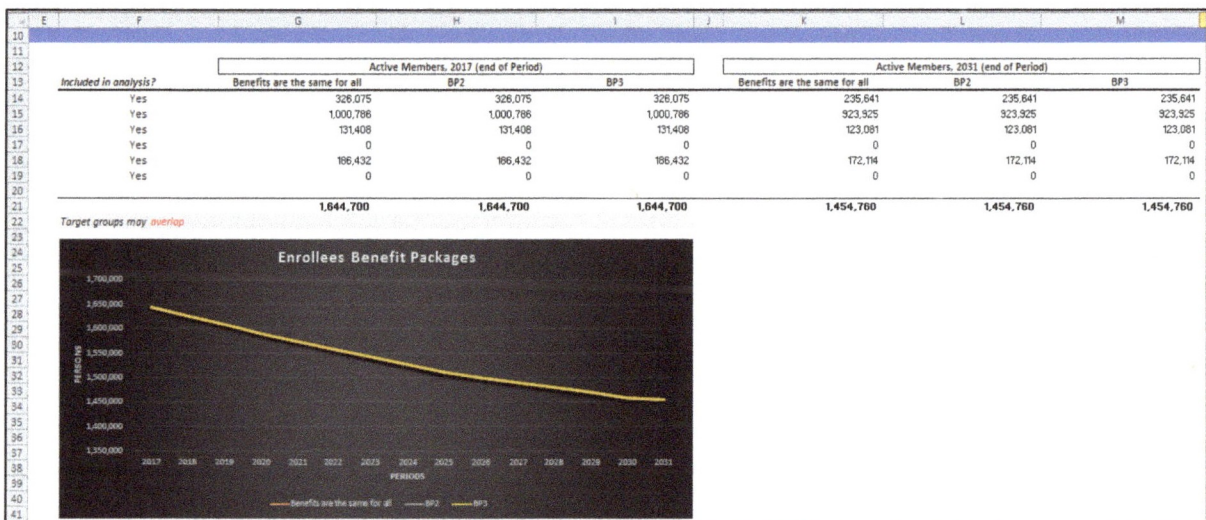

Expenditures and Revenues Projection

In this partition (Figure 232), the basis of expenditures can be defined as total cost, outpatient costs, or inpatient costs in the drop-down menu of **cell B46** (Figure 233).

Figure 232: Preview of Expenditures and Revenues Projections Partition in the Dashboard Worksheet

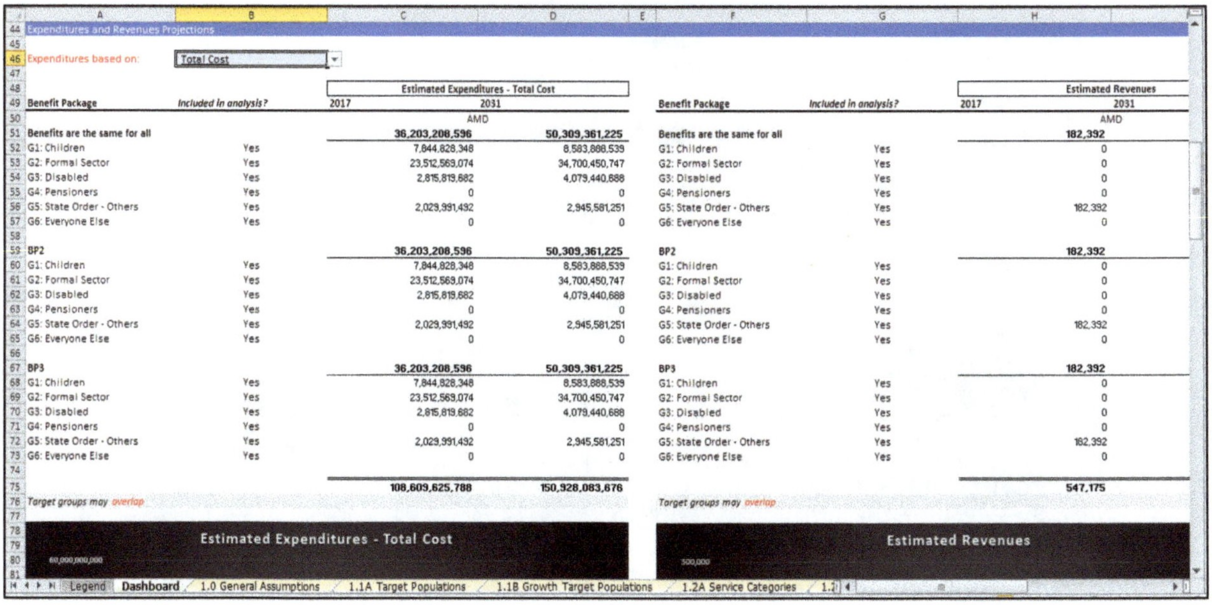

Note: AMD = Armenian dram.

Figure 233: Input Cell for Basis of Expenditures in the Expenditures and Revenues Projections Partition

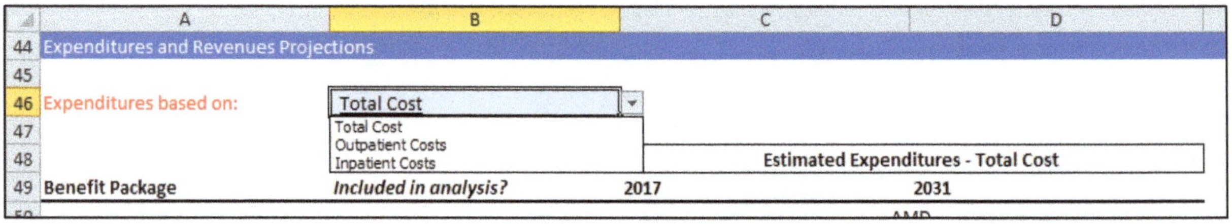

This portion of the Dashboard shows data table and chart specified at the end of the first period and last period by *benefit package* and *target groups* for *estimated expenditures* (Figure 234), *estimated revenues* (Figure 235), *cash flow* (Figure 236), *expenditures per enrollee* (Figure 237), *revenues per enrollee* (Figure 238), and *cash flow per enrollee* (Figure 239).

Figure 234: Estimated Expenditures Table and Chart in the Expenditures and Revenues Projections Partition

Benefit Package	Included in analysis?	Estimated Expenditures - Total Cost	
		2017	2031
		AMD	
Benefits are the same for all		36,203,208,596	50,309,361,225
G1: Children	Yes	7,844,828,348	8,583,888,539
G2: Formal Sector	Yes	23,512,569,074	34,700,450,747
G3: Disabled	Yes	2,815,819,682	4,079,440,688
G4: Pensioners	Yes	0	0
G5: State Order - Others	Yes	2,029,991,492	2,945,581,251
G6: Everyone Else	Yes	0	0
BP2		36,203,208,596	50,309,361,225
G1: Children	Yes	7,844,828,348	8,583,888,539
G2: Formal Sector	Yes	23,512,569,074	34,700,450,747
G3: Disabled	Yes	2,815,819,682	4,079,440,688
G4: Pensioners	Yes	0	0
G5: State Order - Others	Yes	2,029,991,492	2,945,581,251
G6: Everyone Else	Yes	0	0
BP3		36,203,208,596	50,309,361,225
G1: Children	Yes	7,844,828,348	8,583,888,539
G2: Formal Sector	Yes	23,512,569,074	34,700,450,747
G3: Disabled	Yes	2,815,819,682	4,079,440,688
G4: Pensioners	Yes	0	0
G5: State Order - Others	Yes	2,029,991,492	2,945,581,251
G6: Everyone Else	Yes	0	0
		108,609,625,788	150,928,083,676

Target groups may *overlap*

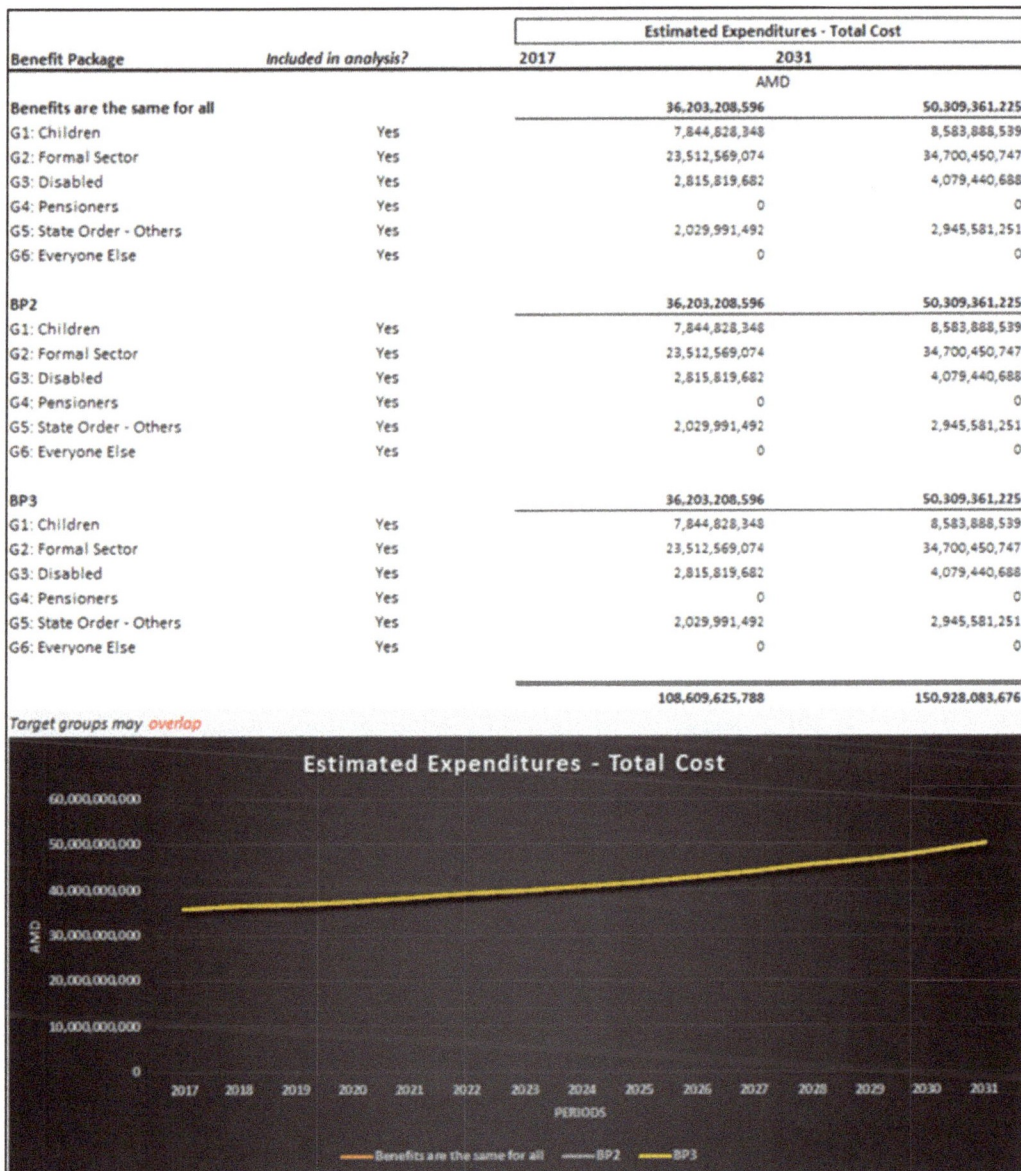

Note: AMD = Armenian dram.

Figure 235: Estimated Revenues Table and Chart in the Expenditures and Revenues Projections Partition

Benefit Package	Included in analysis?	Estimated Revenues	
		2017	2031
		AMD	
Benefits are the same for all		182,392	247,286
G1: Children	Yes	0	0
G2: Formal Sector	Yes	0	0
G3: Disabled	Yes	0	0
G4: Pensioners	Yes	0	0
G5: State Order - Others	Yes	182,392	247,286
G6: Everyone Else	Yes	0	0
BP2		182,392	247,286
G1: Children	Yes	0	0
G2: Formal Sector	Yes	0	0
G3: Disabled	Yes	0	0
G4: Pensioners	Yes	0	0
G5: State Order - Others	Yes	182,392	247,286
G6: Everyone Else	Yes	0	0
BP3		182,392	247,286
G1: Children	Yes	0	0
G2: Formal Sector	Yes	0	0
G3: Disabled	Yes	0	0
G4: Pensioners	Yes	0	0
G5: State Order - Others	Yes	182,392	247,286
G6: Everyone Else	Yes	0	0
		547,175	741,858

Target groups may overlap

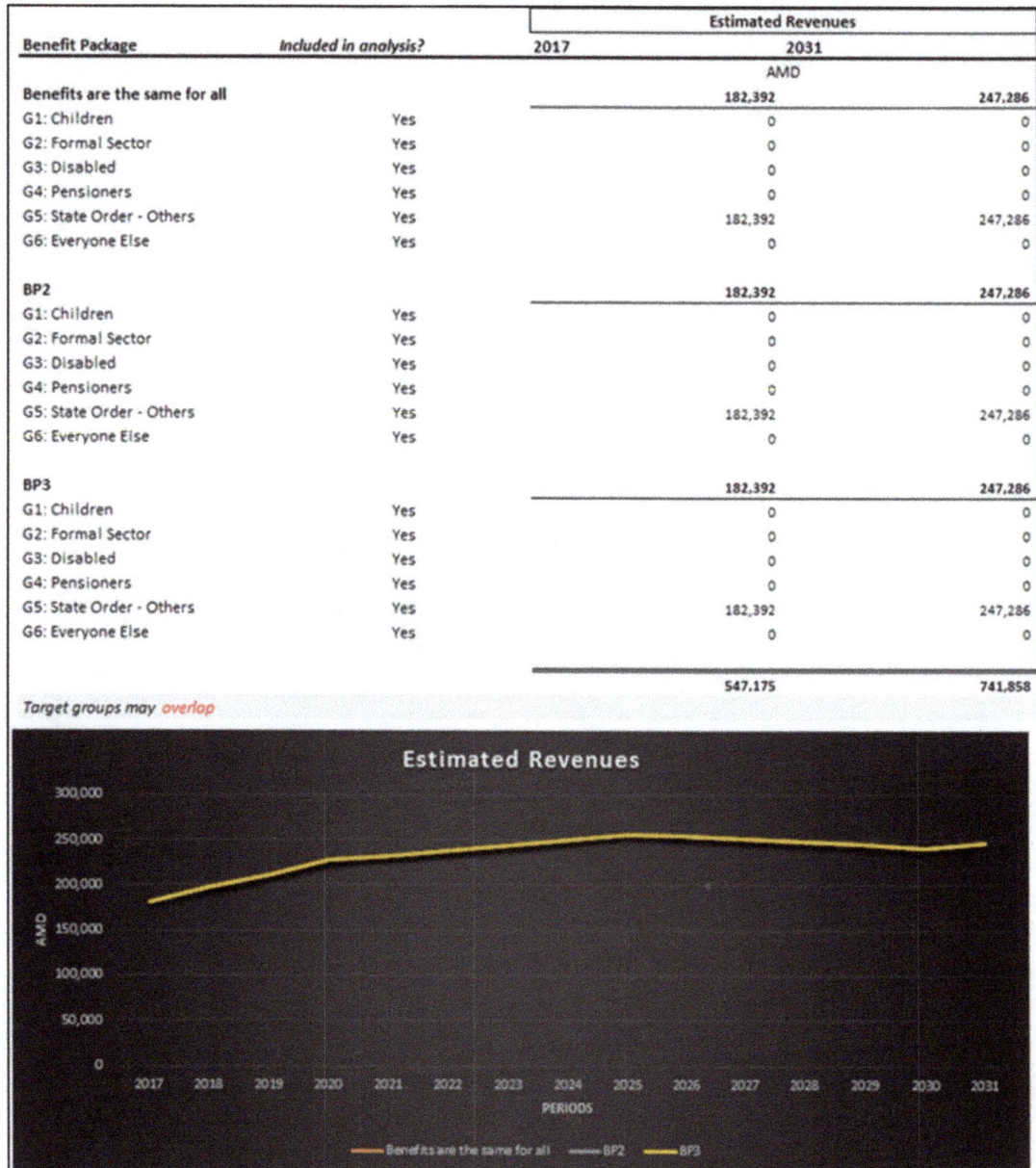

Note: AMD = Armenian dram.

Figure 236: Cash Flow Table and Chart in the Expenditures and Revenues Projections Partition

Benefit Package	Included in analysis?	Cash Flow 2017	2031	Discounted Cash Flow at 2%
			AMD	
Benefits are the same for all		**(36,203,026,204)**	**(50,309,113,939)**	**(531,746,799,787)**
G1: Children	Yes	(7,844,828,348)	(8,583,888,539)	
G2: Formal Sector	Yes	(23,512,569,074)	(34,700,450,747)	
G3: Disabled	Yes	(2,815,819,682)	(4,079,440,688)	
G4: Pensioners	Yes	0	0	
G5: State Order - Others	Yes	(2,029,809,101)	(2,945,333,965)	
G6: Everyone Else	Yes	0	0	
BP2		**(36,203,026,204)**	**(50,309,113,939)**	**(531,746,799,787)**
G1: Children	Yes	(7,844,828,348)	(8,583,888,539)	
G2: Formal Sector	Yes	(23,512,569,074)	(34,700,450,747)	
G3: Disabled	Yes	(2,815,819,682)	(4,079,440,688)	
G4: Pensioners	Yes	0	0	
G5: State Order - Others	Yes	(2,029,809,101)	(2,945,333,965)	
G6: Everyone Else	Yes	0	0	
BP3		**(36,203,026,204)**	**(50,309,113,939)**	**(531,746,799,787)**
G1: Children	Yes	(7,844,828,348)	(8,583,888,539)	
G2: Formal Sector	Yes	(23,512,569,074)	(34,700,450,747)	
G3: Disabled	Yes	(2,815,819,682)	(4,079,440,688)	
G4: Pensioners	Yes	0	0	
G5: State Order - Others	Yes	(2,029,809,101)	(2,945,333,965)	
G6: Everyone Else	Yes	0	0	
		(108,609,078,613)	(150,927,341,818)	

Target groups may *overlap*

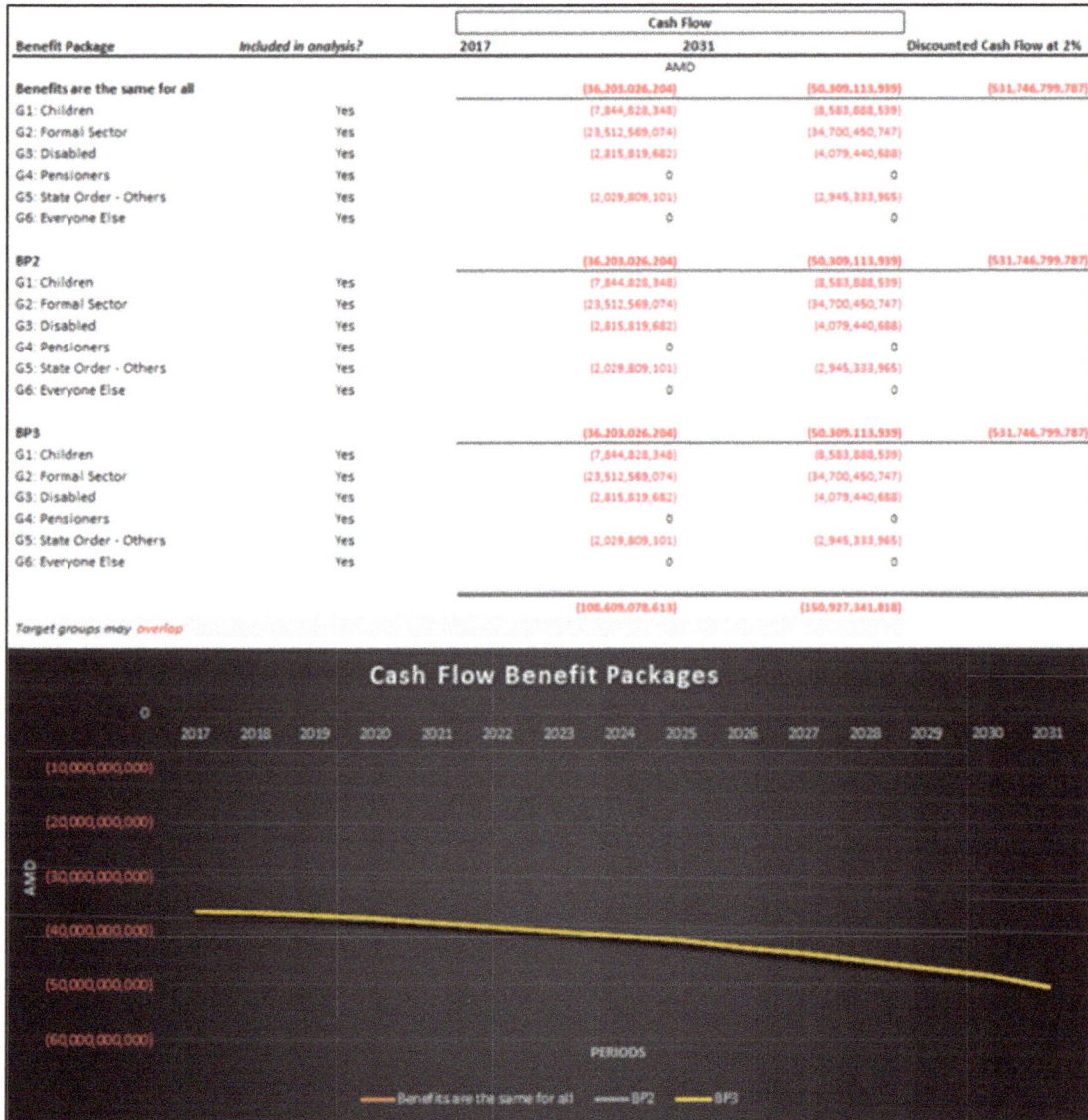

Note: AMD = Armenian dram.

Figure 237: Expenditures per Enrollee–Total Cost Table and Chart in the Expenditures and Revenues Projections Partition

Benefit Package	Included in analysis?	Expenditures per Enrollee - Total Cost	
		2017	2031
		AMD	
Benefits are the same for all		22,012	34,583
G1: Children	Yes	24,058	36,428
G2: Formal Sector	Yes	23,494	37,558
G3: Disabled	Yes	21,428	33,144
G4: Pensioners	Yes	0	0
G5: State Order - Others	Yes	10,889	17,114
G6: Everyone Else	Yes	0	0
BP2		22,012	34,583
G1: Children	Yes	24,058	36,428
G2: Formal Sector	Yes	23,494	37,558
G3: Disabled	Yes	21,428	33,144
G4: Pensioners	Yes	0	0
G5: State Order - Others	Yes	10,889	17,114
G6: Everyone Else	Yes	0	0
BP3		22,012	34,583
G1: Children	Yes	24,058	36,428
G2: Formal Sector	Yes	23,494	37,558
G3: Disabled	Yes	21,428	33,144
G4: Pensioners	Yes	0	0
G5: State Order - Others	Yes	10,889	17,114
G6: Everyone Else	Yes	0	0

Target groups may overlap

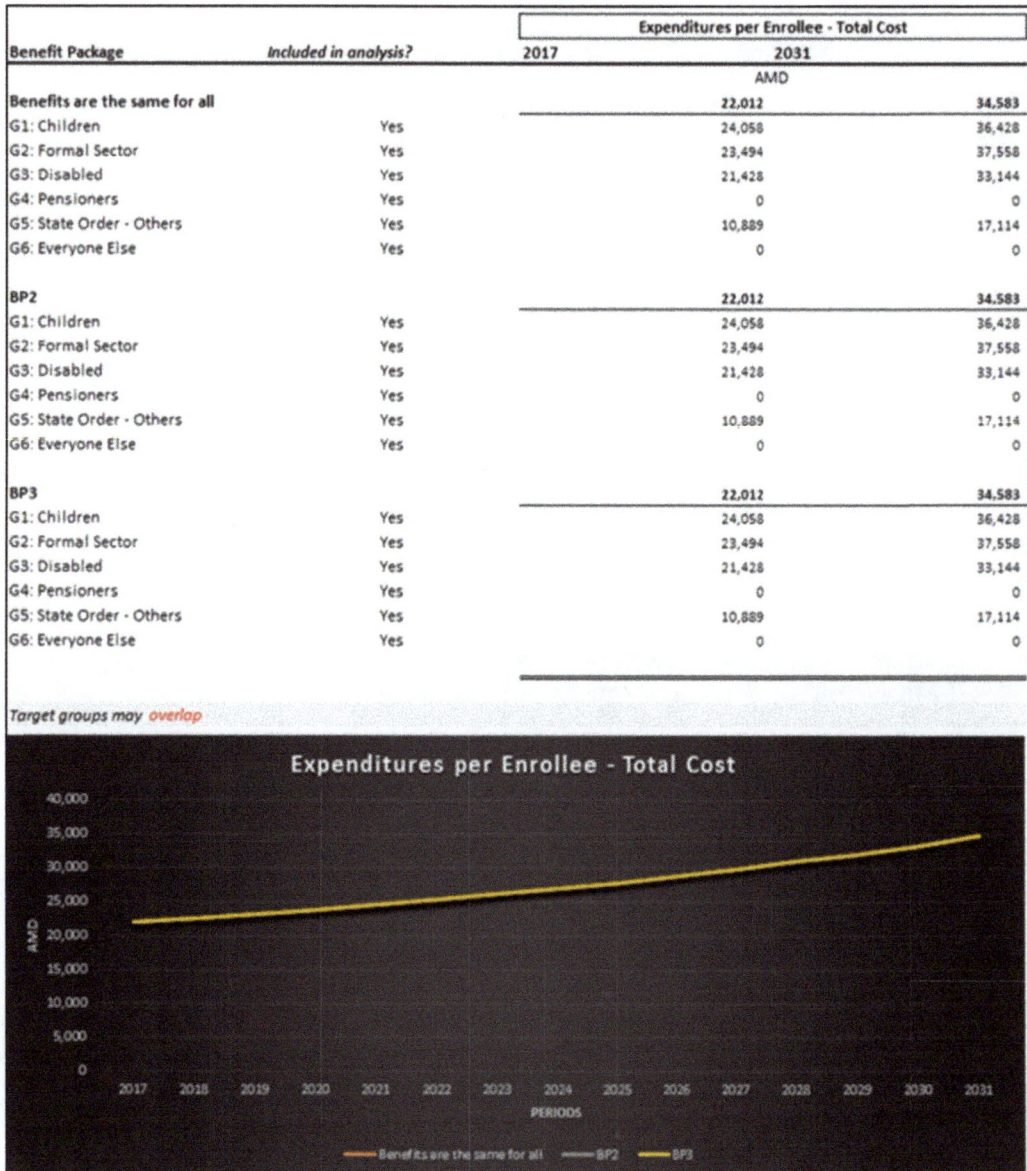

Note: AMD = Armenian dram.

Figure 238: Revenues per Enrollee Table and Chart in the Expenditures and Revenues Projections Partition

Benefit Package	Included in analysis?	Revenues per Enrollee	
		2017	2031
		AMD	
Benefits are the same for all		**4**	**4**
G1: Children	Yes	25	38
G2: Formal Sector	Yes	0	0
G3: Disabled	Yes	0	0
G4: Pensioners	Yes	0	0
G5: State Order - Others	Yes	0	0
G6: Everyone Else	Yes	0	0
BP2		**4**	**4**
G1: Children	Yes	25	38
G2: Formal Sector	Yes	0	0
G3: Disabled	Yes	0	0
G4: Pensioners	Yes	0	0
G5: State Order - Others	Yes	0	0
G6: Everyone Else	Yes	0	0
BP3		**4**	**4**
G1: Children	Yes	25	38
G2: Formal Sector	Yes	0	0
G3: Disabled	Yes	0	0
G4: Pensioners	Yes	0	0
G5: State Order - Others	Yes	0	0
G6: Everyone Else	Yes	0	0

Target groups may overlap

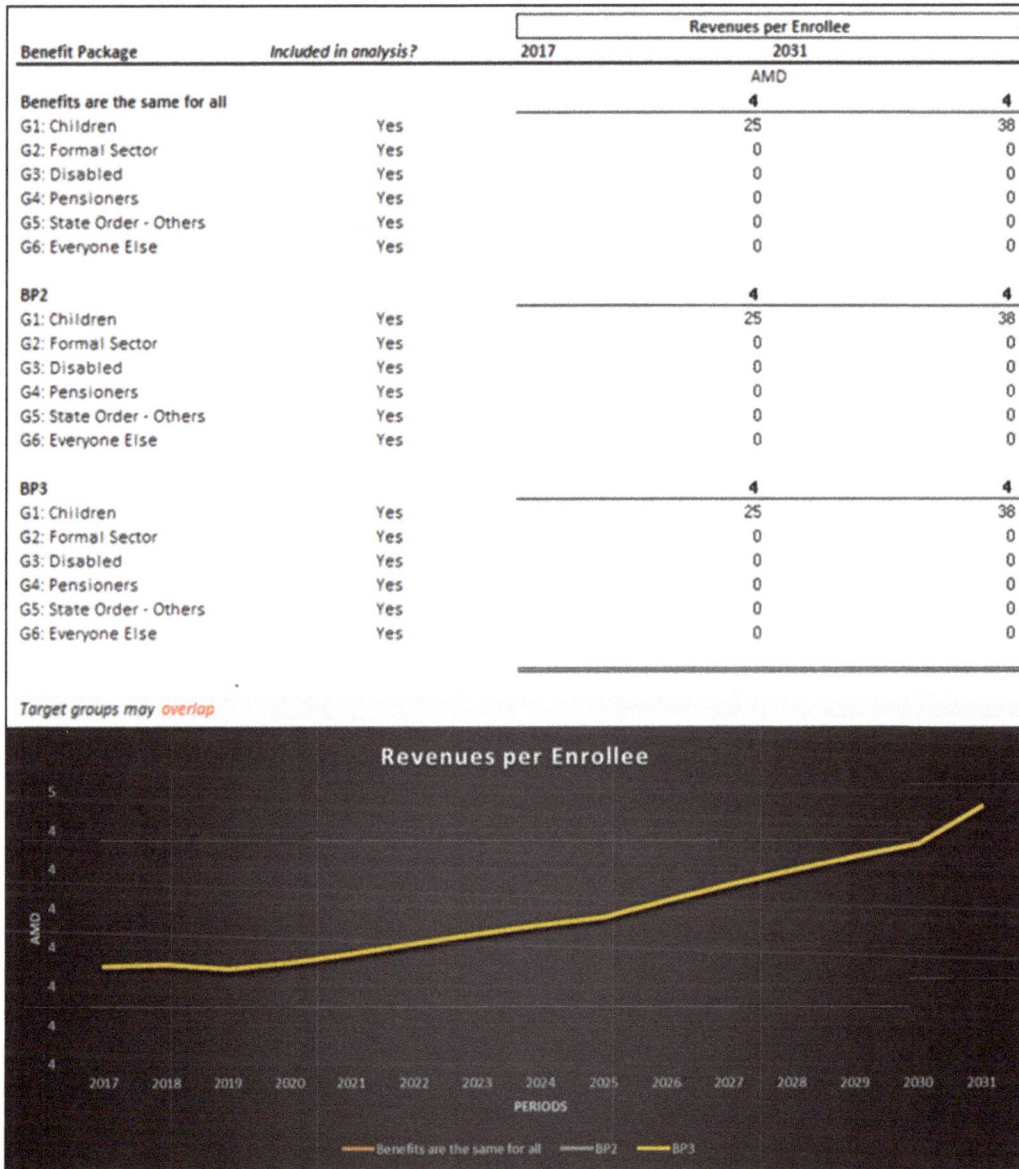

Note: AMD = Armenian dram.

Figure 239: Cash Flow per Enrollee Table and Chart in the Expenditures and Revenues Projections Partition

Benefit Package	Included in analysis?	Cash Flow per Enrollee	
		2017	2031
		AMD	
Benefits are the same for all		(22,012)	(34,582)
G1: Children	Yes	(24,058)	(36,428)
G2: Formal Sector	Yes	(23,494)	(37,558)
G3: Disabled	Yes	(21,428)	(33,144)
G4: Pensioners	Yes	0	0
G5: State Order - Others	Yes	(10,888)	(17,113)
G6: Everyone Else	Yes	0	0
BP2		(22,012)	(34,582)
G1: Children	Yes	(24,058)	(36,428)
G2: Formal Sector	Yes	(23,494)	(37,558)
G3: Disabled	Yes	(21,428)	(33,144)
G4: Pensioners	Yes	0	0
G5: State Order - Others	Yes	(10,888)	(17,113)
G6: Everyone Else	Yes	0	0
BP3		(22,012)	(34,582)
G1: Children	Yes	(24,058)	(36,428)
G2: Formal Sector	Yes	(23,494)	(37,558)
G3: Disabled	Yes	(21,428)	(33,144)
G4: Pensioners	Yes	0	0
G5: State Order - Others	Yes	(10,888)	(17,113)
G6: Everyone Else	Yes	0	0

Target groups may overlap

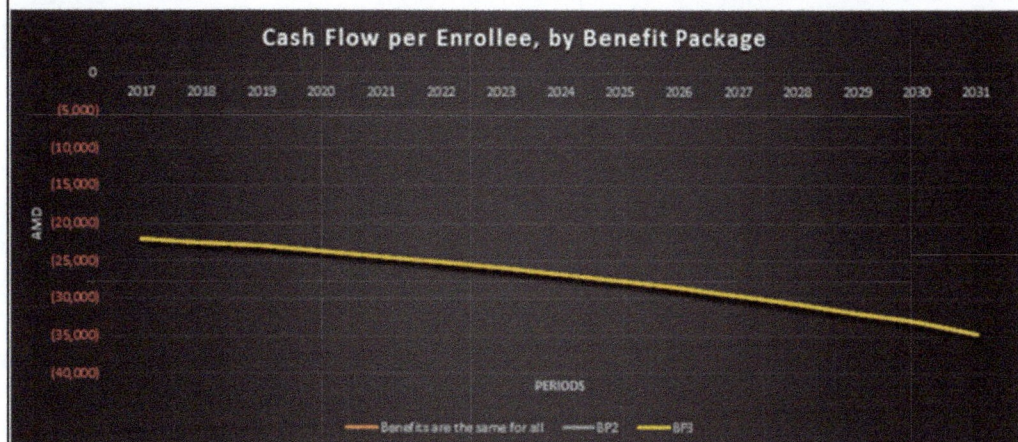

Note: AMD = Armenian dram.

Ratios

In this partition (Figure 240), the Dashboard shows the data table and consequent chart specified at the end of the first period and last period by the *benefit package* and *target groups* for *revenue as percent of expenditures* (Figure 241), as well as *cash flow as percent of revenues* (Figure 242).

Figure 240: Preview of the Ratios Partition in the Dashboard Worksheet

Benefit Package	Included in analysis?	Revenue as % of Expenditures - Total Cost			Benefit Package	Included in analysis?	Cash Flow as % of Revenues	
		2017	2031				2017	2031
		AMD					AMD	
Benefits are the same for all		0%	0%		Benefits are the same for all		-19849063%	-20344498%
G1: Children	Yes	0%	0%		G1: Children	Yes	0%	0%
G2: Formal Sector	Yes	0%	0%		G2: Formal Sector	Yes	0%	0%
G3: Disabled	Yes	0%	0%		G3: Disabled	Yes	0%	0%
G4: Pensioners	Yes	0%	0%		G4: Pensioners	Yes	0%	0%
G5: State Order - Others	Yes	0%	0%		G5: State Order - Others	Yes	-1112485%	-1191063%
G6: Everyone Else	Yes	0%	0%		G6: Everyone Else	Yes	0%	0%
BP2		0%	0%		BP2		-19849063%	-20344498%
G1: Children	Yes	0%	0%		G1: Children	Yes	0%	0%
G2: Formal Sector	Yes	0%	0%		G2: Formal Sector	Yes	0%	0%
G3: Disabled	Yes	0%	0%		G3: Disabled	Yes	0%	0%
G4: Pensioners	Yes	0%	0%		G4: Pensioners	Yes	0%	0%
G5: State Order - Others	Yes	0%	0%		G5: State Order - Others	Yes	-1112485%	-1191063%
G6: Everyone Else	Yes	0%	0%		G6: Everyone Else	Yes	0%	0%
BP3		0% Include in analysis?			BP3		-19849063%	-20344498%
G1: Children	Yes	0%	0%		G1: Children	Yes	0%	0%
G2: Formal Sector	Yes	0%	0%		G2: Formal Sector	Yes	0%	0%
G3: Disabled	Yes	0%	0%		G3: Disabled	Yes	0%	0%
G4: Pensioners	Yes	0%	0%		G4: Pensioners	Yes	0%	0%
G5: State Order - Others	Yes	0%	0%		G5: State Order - Others	Yes	-1112485%	-1191063%
G6: Everyone Else	Yes	0%	0%		G6: Everyone Else	Yes	0%	0%

Legend   Dashboard   1.0 General Assumptions   1.1A Target Populations   1.1B Growth Target Populations   1.2A Service Categories

Note: AMD = Armenian dram.

Figure 241: Revenues as Percentage of Expenditures Table and Chart in the Ratios Partition

Benefit Package	Included in analysis?	Revenue as % of Expenditures - Total Cost		
		2017	2031	
			AMD	
Benefits are the same for all			0%	0%
G1: Children	Yes		0%	0%
G2: Formal Sector	Yes		0%	0%
G3: Disabled	Yes		0%	0%
G4: Pensioners	Yes		0%	0%
G5: State Order - Others	Yes		0%	0%
G6: Everyone Else	Yes		0%	0%
BP2			0%	0%
G1: Children	Yes		0%	0%
G2: Formal Sector	Yes		0%	0%
G3: Disabled	Yes		0%	0%
G4: Pensioners	Yes		0%	0%
G5: State Order - Others	Yes		0%	0%
G6: Everyone Else	Yes		0%	0%
BP3			0% Include in analysis?	
G1: Children	Yes		0%	0%
G2: Formal Sector	Yes		0%	0%
G3: Disabled	Yes		0%	0%
G4: Pensioners	Yes		0%	0%
G5: State Order - Others	Yes		0%	0%
G6: Everyone Else	Yes		0%	0%

Target groups may overlap

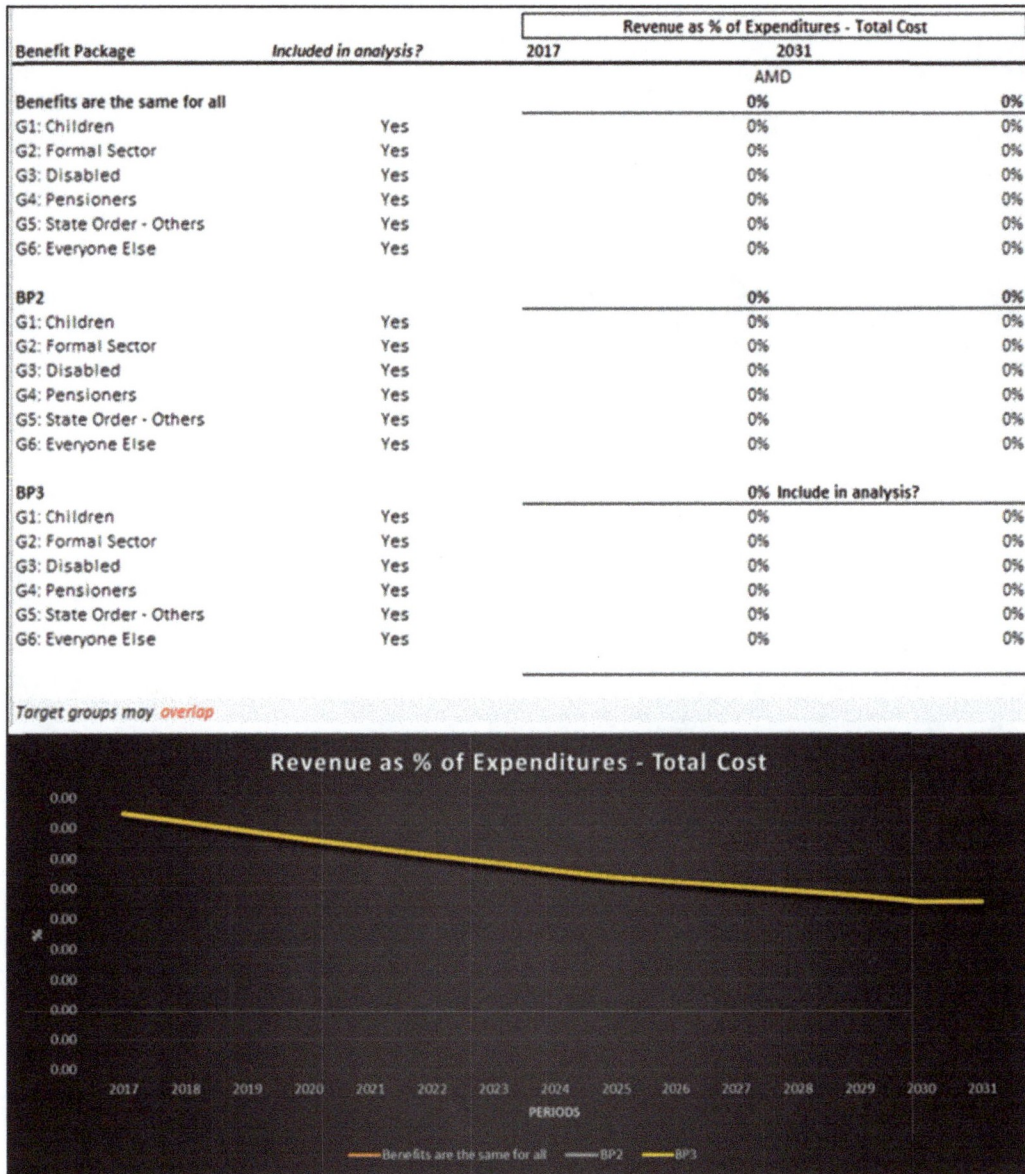

Note: AMD = Armenian dram.

Figure 242: Cash Flow as Percentage of Revenues Table and Chart in the Ratios Partition

Benefit Package	Included in analysis?	Cash Flow as % of Revenues	
		2017	2031
		AMD	
Benefits are the same for all		-19849063%	-20344498%
G1: Children	Yes	0%	0%
G2: Formal Sector	Yes	0%	0%
G3: Disabled	Yes	0%	0%
G4: Pensioners	Yes	0%	0%
G5: State Order - Others	Yes	-1112885%	-1191063%
G6: Everyone Else	Yes	0%	0%
BP2		-19849063%	-20344498%
G1: Children	Yes	0%	0%
G2: Formal Sector	Yes	0%	0%
G3: Disabled	Yes	0%	0%
G4: Pensioners	Yes	0%	0%
G5: State Order - Others	Yes	-1112885%	-1191063%
G6: Everyone Else	Yes	0%	0%
BP3		-19849063%	-20344498%
G1: Children	Yes	0%	0%
G2: Formal Sector	Yes	0%	0%
G3: Disabled	Yes	0%	0%
G4: Pensioners	Yes	0%	0%
G5: State Order - Others	Yes	-1112885%	-1191063%
G6: Everyone Else	Yes	0%	0%

Target groups may overlap

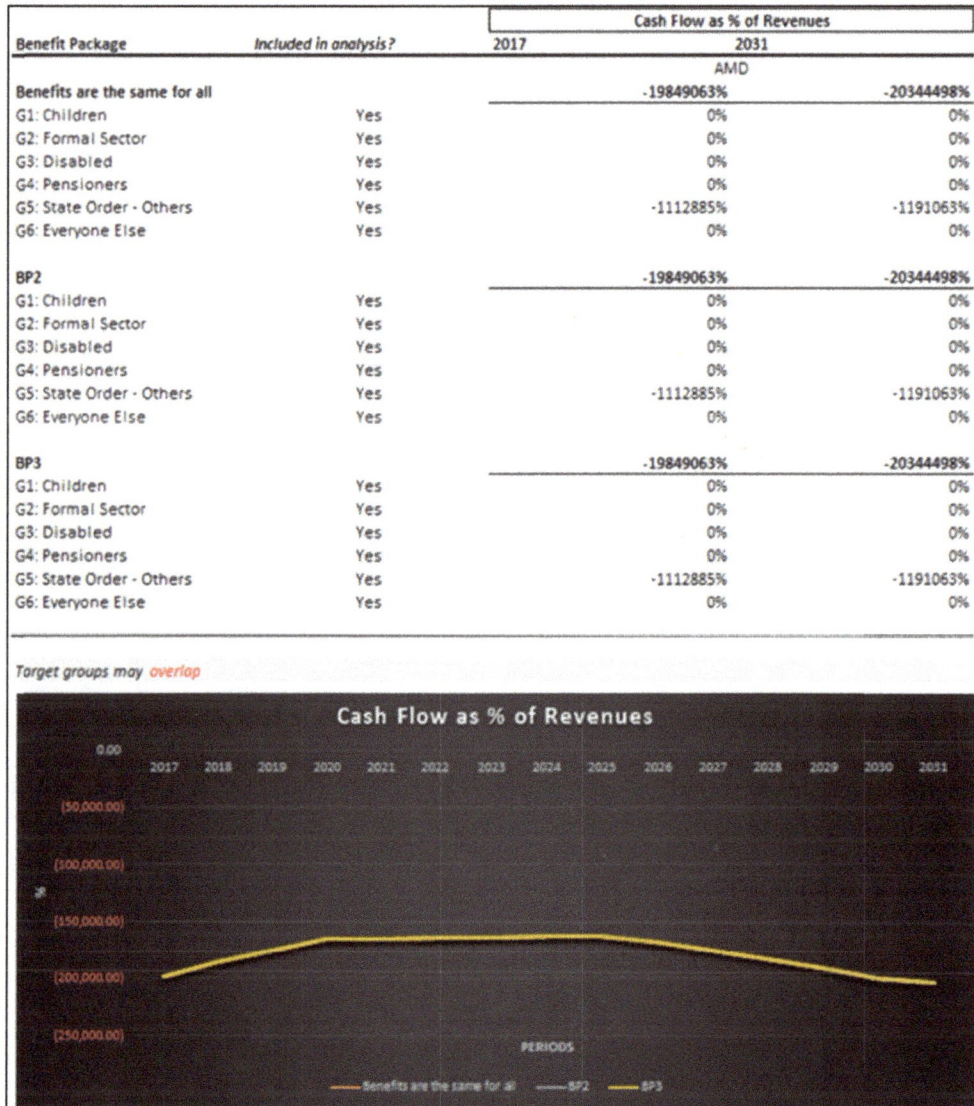

Note: AMD = Armenian dram.

D.   Results of Baseline Scenario Viewed Using the Dashboard Worksheet

The default settings in the sample SLAM Excel file shows the following results in the "Dashboard" worksheet.

Projections of the Target Populations and Active Members

Because the same growth percentages are applied to various member types, the larger groups will grow faster.

The target population is the population from which the health insurance program draws its members (Figure 243). If the uptake and the retention were both 100%, then the total of active members of the various member types would equal the target populations. However, while the uptake is assumed to be 100% of the target group growth, the retention rate is less than the desired retention rate of 100% per annum; hence the number of active members is lower (Figure 244).

Figure 243: Projections of Target Populations in the Dashboard Worksheet

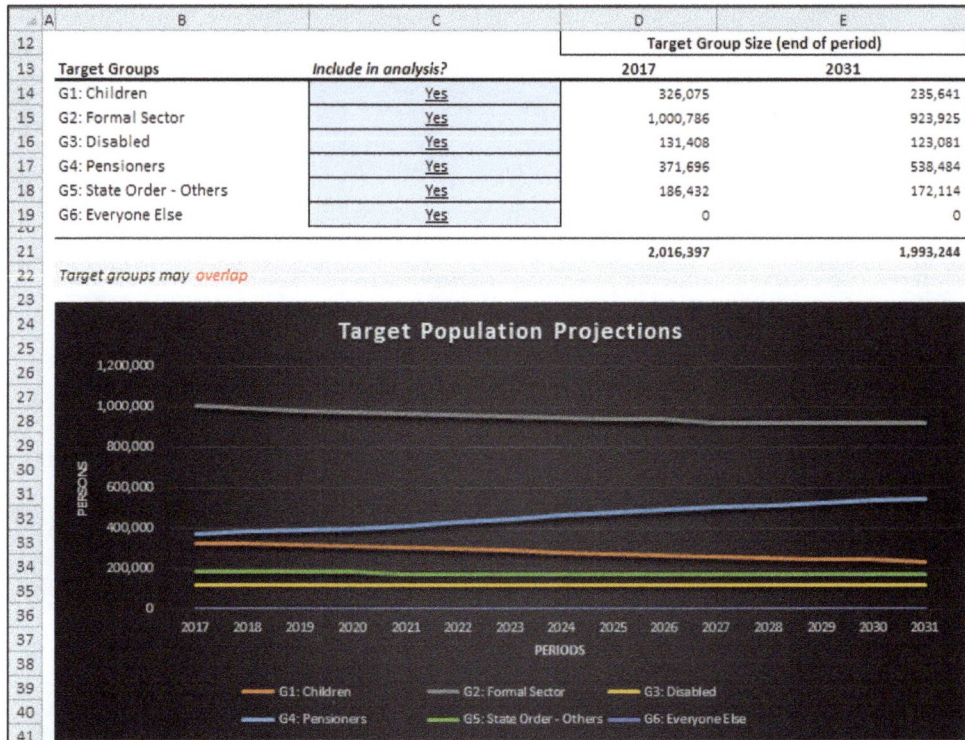

Figure 244: Projections of Active Members in the Dashboard Worksheet

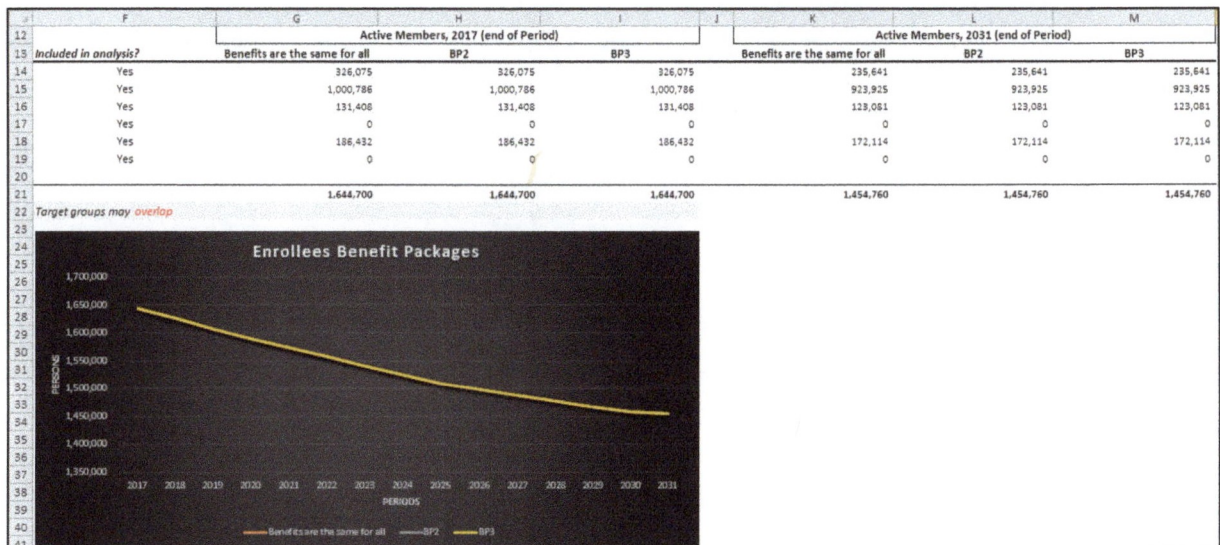

Projections of the Health Expenditures

The projected health services under the baseline scenario show that expenditures are growing (Figure 245). A review of the assumptions set will show that two factors led to this growth: increased numbers of active members and increasing expenditures per enrollee.

Figure 245: Projections of Health Expenditures in the Dashboard Worksheet

Benefit Package	Included in analysis?	Estimated Expenditures - Total Cost	
		2017	2031
		AMD	
Benefits are the same for all		36,203,208,596	50,309,361,225
G1: Children	Yes	7,844,828,348	8,583,888,539
G2: Formal Sector	Yes	23,512,569,074	34,700,450,747
G3: Disabled	Yes	2,815,819,682	4,079,440,688
G4: Pensioners	Yes	0	0
G5: State Order - Others	Yes	2,029,991,492	2,945,581,251
G6: Everyone Else	Yes	0	0
BP2		36,203,208,596	50,309,361,225
G1: Children	Yes	7,844,828,348	8,583,888,539
G2: Formal Sector	Yes	23,512,569,074	34,700,450,747
G3: Disabled	Yes	2,815,819,682	4,079,440,688
G4: Pensioners	Yes	0	0
G5: State Order - Others	Yes	2,029,991,492	2,945,581,251
G6: Everyone Else	Yes	0	0
BP3		36,203,208,596	50,309,361,225
G1: Children	Yes	7,844,828,348	8,583,888,539
G2: Formal Sector	Yes	23,512,569,074	34,700,450,747
G3: Disabled	Yes	2,815,819,682	4,079,440,688
G4: Pensioners	Yes	0	0
G5: State Order - Others	Yes	2,029,991,492	2,945,581,251
G6: Everyone Else	Yes	0	0
		108,609,625,788	150,928,083,676

Target groups may overlap

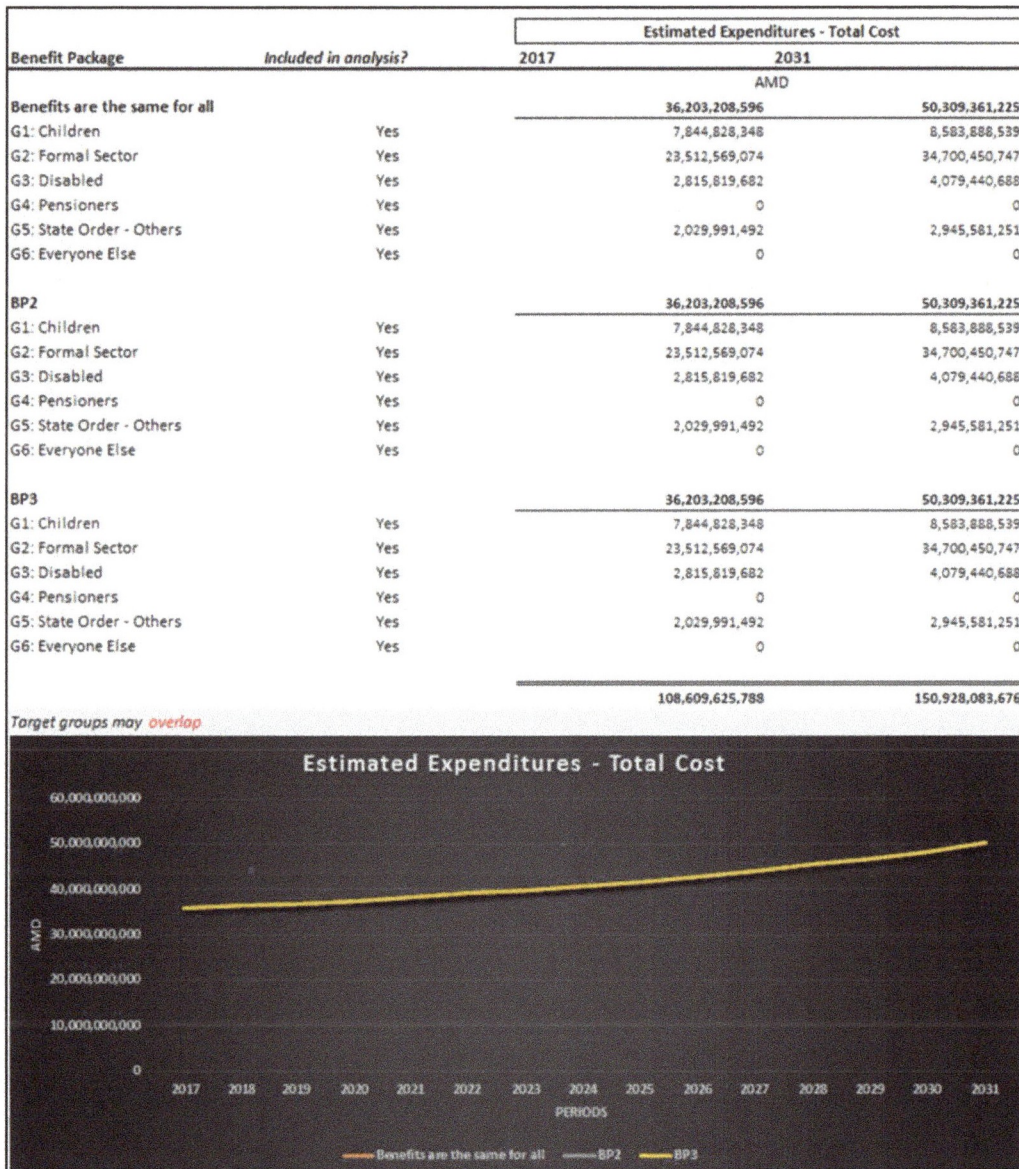

Note: AMD = Armenian dram.

Projections of Revenues from Premiums

The estimated revenues from premiums, assuming benefits are the same for all, are 182,392 in 2017 and 247,286 in 2031 (Figure 246). In case there are hikes in the provided line graph in future studies, these increases could correspond to any premium adjustments made in the scenario analysis. Since there are no defined B2 and B3 differences with the first benefit package in the sample Excel file in used in this manual, the estimated revenues for B2 and B3 are the same as B1 (benefits are the same for all members).

Figure 246: Projections of Revenues from Premiums in the Dashboard Worksheet

Benefit Package	Included in analysis?	Estimated Revenues	
		2017	2031
		AMD	
Benefits are the same for all		182,392	247,286
G1: Children	Yes	0	0
G2: Formal Sector	Yes	0	0
G3: Disabled	Yes	0	0
G4: Pensioners	Yes	0	0
G5: State Order - Others	Yes	182,392	247,286
G6: Everyone Else	Yes	0	0
BP2		182,392	247,286
G1: Children	Yes	0	0
G2: Formal Sector	Yes	0	0
G3: Disabled	Yes	0	0
G4: Pensioners	Yes	0	0
G5: State Order - Others	Yes	182,392	247,286
G6: Everyone Else	Yes	0	0
BP3		182,392	247,286
G1: Children	Yes	0	0
G2: Formal Sector	Yes	0	0
G3: Disabled	Yes	0	0
G4: Pensioners	Yes	0	0
G5: State Order - Others	Yes	182,392	247,286
G6: Everyone Else	Yes	0	0
		547,175	741,858

Target groups may overlap

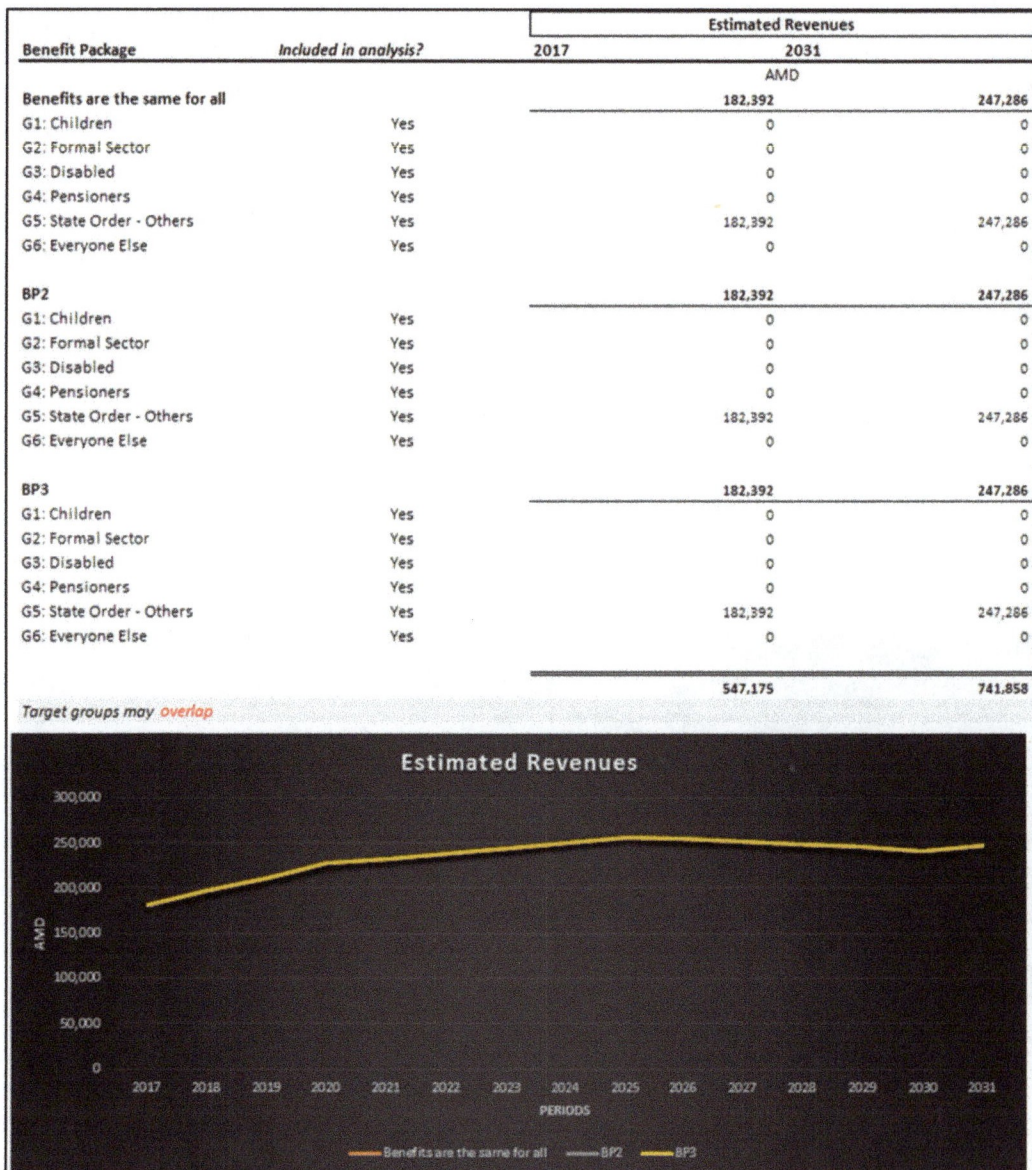

Note: AMD = Armenian dram.

Projection of Cash Flows

The figures here show the projections under the Baseline Scenario assumptions of the cash flows (Figures 247 and 248), cash per Active Member (Figure 249), and ratio of the cost over revenues together with the number of Active Members (Figure 250).

Figure 247: Projections of Cash Flow in the Dashboard Worksheet

Benefit Package	Included in analysis?	Cash Flow		Discounted Cash Flow at 2%
		2017	2031	
			AMD	
Benefits are the same for all		(36,203,026,204)	(50,309,113,939)	(531,746,799,787)
G1: Children	Yes	(7,844,828,348)	(8,583,888,539)	
G2: Formal Sector	Yes	(23,512,569,074)	(34,700,450,747)	
G3: Disabled	Yes	(2,815,819,682)	(4,079,440,688)	
G4: Pensioners	Yes	0	0	
G5: State Order - Others	Yes	(2,029,809,101)	(2,945,333,965)	
G6: Everyone Else	Yes	0	0	
BP2		(36,203,026,204)	(50,309,113,939)	(531,746,799,787)
G1: Children	Yes	(7,844,828,348)	(8,583,888,539)	
G2: Formal Sector	Yes	(23,512,569,074)	(34,700,450,747)	
G3: Disabled	Yes	(2,815,819,682)	(4,079,440,688)	
G4: Pensioners	Yes	0	0	
G5: State Order - Others	Yes	(2,029,809,101)	(2,945,333,965)	
G6: Everyone Else	Yes	0	0	
BP3		(36,203,026,204)	(50,309,113,939)	(531,746,799,787)
G1: Children	Yes	(7,844,828,348)	(8,583,888,539)	
G2: Formal Sector	Yes	(23,512,569,074)	(34,700,450,747)	
G3: Disabled	Yes	(2,815,819,682)	(4,079,440,688)	
G4: Pensioners	Yes	0	0	
G5: State Order - Others	Yes	(2,029,809,101)	(2,945,333,965)	
G6: Everyone Else	Yes	0	0	
		(108,609,078,613)	(150,927,341,818)	

Target groups may overlap

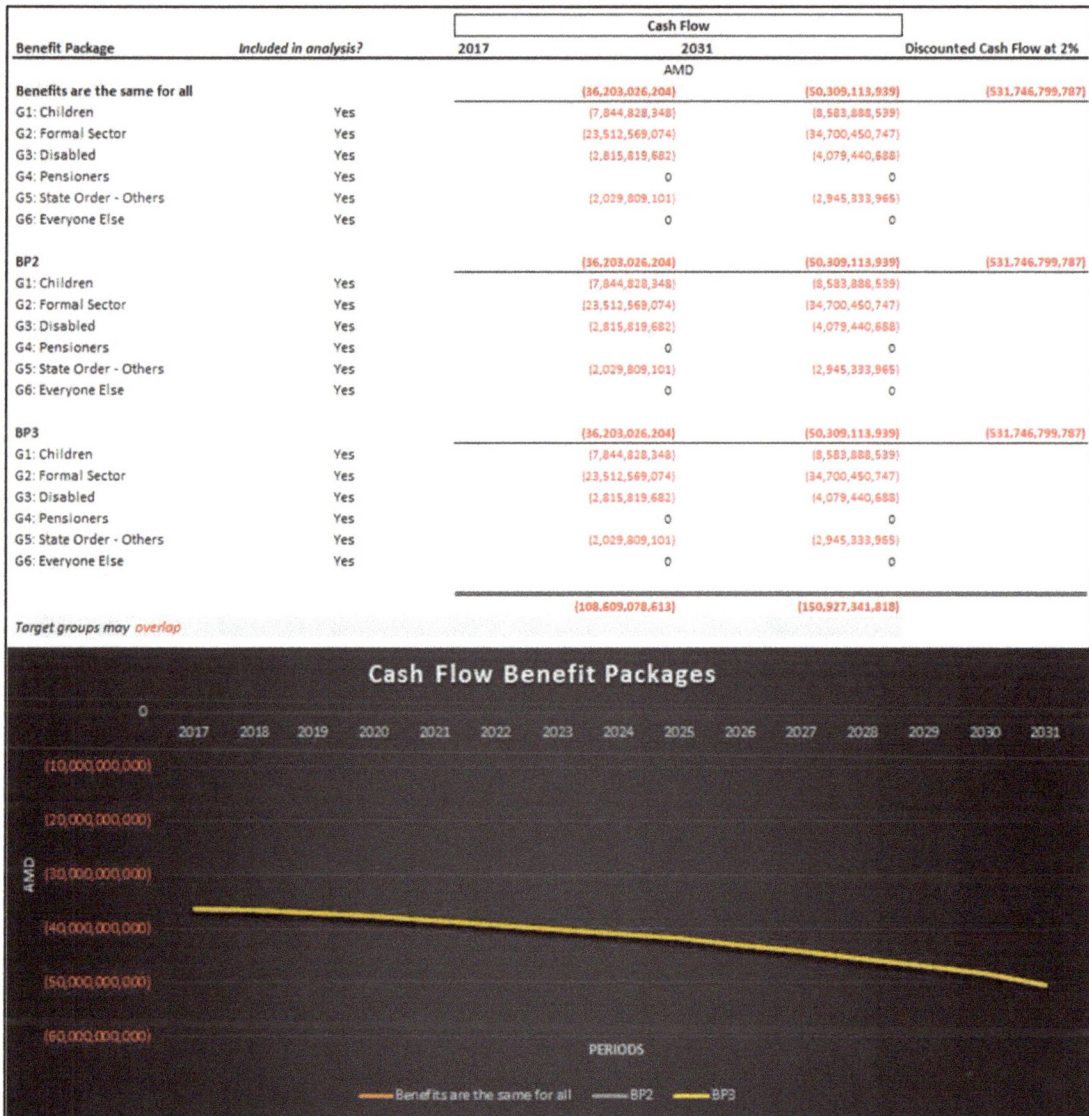

Note: AMD = Armenian dram.

Figure 248: Projections of Cash Flow per Active Member in the Dashboard Worksheet

Benefit Package	Included in analysis?	Cash Flow per Enrollee	
		2017	2031
		AMD	
Benefits are the same for all		(22,012)	(34,582)
G1: Children	Yes	(24,058)	(36,428)
G2: Formal Sector	Yes	(23,494)	(37,558)
G3: Disabled	Yes	(21,428)	(33,144)
G4: Pensioners	Yes	0	0
G5: State Order - Others	Yes	(10,888)	(17,113)
G6: Everyone Else	Yes	0	0
BP2		(22,012)	(34,582)
G1: Children	Yes	(24,058)	(36,428)
G2: Formal Sector	Yes	(23,494)	(37,558)
G3: Disabled	Yes	(21,428)	(33,144)
G4: Pensioners	Yes	0	0
G5: State Order - Others	Yes	(10,888)	(17,113)
G6: Everyone Else	Yes	0	0
BP3		(22,012)	(34,582)
G1: Children	Yes	(24,058)	(36,428)
G2: Formal Sector	Yes	(23,494)	(37,558)
G3: Disabled	Yes	(21,428)	(33,144)
G4: Pensioners	Yes	0	0
G5: State Order - Others	Yes	(10,888)	(17,113)
G6: Everyone Else	Yes	0	0

Target groups may overlap

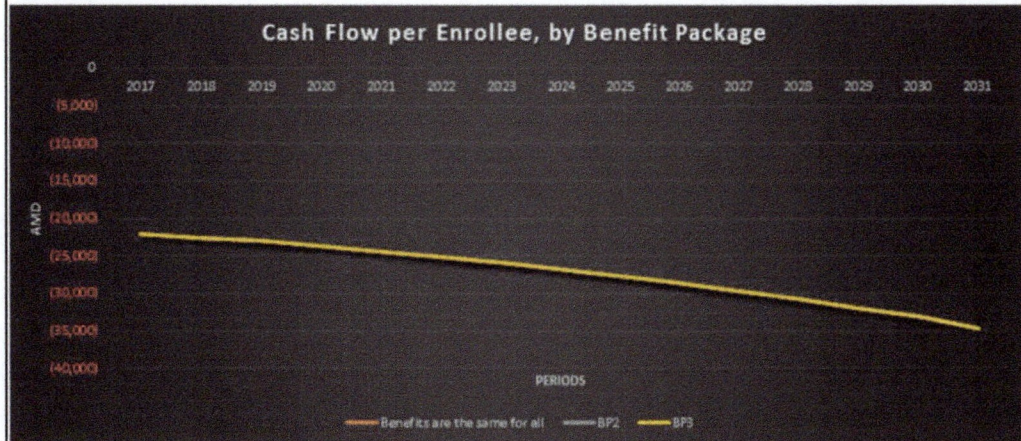

Note: AMD = Armenian dram.

Figure 249: Projections of Cash per Active Member in the Dashboard Worksheet

Benefit Package	Included in analysis?	Expenditures per Enrollee - Total Cost	
		2017	2031
		AMD	
Benefits are the same for all		22,012	34,583
G1: Children	Yes	24,058	36,428
G2: Formal Sector	Yes	23,494	37,558
G3: Disabled	Yes	21,428	33,144
G4: Pensioners	Yes	0	0
G5: State Order - Others	Yes	10,889	17,114
G6: Everyone Else	Yes	0	0
BP2		22,012	34,583
G1: Children	Yes	24,058	36,428
G2: Formal Sector	Yes	23,494	37,558
G3: Disabled	Yes	21,428	33,144
G4: Pensioners	Yes	0	0
G5: State Order - Others	Yes	10,889	17,114
G6: Everyone Else	Yes	0	0
BP3		22,012	34,583
G1: Children	Yes	24,058	36,428
G2: Formal Sector	Yes	23,494	37,558
G3: Disabled	Yes	21,428	33,144
G4: Pensioners	Yes	0	0
G5: State Order - Others	Yes	10,889	17,114
G6: Everyone Else	Yes	0	0

Target groups may overlap

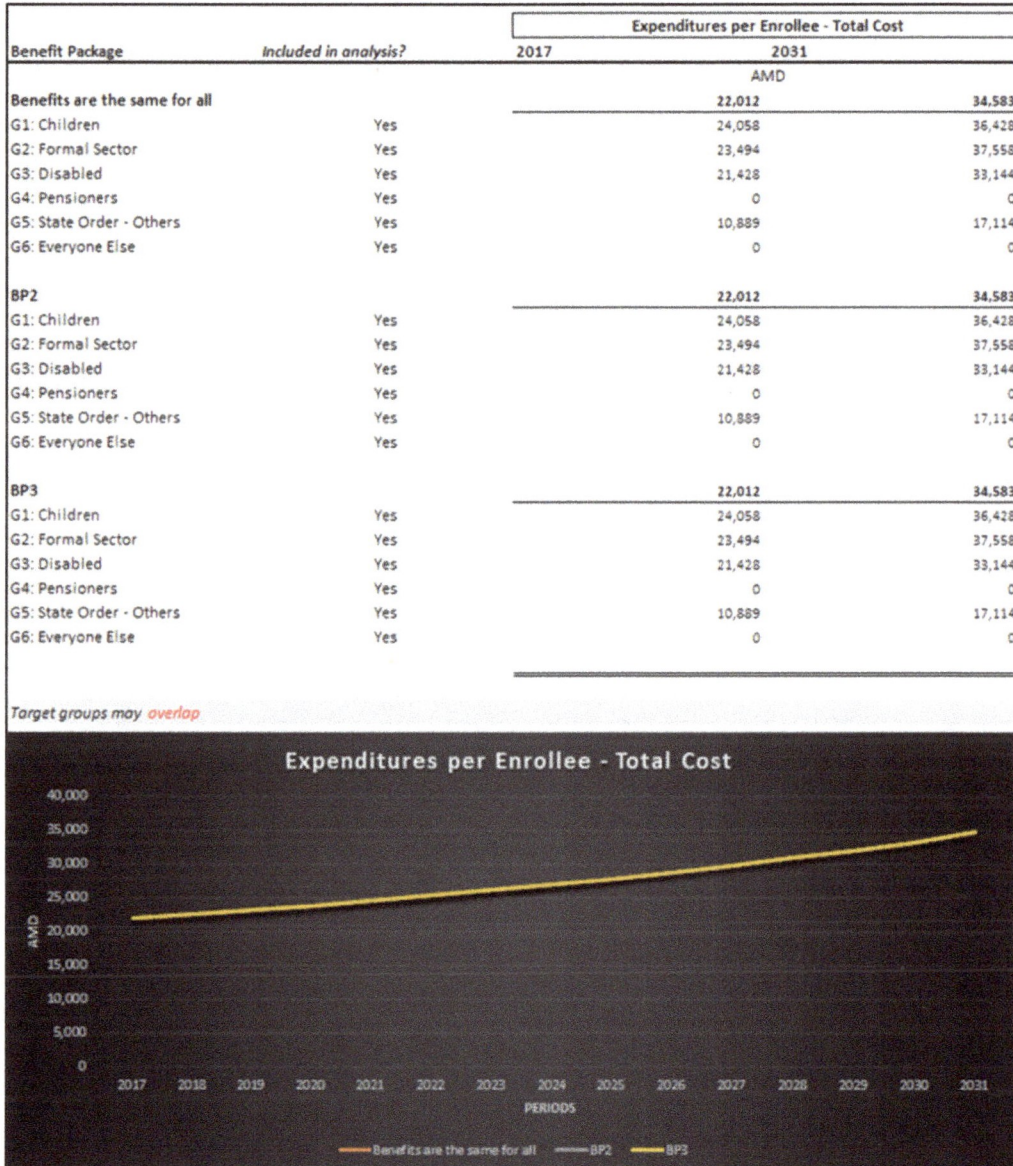

Note: AMD = Armenian dram.

Figure 250: Ratio of the Cost Over Revenues Together with the Number of Active Members in the Dashboard Worksheet

Benefit Package	Included in analysis?	Revenues per Enrollee	
		2017	2031
		AMD	
Benefits are the same for all		4	4
G1: Children	Yes	25	38
G2: Formal Sector	Yes	0	0
G3: Disabled	Yes	0	0
G4: Pensioners	Yes	0	0
G5: State Order - Others	Yes	0	0
G6: Everyone Else	Yes	0	0
BP2		4	4
G1: Children	Yes	25	38
G2: Formal Sector	Yes	0	0
G3: Disabled	Yes	0	0
G4: Pensioners	Yes	0	0
G5: State Order - Others	Yes	0	0
G6: Everyone Else	Yes	0	0
BP3		4	4
G1: Children	Yes	25	38
G2: Formal Sector	Yes	0	0
G3: Disabled	Yes	0	0
G4: Pensioners	Yes	0	0
G5: State Order - Others	Yes	0	0
G6: Everyone Else	Yes	0	0

Target groups may *overlap*

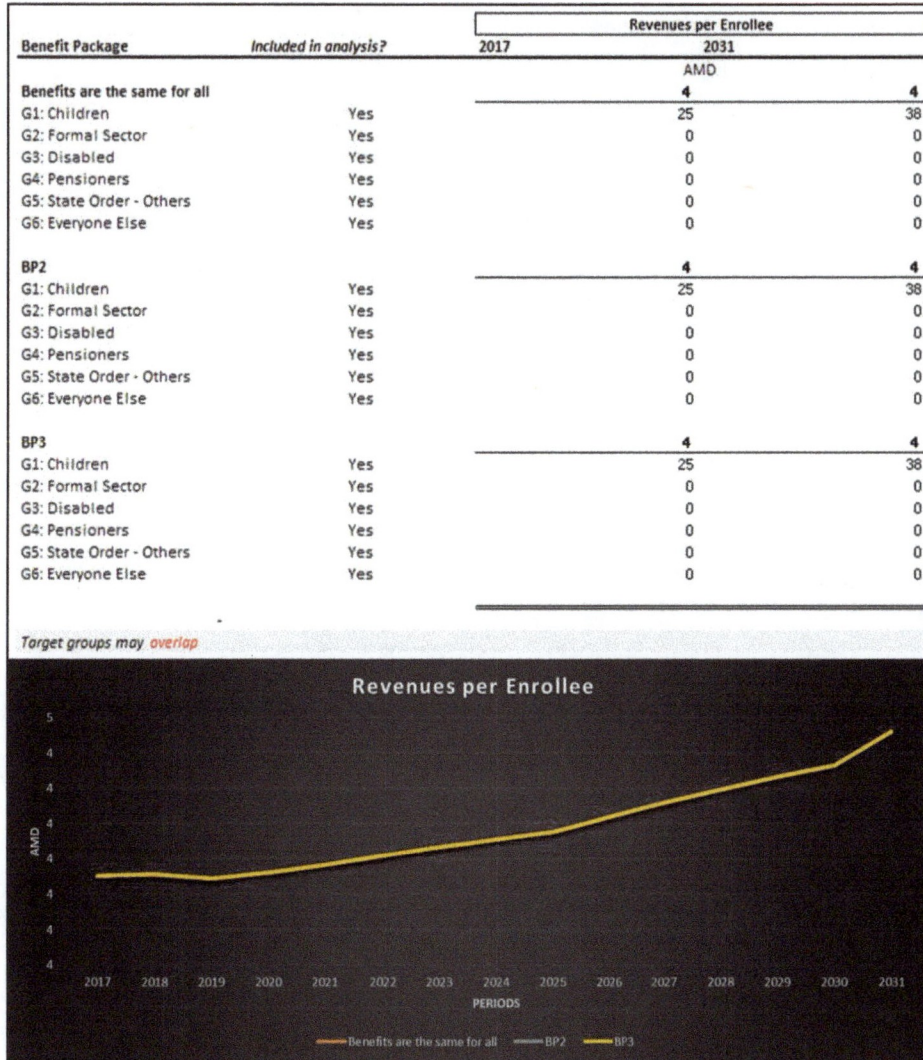

Note: AMD = Armenian dram.

Based on the assumptions set for the baseline scenario, the graphs show the worsening cash flow both in absolute terms as well as per Active Member.

As the incidences of health services provided to the members do not change over time under the baseline scenario (see *Assumption 20),* the worsening of the cash flow is due to two factors. First, the growth in the number of members causes increasingly negative cash flow. Second, while the inflation rates for expenditures and for revenues are equal on a percentage annual basis, the fact that the expenditures per active member started higher compared to the revenues per active member means that the difference per enrollee increases over time.

Analysts are also allowed to determine the discounted cash flows set at the discount rate inputted in the 1.0 General Assumptions worksheet.

Projection of Financial Indicators

Revenue as a percentage of expenditures is a good indicator of how well the premium is set and how well the insurance is performing (Figure 251).

Figure 251: Projection of Financial Indicator: Revenue as a Percentage of Expenditures in the Dashboard Worksheet

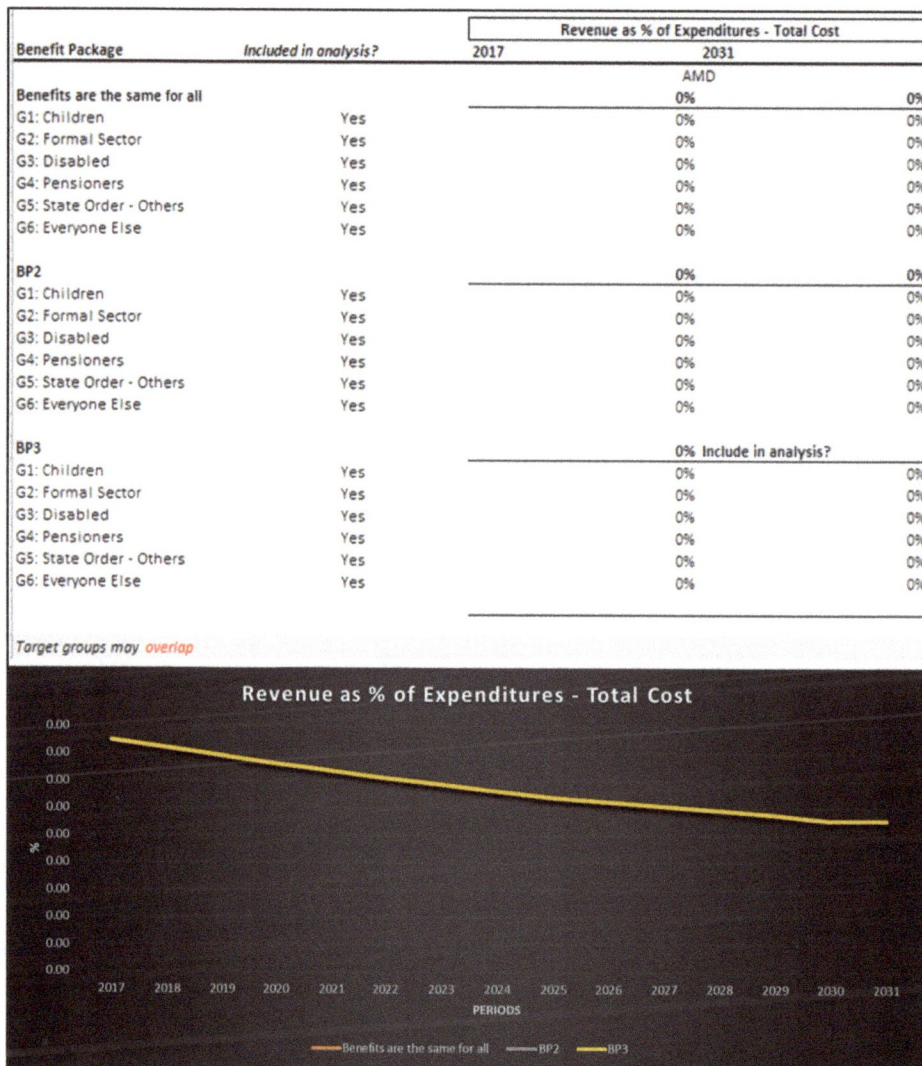

Benefit Package	Included in analysis?	Revenue as % of Expenditures - Total Cost	
		2017	2031
		AMD	
Benefits are the same for all		0%	0%
G1: Children	Yes	0%	0%
G2: Formal Sector	Yes	0%	0%
G3: Disabled	Yes	0%	0%
G4: Pensioners	Yes	0%	0%
G5: State Order - Others	Yes	0%	0%
G6: Everyone Else	Yes	0%	0%
BP2		0%	0%
G1: Children	Yes	0%	0%
G2: Formal Sector	Yes	0%	0%
G3: Disabled	Yes	0%	0%
G4: Pensioners	Yes	0%	0%
G5: State Order - Others	Yes	0%	0%
G6: Everyone Else	Yes	0%	0%
BP3		0% Include in analysis?	
G1: Children	Yes	0%	0%
G2: Formal Sector	Yes	0%	0%
G3: Disabled	Yes	0%	0%
G4: Pensioners	Yes	0%	0%
G5: State Order - Others	Yes	0%	0%
G6: Everyone Else	Yes	0%	0%

Target groups may overlap

Note: AMD = Armenian dram.

Another financial indicator is cash flow as a percentage of revenues from premiums (Figure 252). This ratio is also quite stable, except for the different periodic adjustments in the inflation between expenditures and premiums.

Forecasting projected cash flow by various member types allows determination of which member group type(s) are the major contributors to the positive or negative cash flow of the health insurance program.

In case there are hikes in the provided line graph in future studies, these increases could correspond to any expenditures and premium adjustments made in the scenario analysis.

Figure 252: Projection of Financial Indicator: Cash Flow as a Percentage of Revenues from Premiums in the Dashboard Worksheet

Benefit Package	Included in analysis?	Cash Flow as % of Revenues	
		2017	2031
		AMD	
Benefits are the same for all		-19849063%	-20344498%
G1: Children	Yes	0%	0%
G2: Formal Sector	Yes	0%	0%
G3: Disabled	Yes	0%	0%
G4: Pensioners	Yes	0%	0%
G5: State Order - Others	Yes	-1112885%	-1191063%
G6: Everyone Else	Yes	0%	0%
BP2		-19849063%	-20344498%
G1: Children	Yes	0%	0%
G2: Formal Sector	Yes	0%	0%
G3: Disabled	Yes	0%	0%
G4: Pensioners	Yes	0%	0%
G5: State Order - Others	Yes	-1112885%	-1191063%
G6: Everyone Else	Yes	0%	0%
BP3		-19849063%	-20344498%
G1: Children	Yes	0%	0%
G2: Formal Sector	Yes	0%	0%
G3: Disabled	Yes	0%	0%
G4: Pensioners	Yes	0%	0%
G5: State Order - Others	Yes	-1112885%	-1191063%
G6: Everyone Else	Yes	0%	0%

Target groups may overlap

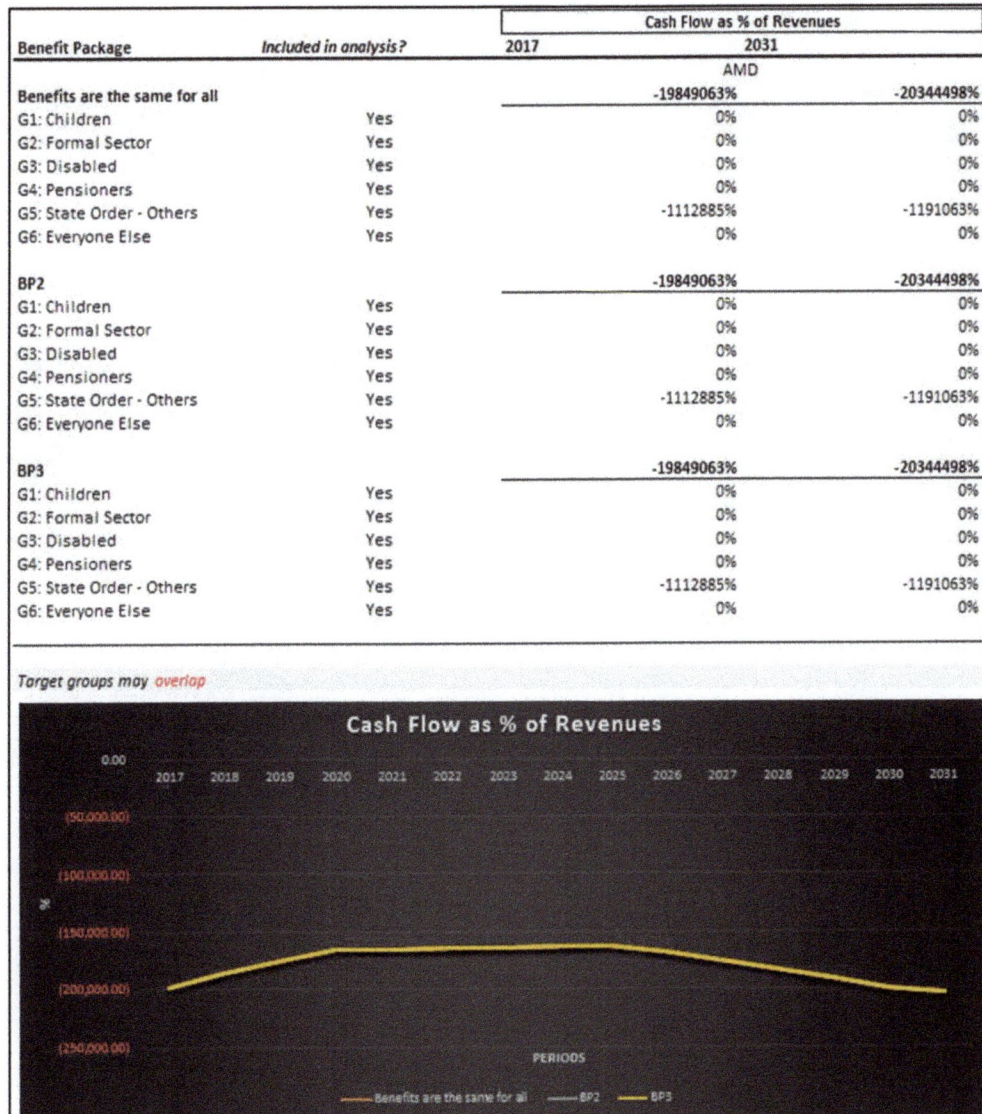

Note: AMD = Armenian dram.

CHAPTER VI

Sensitivity Analysis

The SLAM Excel file allows users to perform sensitivity and scenario analyses using several input parameters, as defined in the baseline scenario. In a sensitivity analysis, a quantitative model input parameter is changed to assess its impact in the model results and its robustness. Sensitive parameters are those whose changes have a large impact on the result. A robust model, meanwhile, is a model where (relatively small) changes in model input parameters have little effect on the result. In a scenario analysis, multiple assumptions can be changed at once (in relation to the baseline scenario) to assess what happens in such a scenario.

Analysts may perform sensitivity analysis using **rows 3–7** of the "Dashboard" worksheet (Figure 253). Specifically, input cells in **column D** allow users to revise the parameters set in the 1.0 General Assumptions worksheet. The user must be careful when setting the parameters and remember that these are on top of the baseline scenario assumptions. **Column H**, meanwhile, allows users to define which group or period the revised parameters will be applied to.

Figure 253: Input cells for Sensitivity and Scenario Analyses in the Dashboard Worksheet

	A	B	C	D	E	F	G	H
1	Dashboard							
2								
3	**Sensitivity Parameters**							
4	Population growth (additional to assumptions, applies each period)			0%		Applies to		G1: Children
5	Inflation, expenditures (additional to assumptions)			0%		Applies to		Each period
6	Inflation, revenues (additional to assumptions)			0%		Applies to		Each period
7	Premium increase (added to the Risk loading, Admin and Profit Margin)			0%		Applies to		First period only

A. Changes in Enrollment Numbers

Cell D4 allows analysts to revise the growth percentages of the Target Group/s. Changes in the growth rates will allow analysts to determine whether increases or reduction in specific Target Groups identified in **cell H4** will yield better cash flow for the health insurance program (Figure 254).

Figure 254: Input Cells for Changes in Enrollment Numbers in the Dashboard Worksheet

	A	B	C	D	E	F	G	H
1	Dashboard							
2								
3	Sensitivity Parameters							
4	Population growth (additional to assumptions, applies each period)			0%		Applies to		G1: Children
5	Inflation, expenditures (additional to assumptions)			0%		Applies to		Each period
6	Inflation, revenues (additional to assumptions)			0%		Applies to		Each period
7	Premium increase (added to the Risk loading, Admin and Profit Margin)			0%		Applies to		First period only

B.   Changes in Expenditures Inflation

As shown in Figure 255, **cell D5** provides the analyst space to input additional assumptions on the health expenditures (e.g., members accessing more expensive health services or getting more expensive treatments). **Cell H5**, on the other hand, allows analysts to consider a single increase of expenditures ("first period only") or periodical increases ("each period").

Figure 255: Input Cells for Changes in Expenditures Inflation in the Dashboard Worksheet

	A	B	C	D	E	F	G	H
1	Dashboard							
2								
3	Sensitivity Parameters							
4	Population growth (additional to assumptions, applies each period)			0%		Applies to		G1: Children
5	Inflation, expenditures (additional to assumptions)			0%		Applies to		Each period
6	Inflation, revenues (additional to assumptions)			0%		Applies to		Each period
7	Premium increase (added to the Risk loading, Admin and Profit Margin)			0%		Applies to		First period only

Changes in inflation will allow analysts to determine whether positive cash flow will be realized when health expenditures are reduced.

C.   Changes in Revenues Inflation

As shown in Figure 256, **cell D6** provides the analyst space to input additional assumptions on premium increase, while **cell H6** allows analysts to consider a single increase of premium ("first period only") or periodical increases ("each period") to compute when the health insurance program will reach a positive cash flow in case negative estimates were derived in the baseline scenario.

Figure 256: Input Cells for Changes in Revenues Inflation in the Dashboard Worksheet

	A	B	C	D	E	F	G	H
1	Dashboard							
2								
3	Sensitivity Parameters							
4	Population growth (additional to assumptions, applies each period)			0%		Applies to		G1: Children
5	Inflation, expenditures (additional to assumptions)			0%		Applies to		Each period
6	Inflation, revenues (additional to assumptions)			0%		Applies to		Each period
7	Premium increase (added to the Risk loading, Admin and Profit Margin)			0%		Applies to		First period only

D.   Changes in Premium Rates

The program also allows analysts to input an additional premium rate on top of the estimated risk loading rates, administrative costs, and profit margins in **cell D7**. As with the inflation sensitivity analyses, users may choose to apply the additional rates to "first period only" or "each period" of the projection in **cell H7** (Figure 257).

Figure 257: Input Cells for Changes in Premium Rates in the Dashboard Worksheet

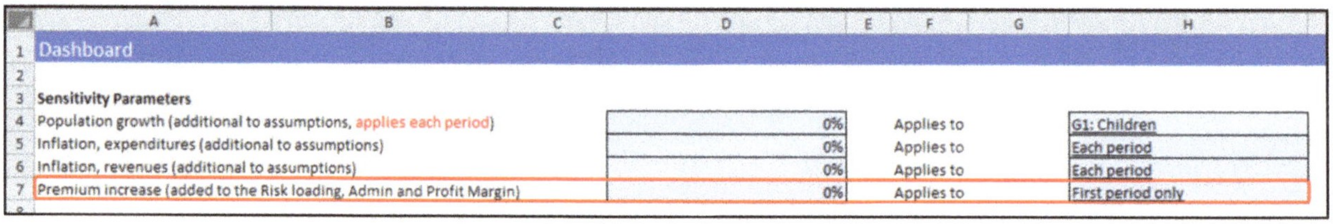

	A	B	C	D	E	F	G	H
1	Dashboard							
2								
3	**Sensitivity Parameters**							
4	Population growth (additional to assumptions, applies each period)			0%		Applies to		G1: Children
5	Inflation, expenditures (additional to assumptions)			0%		Applies to		Each period
6	Inflation, revenues (additional to assumptions)			0%		Applies to		Each period
7	Premium increase (added to the Risk loading, Admin and Profit Margin)			0%		Applies to		First period only

CHAPTER VII

Summary of Use and Potential

To reach positive cash flow, a review of the benefit package is often preferred over a review of the premiums. The SLAM allows managers of health insurance schemes to perform actuarial analysis and projections of current program operations. The objective is to help analysts compare various programs using different financial indicators. The actuarial model permits using the present policy and make projections toward the future to assess the financial sustainability of the health insurance operations. The SLAM will aid program managers to determine whether there could be significant cash flow problems that may grow simultaneously with the projected growth of the health insurance program.

Actuarial projections could show that in some cases, continuing businesses-as-usual is not an option for the sustainability of the health insurance scheme. Thus, expenditures must be examined, increases in premium rates should be considered, and membership expansion should be assessed.

It must be noted that while SLAM can assist in the day-to-day management of health insurance programs, health insurance and actuarial experts are still needed for in-depth assessments and reviews of these insurance schemes. The SLAM will be a useful tool to considerably speed up the review process of the program and increase transparency among analysts.

Appendix

Defining the General Security Settings in Microsoft Excel

The following steps can check the general settings in Microsoft Excel:

Step 1: Select the <u>File</u> menu (Figure A1) in the upper left corner of the Excel file.

Figure A1: The File Menu in Microsoft Excel

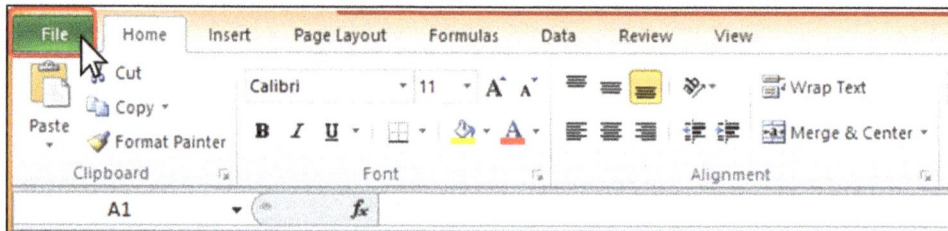

Step 2: In the file menu, select the <u>Options</u> button, which gives access to the Excel Options window (Figure A2).

Figure A2: Options Button in the Microsoft Excel File Menu

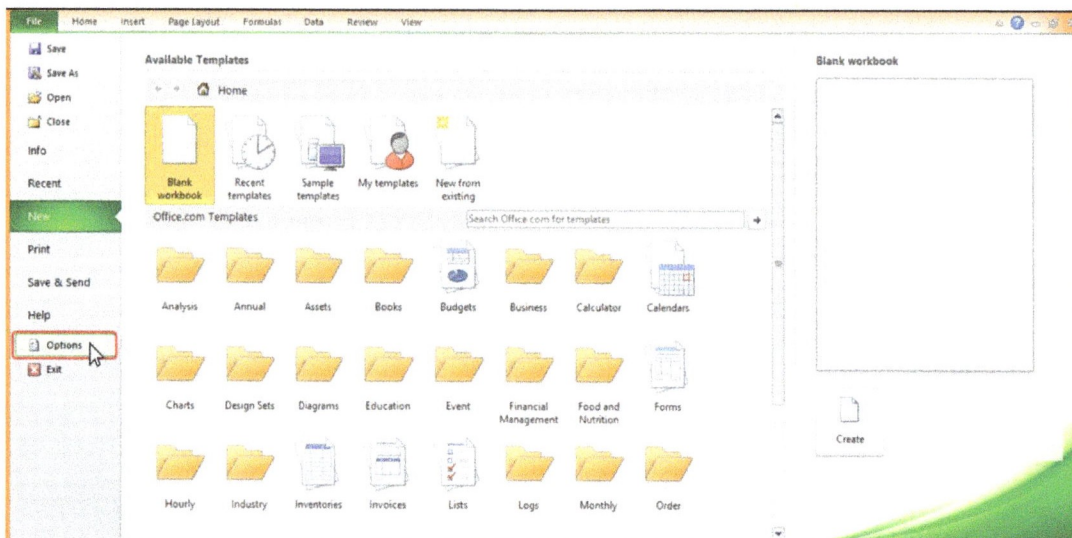

Step 3: In the Excel Options window (Figure A3), (i) choose **Trust Center** button in the side panel, then (ii) select the **Trust Center Settings** button under the Microsoft Excel Trust Center" section, which gives access to the Trust Center window.

Figure A3: Microsoft Excel Options Window and Opening the Trust Center Settings

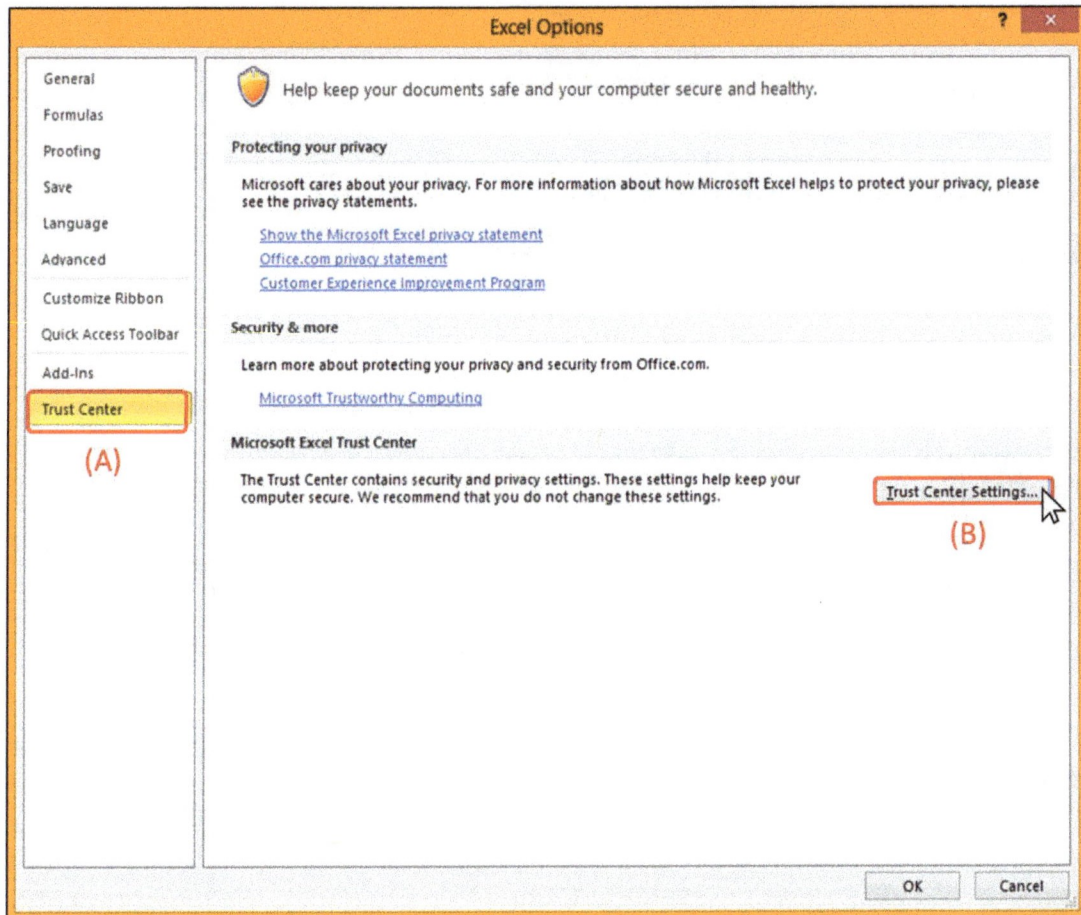

Step 4: In the Trust Center window (Figure A4), (i) choose Macro Settings button in the side panel, (ii) select the Disable all macros with notification bullet under the Macro Settings section, and (iii) press the OK button.

Figure A4: Trust Center Window and Disabling All Macros with Notification

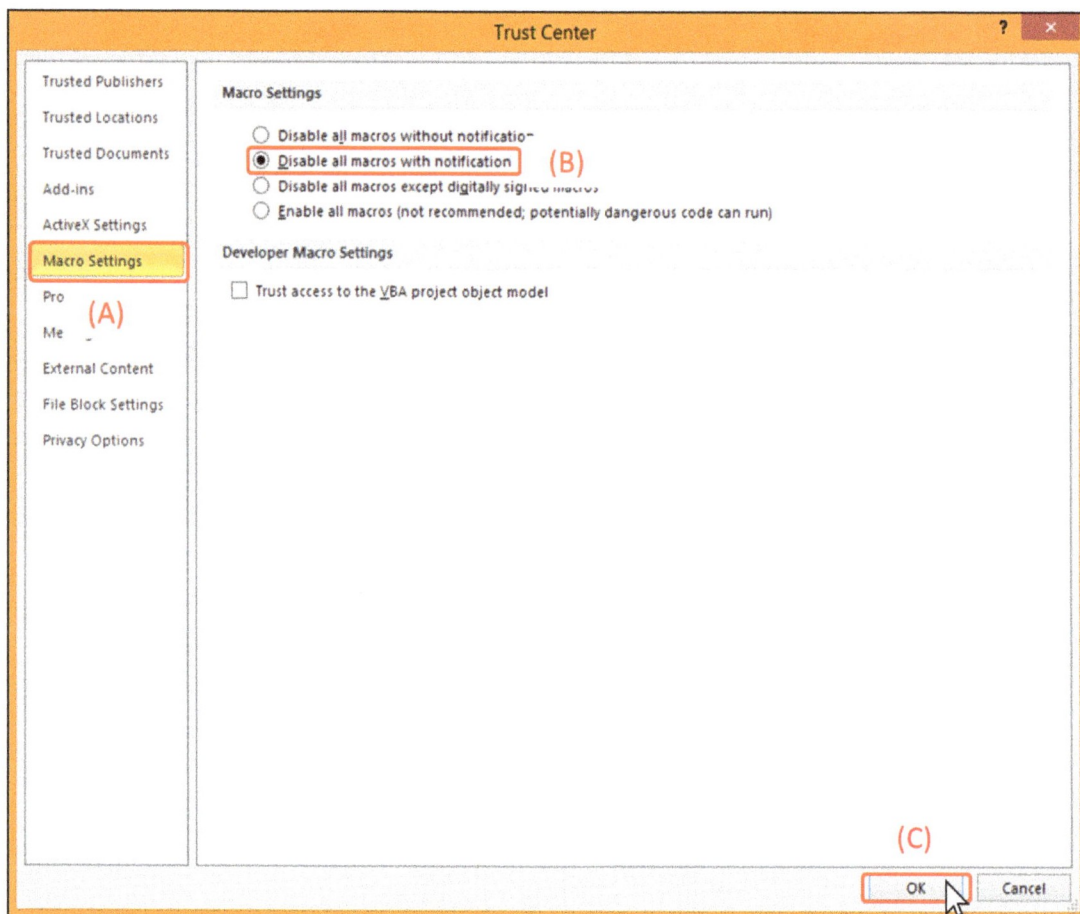

The next time an Excel file with macros is opened, a security warning message bar will be displayed (Figure A5).

Figure A5: Security Warning Message Bar

The SLAM Excel file should now be working. Note, however, that in some older versions of Excel, only selecting Enable Content seems to work after saving the file and reopening the file.

Glossary

actuarial analysis   –   form of statistical analysis typically conducted using health-related financial cost data in the context of calculating insurance premium rates or otherwise determining expenditure needs. It entails estimation of average healthcare expenditures of a risk pool so that financing needs can be estimated to ensure that revenues balance expected outlays

actuarial soundness   –   financial sustainability; implies that expected expenditures (including administrative costs and any reserve requirements) for a risk pool be less than or equal to expected revenues

administrative loading   –   represents the costs for running the health insurance program; it is typically defined as a percentage of the expected health payouts, a fixed amount or a combination of both

benefit package   –   includes what services are covered at which healthcare facilities, what approvals are needed to obtain insurance benefits, and the limitation of the insurance coverage, among others

claim   –   an event reported by the policy holder for which she/he demands economic compensation

claim frequency   –   number of claims divided by the duration, for some group of policies in force during a specific time period

claims severity
(average cost per claim)   –   total claim amount divided by the number of claims

combined ratio   –   ratio of the claim amount plus administrative expenses to the earned premium

dropout rate   –   proportion of members who lost insurance membership out of target populations

duration of a policy   –   amount of time the policy is in force, usually measured in years

earned premium   –   amount of the premium income that covers risks during the period under study. Commonly, premiums are assumed to be earned *pro rata temporis*, i.e., linearly with time. This means that the earned premium is the duration, measured in years, times the annual premium

eligible member   –   an individual who can obtain health insurance benefits after satisfying the compulsory membership requirements

enrollment	–	process by which a member is signed up in the health insurance program
gross premium	–	pure premium (defined below) plus operational expenses of the insurance program, profit margins and risk loading
group enrollment	–	type of health insurance enrollment scheme which provides coverage to a group of members, usually comprised of company employees or members of an organization, e.g., cooperatives
health insurance	–	insurance against loss through illness or injury of the insured; especially insurance providing compensation for medical expenses and often income for disability
health needs	–	latent needs of the population in terms of healthcare services they need
health service	–	services that are obtained from a hospital, clinic, or other types healthcare provider; this may include but not limited to consultation, a night spent at a health facility, a delivery, or surgery
health service category	–	groupings by which the health services covered by health insurance packages are organized into
insurance	–	coverage by contract whereby one party undertakes to indemnify or guarantee another against loss by a specified contingency or peril
key ratios	–	claim frequency, claim severity, pure premium and loss ratio
loss ratio	–	claim amount divided by the earned premium
mandatory enrollment	–	process of enrolling selected/targeted uninsured people automatically in a health insurance plan
profit margin	–	represents the profit of the health insurance program; it is typically defined as a percentage of the expected health payouts or a percentage of the positive operational cash flow
pure premium	–	total claim amount divided by the duration; it is the product of the claim frequency and the claim severity
retention rate	–	percentage of members of the target population that re-enrols at the end the specified period of enrollment (i.e., is still there at the beginning of the next period).
risk loading	–	represents the uncertainty of actuarial estimates, the probability and size of the estimate being smaller than the actual payout; it also shows how big the risk is in the opinion of the insurer is willing to run; this is typically defined as a percentage of the expected health payouts
risk pool	–	the group of health insurance members who together share the risks (e.g., the risk of financial costs due to hospitalization)
target population	–	the population that is considered for insurance coverage
uptake	–	enrollment in the health insurance program

References

M. Cichon et al. 1999. *Modelling in Health Care Finance: A Compendium of Quantitative Techniques for Health Care Financing.* Geneva: International Labour Office.

D. Cotlear et al. 2015. Managing Money: Financing the Bottom-Up Expansion of Universal Health Coverage. In *Going Universal: How 24 Developing Countries are Implementing Universal Health Coverage from the Bottom Up.* Washington, DC: World Bank.

H. Wang et al. 2012. Health Insurance Handbook: How to Make it Work. *World Bank Working Paper.* 219. Washington, DC: World Bank.

www.ingramcontent.com/pod-product-compliance
Lightning Source LLC
Chambersburg PA
CBHW050042220326
41599CB00045B/7258